Homer's The Iliad and The Odyssey
A Biography

Alberto Manguel is a world-renowned writer, translator and editor of literary anthologies. His works include *A History of Reading*, published in 1997 and his novel, *Stevenson Under the Palm Trees*, in 2005.

Other titles in the *Books That Shook the World* series:

Homer's
The Iliad and
The Odyssey

A Biography

ALBERTO MANGUEL

Atlantic Books
LONDON

To Craig, in Ithaca

First published in hardback in Great Britain in 2007 by Atlantic Books,
an imprint of Grove Atlantic Ltd.

This paperback edition published in Great Britain in 2008 by Atlantic Books.

Copyright © Alberto Manguel 2007

1 3 5 7 9 8 6 4 2

A CIP catalogue record for this book is available from the British Library

ISBN 978 1 84354 403 6

Designed by Richard Marston

Typeset by Avon DataSet Ltd, Bidford on Avon, Warwickshire

Printed in Great Britain by Clays Ltd, St Ives plc

Atlantic Books
An imprint of Grove Atlantic Ltd
Ormond House
26–27 Boswell Street
London WC1N 3JZ

www.atlantic-books.co.uk

CONTENTS

ACKNOWLEDGEMENTS

Several readers have helped me in my research: Antonio Basanta Reyes, Carmen Criado, Silvia Di Segni Obiols, Lucie Pabel, Gottwalt Pankow, Arturo Ramoneda, Marta Royo, Jean-Christophe Saladin, Guillermo Schavelzon, Takis Théodoropoulos, Mario Claudio Vicario: to them my deepest thanks. Special thanks to Louisa Joyner for her care, patience and enthusiasm, and to Meg Davies for her precise and intelligent indexing. Also, to Toby Mundy of Grove Atlantic for suggesting the book in the first place, and to Bruce Westwood and the staff of WCA, who were the first enthusiastic emissaries.

A NOTE ON TRANSLATIONS AND EDITIONS

To simplify the reading, I've preferred to use common versions of the Homeric names, 'Ulysses' rather than 'Odysseus' and 'Achilles' rather than 'Akhilleus'. As Samuel Butler noted, 'Neither do I think that Hekabe will supersede Hecuba, till "What's Hecuba to him or he to Hecuba?" is out of date.'[1] (Though in our forgetful times, Butler may have to wait less time than he thought…)

I am aware that I use the term 'Greek' incorrectly. The allied forces against Troy were composed of Achaeans, Danaans and Argives, not of homogenous 'Greeks', a name that was not invented until the expansion of the Roman Empire. However, in the context of this book, I use 'Greek' as a kind of shorthand. Neither does the word 'Hellenic' (which I have used once or twice) properly cover the historical and geographical ground of Homer's stories, only a limited territory in southern Thessaly.

The numbering of Homer's lines differs in the various translations. Throughout the book, I have used the versions of the *Iliad* and the *Odyssey* translated by Robert Fagles and published in 1992 and 2004 respectively by Penguin Classics, which, to my taste, are among the best and most graceful. Other translations of foreign works quoted, unless otherwise stated, are my own.

Concerning the task of a literary critic, A. E. Housman had this to say: 'Knowledge is good, method is good, but one thing beyond all others is necessary; and that is to have a head, not a pumpkin, on your shoulders, and brains, not pudding, in your head.' I have long had occasion to doubt whether I fulfil either requirement.

Alberto Manguel
Mondion
August 2006

INTRODUCTION

'Every great work of literature is either the *Iliad* or
the *Odyssey*.'

Raymond Queneau, Preface to Flaubert's
Bouvard et Pécuchet, 1947

It seems fitting that the two books which, more than any
others, have fed the imagination of the Western world for over
two and a half millennia, should have no clear starting-point
and no identifiable creator. Homer begins long before Homer.
In all probability, the *Iliad* and the *Odyssey* drifted into being
gradually, indefinably, more like popular myths than formal
literary productions, through the untraceable process of
ancient ballads sifting and blending until acquiring a coherent
narrative shape, ballads sung in tongues that were already
archaic when the poet (or poets) whom tradition agreed to call
Homer was at work in the eighth century BC. For many centuries, the poor, blind singer begging his way through ancient
Greece was generally regarded as the author of the *Iliad* and
the *Odyssey*; in time, he came to be replaced by a kind of
inspired spirit, part fable and part allegory, the ghost of Poetry

Past. Eventually, so widespread became the notion of an apoc-ryphal Homer, that in the 1850s Gustave Flaubert was able to mock it in his *Dictionary of Clichés*, a handbook that purported to offer to the bourgeoisie a correct social response for every uttering. 'HOMER: Never existed'.[1]

We don't know anything about Homer. It is otherwise with Homer's books. In a very real sense, the *Iliad* and the *Odyssey* are familiar to us prior to opening the first page. Even before we begin to follow the changing moods of Achilles or admire the wit and courage of Ulysses, we have learned to expect that somewhere in these stories of war in time and travel in space we will be told the experience of every human struggle and every human displacement. Two of our oldest metaphors tell us that all life is a battle and that all life is a journey; whether the *Iliad* and the *Odyssey* drew on this knowledge or whether this knowledge was drawn from the *Iliad* and the *Odyssey* is, in the final count, unimportant, since a book and its readers are both mirrors that reflect one another endlessly. Whatever their nebulous origins, most scholars now assume that the poems ascribed to Homer began as scattered compositions of various kinds that even-tually coalesced and became perfectly interwoven to form the two lengthy stories we now know: one describing the tragedy of a single place, Troy, which is fought over by many men; the other telling the homecoming adventures of a single man, Ulysses, who makes his way back through many dangerous places. For Homer's future readers, Troy came to stand for all cities and Ulysses for every man.

The biography of a book is not the biography of the man who wrote it. Except that, in the case of Homer and his poems, one goes hand in hand with the other, since it is impossible to know which came first: the blind bard who sang of the destruction of the Trojan city and of the longing of a Greek king for his home, or the stories of the lure of war and the search for peace, which required an author to justify their existence. Writers and their work establish curious relationships in the eyes of their readers. There are books that through inspired wording conjure up a lifelike character who overshadows whoever the author may have really been: Don Quixote and Cervantes, Hamlet and Shakespeare are cases in point. There are writers whose lives, as Oscar Wilde said of himself, are the recipients of their genius, and whose books are only the product of their talent.[2] Homer and his works belong to the former category, but there have been times in their long history when readers chose to consign them to the latter.

No one owns Homer, not even the best of his readers. Each one of our readings is done through layers of previous ones that pile upon the page like seams in a rock until the original text (if there ever was so pure a thing) is hardly visible. So that when we think, upon closing Homer, 'Ah, now I've made the *Iliad* – or the *Odyssey* – mine!' what we mean is that we've made ours a story that many others have long annotated, recast, interpreted, adapted, and that, with their testimonies echoing more or less loudly in our ears, we've tried to impose our tastes and prejudices upon a cacophony of one-man bands, like Keats first looking into Chapman's Homer or Joyce hustling Ulysses through the crowded streets of Dublin. In this attempt, strict adherence to official chronologies isn't useful: readings influence one another back and forth across time, and we mustn't accuse St Augustine of anachronism for studying Homer under Goethe's guidance, or Heraclitus for allowing himself to be prejudiced by the commentaries of George Steiner.

Not only does this palimpsest of readings hide from our eyes the original text (or what most scholars agree is the original text). It is said that an English divine, Richard Whately, waving the King James Bible at a meeting of his diocesan clergy, roared out: 'This is *not* the Bible!' Then, after a long pause: 'This, gentlemen, is only a *translation* of the Bible!'[3] Except for an increasingly small group of scholars upon whom has been bestowed the grace of knowing ancient Greek, the rest of us read not Homer but a translation of Homer. In this our fortunes vary: some may be lucky enough to fall upon Alexander Pope's or Robert Fagles'; others may be doomed to T. S. Brandreth's 'literal' version of 1816 or to the pompous 1948 rendition by F. L. Lucas.

Translation is, in its nature, a questionable craft, and it is very strange how, in certain cases, works such as the *Iliad* and the *Odyssey*, made out of words and therefore seemingly dependent for their success on how those precise words are used, can dispense with them and come across in languages that had not even been invented when the poems first came into being. '*Mênin aeide, théa, Peleiadeo Achilleos…*' 'Sing, O

Goddess, the wrath of Peleian Achilles' is a more or less literal English version of the *Iliad*'s first line. But what did Homer mean by *'aeide'*, 'sing'? What by *'théa'*, 'Goddess'? What by *'mênin'*, 'wrath'? Virginia Woolf noted that 'it is vain and foolish to talk of knowing Greek, since in our ignorance we should be at the bottom of any class of schoolboys, since we do not know how the words sounded, or where precisely we ought to laugh, or how the actors acted, and between this foreign people and ourselves there is not only difference of race and tongue but a tremendous breach of tradition'.[4]

Even among modern languages the 'tremendous breach of tradition' persists. 'Wrath' in English, with its old-fashioned ring that has echoes in Blake's tigers and Steinbeck's grapes, is different from the German *'Zorn'*, full of the military sound and fury evident in Emanuel Geibel's 1848 ballad about the *'heil'gen Zorn ums Vaterland'*, 'holy anger over the Fatherland',[5] or from the French *'colère'* which, in existentialist Paris, Simone de Beauvoir defined as a passion 'born from love to murder love'.[6] Under such bewildering circumstances, what is a reader to do? Read, and bear the questions in mind.

In spite of such uneasy conditions, a good book manages to survive, at times, the most unfaithful of translations. Even when reading 'many soul-destroying things/In folded tablets' (as Brandreth self-accusingly has it),[7] Achilles' anger or Ulysses' longing will somehow succeed in moving us, reminding us of our own endeavours, touching something in us that is not just our own but mysteriously common to humankind. In 1990, the Colombian Ministry of Culture set up a system of itinerant libraries to take books to the inhabitants of distant rural regions. For this purpose, carrier book-bags with capacious pockets were transported on donkeys' backs up into the jungle and the sierra. Here the books were left for several weeks in the hands of a teacher or village elder who became, de facto, the librarian in charge. Most of the books were technical works, agricultural handbooks, collections of sewing patterns and the like, but a few literary works were also included. According to one librarian, the books were always safely accounted for. 'I know of a single instance in which a book was not returned,' she said. 'We had taken, along with the usual practical titles, a Spanish translation of the *Iliad*. When the time came to exchange the book, the villagers refused to give it back. We decided to make them a present of it, but asked them why they wished to keep that particular title. They explained that Homer's story reflected their own: it told of a war-torn country in which mad gods mix with men and women who never know exactly what the fighting is about, or when they will be happy, or why they will be killed.'[8]

In the final book of the *Iliad*, Achilles, who has murdered Hector, who in turn has murdered Patroclus, Achilles' beloved friend, agrees to receive Hector's father, King Priam, come to ransom his son's body. It is one of the most moving, most powerful scenes I know. Suddenly, there is no difference between victim and victor, old and young, father and son. Priam's words stir in Achilles 'a deep desire/to grieve for his own father', and with great tenderness he moves away the hand that the old man has stretched out to grasp the hands of his son's murderer and put them to his lips.

> … And overpowered by memory
> both men gave way to grief. Priam wept freely
> for man-killing Hector, throbbing, crouching
> before Achilles' feet as Achilles wept himself,
> now for his father, now for Patroclus once again,
> and their sobbing rose and fell throughout the house.[9]

At length, Achilles tells Priam that they both must 'put their griefs to rest in their own hearts'.

> So the immortals spun our lives that we, we wretched men
> live on to bear such torments – the gods live free of sorrows.
> There are two great jars that stand on the floor of Zeus's halls
> and hold his gifts, our miseries one, the other blessings.
> When Zeus who loves the lightning mixes gifts for a man,
> now he meets with misfortune, now good times in turn.
> When Zeus dispenses gifts from the jar of sorrows only,
> he makes a man an outcast.[10]

To Achilles, and perhaps to Priam, and perhaps to their readers in the Colombian sierra, this is consolation.

CHAPTER 1

Summaries of the Books

The *Iliad*

Before the beginning of the poem, Menelaus' wife, the beautiful Helen, has been captured by Paris, son of the King of Troy, Priam, and of his wife Hecuba. Among Paris's siblings are Hector, married to Andromache, and the visionary Cassandra. To rescue Helen, Menelaus' brother Agamemnon has laid siege to Troy, at the head of a coalition that includes among its famous warriors Ajax, Diomedes, Ulysses, old Nestor, Patroclus and his friend, the greatest warrior of all, Achilles, son of the goddess Thetis. The siege has lasted ten long years and the gods have become involved in the conflict. Their divine favours are divided: on the side of the Trojans are Aphrodite (whose son, Aeneas, is a Trojan), the sun-god Apollo and the war-god Ares; on the side of the Greeks are Thetis, the goddess of wisdom Athena, the sea-god Poseidon, and Zeus' wife, Hera.

Book I

In the tenth year of the Trojan War, the Greek army, led by Agamemnon, is camped on the shore near the city. The priest of Apollo, Chryses, has asked Agamemnon to allow him to ransom his daughter Chryseis whom Agamemnon has claimed as his slave, and has been rudely rejected. Chryses prays to Apollo to help him, and the god sends a plague upon the Greeks. To pacify the god, it is decided at a general assembly that Agamemnon must return his slave girl. Agamemnon agrees, but demands that he be given Achilles' concubine, Briseis, in exchange. Achilles feels dishonoured and withdraws from the war, taking with him Patroclus and their soldiers. Achilles appeals to his mother for revenge, and the goddess Thetis convinces Zeus to side with the Trojans. Zeus and his wife Hera, who supports the Greeks, have an argument, settled by Hera's son, the smithy-god Hephaestus.

Book II

Agamemnon has a dream which tells him that he will take Troy. He tests the dream by suggesting to his army that they abandon the siege and return home. The plan backfires when the soldiers agree wholeheartedly. The commoner Thersites causes a disruption by rallying against the Greek leaders, but Ulysses restores order. The episode ends with a catalogue of the Greek and Trojan forces.

Book III

The two armies meet on the plain outside Troy and settle on a truce, while Paris and Menelaus agree to fight for Helen. High on the ramparts of Troy, Helen points out the Greek warriors to Priam. Aphrodite saves Paris from being killed and transports him back into the city.

Book IV
The gods intervene again. Hera demands that the truce be broken. Athena persuades Pandarus, fighting on the Trojan side, to shoot at Menelaus, who is wounded.

Book V
Helped by Athena, Diomedes attacks the Trojans, and even attacks Aphrodite, as she tries to help Aeneas, and the god of war Ares himself as he is rallying the Trojans.

Book VI
On the battlefield, the Greek Diomedes meets Glaucus, a Lycean fighting on the Trojan side, and they become friends and refuse to fight. Hector goes back to Troy to sacrifice to Athena. He speaks to Helen and to his wife Andromache, and rebukes Paris for not being out on the field. Paris follows Hector's advice and joins the battle.

Book VII
Paris and Hector return to the fight. Hector challenges Ajax to a duel, but the outcome isn't clear. The Trojans propose a truce so that both camps can bury the dead. In the meantime, following old Nestor's advice, the Greeks fortify the camp.

Book VIII

Zeus encourages the Trojans, but also forbids the other gods to take part in the fighting. The Greeks withdraw to their camp and the Trojans set themselves up outside their city walls.

Book IX

Worried about the advance of the Trojans, Nestor suggests that Agamemnon send Ajax, together with Phoenix (the old tutor of Ulysses and Achilles), to convince Achilles to join the troops again. In spite of being offered Briseis back, as well as Agamemnon's daughter's hand in marriage, he refuses.

Book X

Nestor now suggests that Diomedes and Ulysses go during the night to spy on the Trojans. They capture Dolon, an enemy scout and, based on his information, succeed in killing several Trojans.

Book XI

Led by Hector, the Trojans succeed in pushing the Greeks back to their ships, wounding Agamemnon, Diomedes and Ulysses. Achilles sends Patroclus to find out about one of the wounded whose body he sees being carried away. Nestor asks Patroclus to join the battle himself, and to borrow Achilles' armour in order to frighten the enemy.

Book XII

Before Patroclus can return, Hector opens a breach in the Greek camp wall and passes through with his soldiers.

Book XIII

The armies fight on the beach while the Trojans try to reach the Greek ship. Poseidon encourages the Greeks to fight back. Hector's advance is stopped by Ajax.

Book XIV

Hera lulls Zeus to sleep so that Poseidon can continue to rouse the Greek army. Ajax gives Hector a stunning blow.

Book XV

Zeus wakes and speaks sternly to Hera, who then takes his message to the gods, ordering Poseidon to withdraw and Apollo to heal Hector. Once again, the Trojans drive the Greeks back to their ships.

Book XVI

Patroclus returns to Achilles and borrows his friend's armour. In the meantime, Hector and the Trojans force Ajax and the Greeks back again and set fire to the first Greek ship. Dressed in Achilles' armour, Patroclus repulses the Trojans. Ignoring Achilles' warning not to drive them too far back, Patroclus reaches the walls of Troy and is stunned and disarmed by Apollo himself. The Trojan Euphorbus wounds him and Hector kills him.

Book XVII

Hector removes Patroclus' armour while the Greeks manage to carry his body back to camp. The fighting continues, led by Menelaus and Ajax on the Greek side, Hector and Aeneas on that of the Trojans.

Book XVIII

Achilles hears that Patroclus has been killed. Full of rage and grief, he decides to avenge his friend in battle. Thetis promises him that Hephaestus will make him a new armour, but warns him that his own death must follow Hector's. Patroclus' body is brought into the Greek camp. Hephaestus makes Achilles new arms and a splendid new shield.

Book XIX

Ulysses instigates a reconciliation between Agamemnon and Achilles. Achilles puts on his new armour. His faithful horse Xanthus foretells his death.

Book XX

Zeus reverses his decision, and allows the gods to intervene. Achilles begins a furious attack on the Trojans. Aeneas is rescued by Poseidon, Hector by Apollo. The Trojans retreat.

Book XXI

But the retreat is hampered by the river Scamander. As Achilles fills the body with corpses, the river rises angrily against him, but Hephaestus checks the swell with his fire.

The gods begin to fight among themselves: Athena wounds Ares and Aphrodite. The gods now retreat to Olympus, but Apollo distracts Achilles, allowing the Trojans to take refuge behind the walls of their city.

Book XXII

Achilles finds Hector alone outside the walls, waiting for him. As Achilles approaches, Hector tries to run away from him. The gods intervene once more: Apollo withdraws his help and Athena induces Hector to fight and Achilles kills him. He then ties Hector's body to a chariot and drags it behind him into the camp of the Greeks. Priam and his family watch in horror.

Book XXIII

During the night, Achilles is visited by the ghost of Patroclus, who demands a swift burial. The next day, Achilles gives his friend a magnificent funeral, followed by athletic games.

Book XXIV

For eleven days, Hector's body has lain unburied. Following advice from the gods, Priam visits the Greek camp and offers Achilles a ransom for his son's body. Achilles at length accepts and, after a shared meal, Priam returns to Troy with Hector's remains. The poem ends with the funeral of Hector, while the Trojan women, led by Andromache, weep and lament their dead.

The *Odyssey*

The poem starts ten years after the fall of Troy. During the sack of the city, the disrespectful behaviour of some of the Greeks annoyed the gods, especially Athena who, having favoured the Greek side throughout the war, now has raised terrible storms to hinder their return. Though Athena is still well disposed towards Ulysses, he has not been allowed to return to Ithaca, where his faithful wife Penelope has been trying for seven years to ward off a crowd of suitors. Poseidon and the sun-god have sought to punish Ulysses (who, during his travels, has blinded Poseidon's son Polyphemus and whose companions have slaughtered the sun-god's cattle for food). He is now stranded on a faraway island, the prisoner of the nymph Calypso who has chosen him as her lover.

Book I

At a gathering of the gods, Athena asks Zeus why he has forgotten Ulysses. Zeus answers that it is Poseidon's anger that has prevented Ulysses from returning to Ithaca, but that now, since Poseidon is away visiting the Ethiopians, Ulysses can begin the journey home. Athena disguises herself as Mentes, chief of the Taphians, and visits Ulysses' son Telemachus in Ithaca, telling him to take action against his mother's suitors. She instructs him to seek news of his father from King Nestor in Pylos and from King Menelaus in Sparta.

Book II

Telemachus calls an assembly to denounce the suitors. Speeches are made but public opinion is not sufficiently roused against them. As a result, Telemachus leaves for Pylos in secret, accompanied by Athena, who disguises herself this time as Mentor, a friend of Ulysses.

Book III

King Nestor tells Telemachus about the return of other Greek heroes who fought at Troy, such as Menelaus and Agamemnon, but can give him no news of Ulysses. He orders his son Pisistratus to accompany Telemachus to Sparta.

Book IV

At the court of Menelaus, Telemachus and his companions are entertained by the king and by his wife Helen, now restored to her throne. Menelaus tells them that, during his voyage back from Troy, the Old Man of the Sea informed him that Ulysses was being held captive by the nymph Calypso. Meanwhile, back in Ithaca, the suitors and Penelope learn of Telemachus' departure. The suitors plan to ambush him on his return and kill him.

Book V

At a gathering of the gods, Hermes is sent to tell Calypso that she must release Ulysses. Calypso then, sorrowfully, provides him with wood to build a boat. Ulysses sails away but, after only seventeen days, Poseidon discovers him and wrecks the boat in a storm. Naked and wounded, Ulysses manages to reach the land of the Phaeacians.

Book VI

Ulysses is discovered by Princess Nausicaa and her maids who are washing clothes and playing ball on the beach. Ulysses begs her for hospitality; she gives him something to wear and tells him to go to her father's palace.

Book VII

Ulysses asks Nausicaa's parents, King Alcinous and Queen Arete, to help him. Without revealing his identity, he tells them only part of his story. The king suggests that he stay and marry Nausicaa.

Book VIII

King Alcinous offers his guest a lavish party. The blind bard Demodocus sings about Ulysses and his quarrel with Achilles, and later about the ploy of the wooden horse. Ulysses weeps at the memory. During an athletics exhibition, he is taunted and forced to demonstrate his strength.

Book IX

At last, Ulysses reveals his name and tells his full story: how he and his companions left Troy on twelve ships, raided the Trojan allies in Thrace, reached the land of the lotus-eaters, and finally landed on the island of the Cyclops where they were captured by the Cyclops Polyphemus and kept in his cave to be eaten one by one. Ulysses explains how he succeeded in blinding Polyphemus, how he told his victim that his name was 'Nobody' and how he escaped from the cave holding onto the belly of a ram. When, before leaving, he revealed his real name, Polyphemus swore that he would ask his father Poseidon to avenge him.

Book X

Ulysses continues his story: he and his companions reached the floating island of the god Aeolus, who gave them a bag containing all the winds except the west wind, to help them on their course. While Ulysses slept, his companions opened the bags and their ships were blown back to the god's island, who refused to assist them again. They reached the land of the giant Laestrygonians, who destroyed eleven of their ships. On the surviving ship, Ulysses and his companions arrived at the island of the enchantress Circe who turned some of the men into swine and took Ulysses as her lover. After a year on the island, Ulysses asked to be allowed to leave. Circe explained to him that he had first to travel to the Underworld and ask the ghost of the seer Tiresias for instructions.

Book XI

Ulysses tells of his visit to the Underworld: after he and his companions had conjured up the dead, the ghost of Tiresias told him that, even after reaching Ithaca, he would continue to travel. Among the ghosts, Ulysses spoke to his dead mother, to King Agamemnon, to Achilles and to Hercules.

Book XII

Ulysses concludes his story: after having lost some of the men to the monster Scylla, and after passing the whirlpool Charybdis and sailing past the luring sirens, Ulysses and his companions reached the island where the sun-god kept his cattle. Though they had been told not to touch the herd, hunger forced the men to kill and eat a few. The god complained to Zeus who, as a punishment, destroyed their ships with a thunderbolt. Ulysses was the only one to survive. On a beam from his ship, he drifted for nine days until, at last, he reached Calypso's island. The rest of the story, the king knows.

Book XIII

King Alcinous sends Ulysses off laden with rich gifts. Ulysses falls asleep and the Phaeacian sailors deposit him on the shore of Ithaca. Athena appears, disguised as a young man, and though he tries to hide his identity, she tells him that she knows who he is and that she will help him against the suitors. Athena dresses Ulysses up as an old beggar.

Book XIV

Ulysses in disguise is greeted by the swineherd Eumaeus, and makes up stories about himself to entertain his host.

Book XV

Telemachus leaves Menelaus and Helen, and returns home. He brings with him the seer Theoclymenus. Back in Ithaca,

Eumaeus tells Ulysses the story of his life. Telemachus avoids falling into the hands of the suitors.

Book XVI
Telemachus comes to the swineherd's hut and Ulysses reveals himself to him. He explains that they must be careful if they are to succeed against the suitors. The suitors sail back from their pursuit of Telemachus, and discuss what to do next.

Book XVII
Telemachus returns to the palace and speaks with Penelope. In the meantime, the goatherd Melanthius, an ally of the suitors, seeing Ulysses with Eumaeus, insults the man he takes to be a beggar. As they approach the palace, Ulysses' dog Argos recognizes his master and dies of a broken heart. Ulysses begs the suitors for food; one of their leaders, Antinous, throws a stool at him instead.

Book XVIII
Irus, a professional beggar, taunts Ulysses, who knocks him out in a boxing match. Penelope appears and receives gifts from the suitors. One of the maids mocks Ulysses who threatens to tell Telemachus of her behaviour. Another of the leading suitors, Eurymachus, insults Ulysses. When Ulysses answers back, Eurymachus throws a stool at him but hits the wine-steward instead.

Book XIX

Led by Athena, Ulysses and Telemachus remove the weapons from the hall. The maid insults Ulysses again. Ulysses tells Penelope that he once entertained her husband and that he is now not far away. The old nurse Eurycleia washes his feet and recognizes him because of a scar. Ulysses begs her not to tell. Penelope explains that, on the following night, she will allow the suitors to try shooting with Ulysses' bow.

Book XX

Ulysses lies awake impatiently. The loyal cowherd Philoetius appears. Another of the suitors, Ctesippus, flings an ox-foot at Ulysses to mock him. Seeing the suitors overcome by wild laughter, Theoclymenus tells them they are all marked for death.

Book XXI

Penelope brings out Ulysses' bow and announces the test: they are to bend the bow and shoot an arrow through several axes. All the suitors try and fail, except Antinous, who postpones his turn. Ulysses reveals himself to Eumaeus and Philoetius. As Penelope leaves the hall, he grabs hold of the bow and shoots through the axes.

Book XXII

Ulysses shoots Antinous and reveals his identity to the suitors. Helped by Telemachus, Eumaeus and Philoetius, the slaughter of the suitors begins. The treacherous Melanthius brings several coats of armour for the suitors, but is caught. Ulysses runs out of arrows, puts on an armour, and finishes off the suitors with spears. In a grisly ending, Melanthius is tortured to death and twelve of the maids are hanged.

Book XXIII

Penelope, told by Eurycleia of Ulysses' return, refuses to believe it. She tests him by telling Eurycleia to move their bed out of their room, knowing that it is too heavy for anyone to budge it. Ulysses becomes angry and, at last, Penelope recognizes her husband. The couple go to bed and tell each other their stories.

Book XXIV

Hermes leads the souls of the suitors into the Underworld where they meet with the ghosts of Agamemnon, Ajax, Patroclus and Achilles. In the meantime, Ulysses visits his father, Laertes, who has retired to a farm and, after some delay, reveals himself to him. The relatives of the suitors plan revenge, but after lending Laertes the strength to kill one of the relatives, Athena, still disguised as Mentor, imposes a lasting peace on Ithaca.

CHAPTER 2

A Life of Homer?

Homer, or another Greek of the same name...

Oscar Wilde, Oscariana, 1910 (post.)

Homer (the overwhelming presence we call 'Homer') is a shadowy figure whose first biographers (or inventors) believed had been born not long after the Sack of Troy, traditionally dated in 1184 BC.[1] Eratosthenes of Cyrene, librarian of Alexandria, who among other achievements quite accurately calculated the circumference of the earth, stated in his *Chronographiae* that Homer was a near contemporary of Hector and Achilles. For the ancient Greeks, there was no question about the reality of Homer. He was simply the greatest of poets, a man of flesh and blood who, in some remote age, had composed the works on which all Greek culture was based; not only the *Iliad* and the *Odyssey* but also a number of other hymns and epics: a poem on Amphiaraus' expedition against Thebes, the so-called *Small Iliad*, the *Phoceis*, the *Cercopes*, the *Battle of the Frogs and Mice*, most of which are now lost and many long discredited. In the fifth century BC, the historian Herodotus doubted the attribution of some of these works to Homer, but never the existence of the man himself.[2] A few decades earlier, Aeschylus, none of whose plays is (as far as we know) based on either the *Iliad* or the *Odyssey*, stated that they were all 'slices from the great banquets of Homer',[3] thereby implying that there were other Homeric poems that had served him as inspiration; if so, they have not come down to us. His fame certainly has. A celebrated allegorical marble relief, carved by Archelaos of Priene in the late second century, depicts Homer being crowned by Time and Space ('*Oikoumene*', the 'Inhabited World') and acclaimed by the Muses of History, Tragedy, Comedy and Poetry, while his 'children', the *Iliad* and the *Odyssey*, kneel by his side. Above the poet's apotheosis, in the upper section of the relief, Zeus appears in the Pantheon, honoured by the other gods. Zeus, 'Father of the Gods', is reflected by Homer, 'Father of Humankind'.[4]

'Father of Humankind' implied the role of father of human history. Each of Homer's two great poems begins after a period of ten years: the *Iliad*, a decade after the commencement of the siege of Troy; the *Odyssey*, a decade after the city's fall. For the Greeks, these ten-year periods may have possessed a magical or legendary quality, marking the dividing line between the time of the gods and the time of humans; Greek history began, in their reckoning, the year of the destruction of Troy. Earlier dates were known and recorded (an inscribed slab known as the Parian marble, now in the Ashmolean Museum in Oxford, notes what would be for us the year 1582 BC as the first date in Greek history), but the fall of the fabled city was regarded as the conventional starting-point of witnessed events. The epic of Gilgamesh and the stories of the ancient Egyptians stir in our prehistory, but Homer and his poems are the beginning of all our stories.

Among the literary works of ancient Greece, the Homeric poems may have been the first to take advantage of the possibilities offered by written language: greater length, since the composition no longer needed to be short enough to be held in the poet's memory; greater consistency, both of plot and character, than that of oral poetry; greater continuity, because the written text permitted comparison with earlier or later narrative passages; greater harmony, since the eye could assist the composing mind by enriching the purely aural rules of versification with those of the physical relationship between the words on the page. Above all, the poem set down in writing allowed the work a wider, more generous reach: he who received the poem no longer needed to share the poet's time and space. An alphabetic writing system had reached Greece not earlier than the ninth or eighth century BC; before that, there was a gap of 200 to 300 years following the collapse of Mycenaean culture and the disappearance of the writing system known as Linear B. The first examples of alphabetically written literary compositions are from the mid-eighth century: the 'Phoenician letters' as Herodotus called them.[5] In Book VI of the *Iliad*, Glaucus tells the story of how his grandfather was sent off with a message to the king of Lycia, instructing him to kill the bearer: '[He] gave him tokens,/murderous signs, scratched in a folded tablet.'[6] It is conceivable that the author of the *Iliad* had recourse to such signs and tablets, and that he composed some of his work in written form. For certain modern scholars,[7] it is possible that the original Ionian composer (or composers) of the *Iliad* and the *Odyssey* wrote out the text of the poems not on tablets but on papyrus scrolls from Egypt. The Ionians of the seventh century BC were enterprising merchants who set up shop as far as the western reaches of the Nile delta and down to the Second Cataract; the names of the most adventurous ones appear engraved on the thigh of one of the colossal statues of Abu Simbel. From Egypt, they brought home the wonderful invention of the papyrus scrolls which, according to Herodotus, they continued to call *diphterai* or 'skins' since their own books were made of vellum. If Homer did indeed write out his poems, then their length was in great measure determined by how much text one of these scrolls could contain: the division of the *Iliad* and the *Odyssey* into twenty-four cantos each is possibly the consequence of this physical limitation.[8]

Before deciding whether Homer composed orally or in writing, it was deemed useful to establish whether he indeed existed in the first place and, if so, where he was born and how his life developed. The location of his birthplace became a much-disputed question and seven cities famously claimed to be the true one: Chios, Smyrna, Colophon, Salamis, Rhodes, Argos and Athens. In time, the question acquired a variety of allegorical interpretations. In the seventeenth century, for instance, the English poet Thomas Heywood saw in the dispute over Homer's birthplace a parable of the poor artist who attains fame only after death:

> Seven cities warr'd for Homer, being dead,
> Who, living, had no roof to shroud his head.[9]

Miguel de Cervantes, instead, recognized in the uncertainty of Homer's birthplace a sign of Fame's equanimity, since it allowed more than one town to share in the poet's glory, as was the case with his Don Quixote 'whose birthplace Cide Hamete was unwilling to state exactly, because he wished that all villages and cities of La Mancha contend amongst them to adopt him and claim him as theirs, as the seven Greek cities contended for Homer'.[10]

One of the oldest traditions affirmed that Homer had come into the world on the island of Chios, and the late-seventh-century BC 'Hymn to Delian Apollo' (attributed in antiquity to Homer) presented itself as the work of 'The blind man who lives in rugged Chios'.[11] Eventually, Chios asserted its pre-eminence, and visitors today are still shown the hollow in a rock about four miles from the island's main town, where Homer and his descendants, known as the Homeridae, were supposed to have sat and sung poems to one another. Two further arguments sustain Chios's candidature. First, the language of the poems is mainly Ionic, spoken by the early Greeks who settled on the west coast of Asia Minor and the adjacent islands, including Chios; although it may have been the conventional language of epic poetry, which Homer adopted for that very reason. Second, especially in the *Iliad*, there are references to the geography of this area, such as the mountain peaks of Samothrace seen from the plain of Troy, that can only be known to someone familiar with the landscape. To compete with Chios, the island of Cos claimed to be Homer's burial-place, a claim that Cyprus in turn contested. Cyprian tradition asserted that a native of Cyprus, a woman called Themisto, was Homer's mother, and that Homer chose to die there where her bones lay buried.[12]

During the third and second centuries BC, perhaps out of a need to lend further detail to Homer's evanescent character, there appeared several spurious biographies attributed, for the sake of verisimilitude, to well-known authors. The longest was thought to be the work of Herodotus (an attribution long proved false) and gave a list of Homer's many travels as well as a detailed genealogy: a woman called Cretheis, not Themisto, is mentioned as Homer's mother.

The *Life of Homer* attributed to Herodotus was written in the fifth or fourth century BC. Its author was perhaps a native of Smyrna, since he gives Smyrna as Homer's birthplace in what is surely an attempt to glorify the city ('That Homer was Aeolian and neither Ionian nor Dorian is proved by me in what I have written,' the author says with admirable confidence). Whatever the nationality of its author, the *Life of Homer*, like Homer's poems, was composed in Ionian Greek[13] and shows a perfect familiarity with the dialect and customs of that area.

According to the story, Homer's grandparents died young

and left their young daughter Cretheis in the care of their friend Cleanax. After a few years, Cretheis fell in love and became pregnant; for fear of scandal, Cleanax dispatched her off to the newly built city of Smyrna. Homer's birth, the author explains, took place exactly 168 years after the War of Troy, by the banks of the river Meles. Cretheis named the boy Melesigenes after the river, as Milton reminds us: 'Blind *Melesigenes* thence *Homer* call'd.'[14] When the time came, Cretheis sent her son to school where, because of his wonderful abilities, he was adopted by the teacher who foretold a brilliant future for him and allowed him the run of the establishment. A visitor to Smyrna convinced Melesigenes to leave the city and take to the sea. From ship to ship, he crisscrossed Poseidon's realm and visited the places his Ulysses would visit later, including, of course, Ithaca. On board, and for the first time, he began to compose poems to the great delight of his companions. From then onwards, the people he met became characters in the works that still lay in the future: the friendly Mentor from Ithaca, the bard Phemius, Mentes, lord of the Taphians, the leathersmith Tychios who made the shield for Ajax. The lively author of the *Life of Homer* accuses others of making things up: for instance, he says that, though the inhabitants of Ithaca claim that it was among them that the poet went blind, it was in fact in Colophon that this happened – a point, he adds, on which all Colophonians agree. Apparently, the change of name from Melesigenes to Homer took place in Cimmeris, where the blind poet proposed to the local senate that, in exchange for bed and board, he would make the town famous with his songs. The senators (in the tradition of most government bodies) refused, arguing that if they set this dangerous precedent, Cimmeris would soon be overrun with blind beggars ('*homers*' in Cimmerian) seeking handouts. To shame them, the poet adopted the name Homer.

In the sixth century BC, the philosopher Heraclitus accepted as a fact that Homer had died of disappointment at not being able to solve a children's riddle about catching lice.[15] The author of the *Life of Homer* disputes this, and has Homer die on the island of Ios, not from being unable to guess a riddle but from 'a weakness of constitution'.[16] Throughout the biography, and with inspired hindsight, the author depicts scenes from the *Odyssey* in Homer's life – Homer's mother cards wool and weaves like a faithful Penelope; the goatherd Glaucos receives Homer hospitably, just as Ulysses will be welcomed home by the faithful swineherd Eumaeus – and builds up the classical picture of Homer as the blind bard, travelling from place to place, singing his marvellous poems.

From very early on, Homer was identified with one of his own characters. For his listeners and readers he was a rhapsodist, composer and performer of epic songs, a 'king of poets' who sometimes was called upon to compete with others. Heraclitus thought that, on one such occasion, Homer had competed with Hesiod in a recital contest.[17] The description of a bard's performance appears in the *Odyssey*, when, at the court of King Alcinous, the blind bard Demodocus sings three stories to the sound of a *kittara* or lyre: first, a 'song whose fame had reached the skies those days', on 'The Strife between Odysseus and Achilles';[18] later, to please the crowds, 'The Love of Ares and Aphrodite';[19] and finally, at Ulysses' leave-taking, the tale of the Wooden Horse and the Sack of Troy.[20] The first and last are wonderful moments of story within story, since Ulysses himself, unrecognized, is part of the audience and weeps at the memory of his retold past. (Another bard, the Ithacan Phemius, is described earlier on, performing for Penelope's suitors at Ulysses' court.)[21]

Of the early bards or rhapsodists we know almost nothing, except that many of them were blind, travelled from town to town, and performed in public places and in royal courts. We know (Homer himself tells us) that they were meant 'to sing the famous deeds of fighting heroes'[22] (Homer's word for 'poet' is *'aoidos'*, 'singer') and that they depended on the generosity of their listeners for bed and board. Reflecting on what he regarded as the exaggerated protraction of the final events in the *Odyssey*, T. E. Lawrence ('Lawrence of Arabia') observed that 'Perhaps the tedious delay of the climax through ten books may be a poor bard's means of prolonging his host's hospitality.'[23]

The traditional role of the poet-singer survived well into our time. In the 1930s, the American Milman Parry and his disciple, Albert Lord, discovered, through their work on the bards of the ex-Yugoslavia, a number of popular singers in Muslim Serbia (*'guzlars'*) steeped in an ancient epic tradition very similar in form and style to that of Homer, whose poems showed a high incidence of 'formulaic' language. In broad terms, Parry and Lord suggested that the *Odyssey* and the *Iliad* might have been sung in a manner resembling that of these Balkan bards whose songs were transmitted orally from generation to generation, and who, with the assistance of a string instrument, improvised on set texts and lent individual intonations and stresses to particular passages of a chosen poem.[24] That is to say, on the basis of established formulae and using stories their audiences knew well, the bards sang poems that turned out to be new on each occasion.

Three centuries after Homer, by the fourth century BC, the accoutrements of the bard had changed. Though he still remained 'the interpreter of the poet's thought',[25] he no longer used a lyre to accompany his words: now he dressed fashionably and carried an emblematic walking-stick. 'I am often envious of you rhapsodists in your profession,' says Socrates, not without a certain irony. 'Your art requires of you to go in fine array, and look as beautiful as you can, and meanwhile you must be conversant with many excellent poets, and especially with Homer, the best and most divine of all.'[26]

How much of their poems the ancient Greek bards invented and how much they performed by rote, how strictly they were supposed to adhere to an original and how the selection of their repertory was made, are questions to which we have no clear answers. Homer, alone among the bards, emerged in the popular imagination as having perfected his art to such an extent that it became the measure of all excellence, never to be surpassed. An undated ordinance attributed to Solon,

Pisistratus or Hipparchus, states that both the *Iliad* and the *Odyssey* should be recited in their entirety at the Panathenaea, a festival held in July in honour of the goddess Athena:[27] Homer was the only poet thus honoured and his biographies filled a popular desire to know more about the celebrated author.

And yet, the fact that Homer has a biography (or several) does not, of course, prove that he existed. 'Some say,' wrote Thomas De Quincey in 1841, 'there never was such a person as Homer.' 'No such person as Homer! On the contrary,' say others, 'there were scores.'[28] It may be that Homer was born not as a man but as a symbol, the name that the ancient bards gave to their own art, turning a timeless activity into a legendary primordial person, into a celebrated common ancestor of all poets, the first and the best. When Parry interviewed the Balkan *guzlars* and asked them for the names of the most admirable among them, several mentioned a master-bard called Isak or Huso, a prodigy who lived longer than any normal man and whose birthplace was disputed. His repertory was immense and it included all the best-known songs, but none of the witnesses had ever attended one of his recitals, only heard about it from other sources.[29] It is possible that Homer was born by much the same process.

What qualities might explain Homer's early celebrity? Homer's poems offered two unifying elements to the scattered Greek cities of Homer's age: common stories and common gods. 'Now in the contest between city and tribe,' noted the historian Gilbert Murray, 'the Olympian gods [Homer's pantheon] had one great advantage. They were not tribal or local, and all other gods were. They were by this time international, with no strong roots anywhere except where one of them could be identified with some local god; they were full of fame and beauty and prestige. They were ready to be made "*Poliouchoi*", "City-holders", of any particular city, still more ready to be "*Hellânioi*", patrons of all Hellas.'[30] Homer's poems became the canonical texts that offered a cosmopolitan view of the gods and heroes; they were the reference against which documentary truths and metaphysical arguments could be tested. Two schools of thought reflected this dual reading. On the one hand, historians argued that the legends were versions, more or less accurate, of factual evidence. The historian Strabo, for example, argued that the *Odyssey* was written to teach geography: 'Homer must be excused (…) if he mixed fantastic elements in his stories because they are meant to inform and instruct.'[31] On the other hand, the philosophers contended that the legends were allegories which concealed a sort of poetic proof. The Stoics in particular used Homer to illustrate and validate their discourse; Aristotle, however, refused to allegorize the mythical stories.[32]

'For the philosopher,' concludes the historian Paul Veyne, 'myth was an allegory of philosophical truths. For the historians, it was a minor deformation of historical truths.'[33] For both, Homer was the unavoidable reference. These two views of Homer echoed far into the future, both in the explorations and discoveries of the numerous schools of archaeologists who, following the early Greek historians, believed that the stories were true and that Homer described the events and their setting with illuminating accuracy, and in the countless allegorical readings that surface in every age, from the versions taught in Roman schools to present-day mirrorings of the *Iliad* and the *Odyssey*.

By the sixth century BC, Homer had become not only the greatest of poets but the master whose view informed the entire Greek conception of the world, both of mortals and of gods, or of mortals who try to be heroes among gods who don't shine for their exemplary conduct. 'Homer and Hesiod,' wrote the philosopher Xenophanes, 'have ascribed to the gods all things that are a shame and a disgrace among mortals, stealing and adultery and cheating on one another.'[34] In this uncertain universe, as Homer made clear, human beings had to depend on their own resources and wit, not on the unreliable divine behaviour. As a cautionary tale, few episodes are more atrocious than the gods' dealings with the Trojan Hector in the *Iliad*. At first, Hector is helped by Zeus and by Apollo; then, at a certain arbitrary point, they abandon him to his own luck. Worse still, the goddess Athena deceives him by passing herself off as one of Hector's own brothers, and encourages him to fight Achilles who she knows will certainly kill him.[35] Homer's gods can be vicious and deceitful.

However, in certain cases (though not by any means in all), the behaviour of Homer's mortal heroes was something to which a just man might aspire. A professional ethos was developed among the Greek warrior class, recognizing that cool-headed tactics and loyal comradeship made for better fighters, and so it became important to study in Homer the errors of Agamemnon, the devotion of Achilles to Patroclus, the resolution of Hector, the mulled-over experience of Nestor, the wily strategies of Ulysses. In this context, a formal education was deemed impossible without reference to Homer's work. The young Alcibiades, during a visit to a grammar-school *c.* 430 BC, asked the teacher for one of Homer's books and, being told that there was none, gave the poor man a blow with his fist.[36] A school without Homer was not a school: worse, it was a learning place without the means of learning excellence.

CHAPTER 3

Among the Philosophers

> [Homer's work] forms a world in itself... which one can
> study to the end of time and still feel that one is inside
> an epitome of the entire literary cosmos.
>
> Northrop Frye, *The Secular Scripture and Other Writings*, 1975

Though Homer might have been 'best and most divine' for Socrates (or rather for Plato, who made Socrates pronounce this encomium), he also presented a philosophical dilemma. In the *Republic*, Plato draws an analogy between human beings and the societies they build, society seen as a reflection of the human soul, divided into the governing, the military and the merchant classes, which loosely correspond to human intelligence, courage and appetite (though this is a gross simplification of Plato's complex and open view.)[1] From this ideal state, the artisans of the false must be banned: that is to say, those who make images of images have no place in a well-regulated world, since they produce nothing that is true. An artist will, for example, create a couch in a picture or in a poem, inspired by the couch a cabinet-maker makes, in turn inspired by the primordial idea of a couch created by the godhead. Even Homer (and here begins Plato's battle with the poet he most admires) cannot be allowed in the ideal republic because, not only does he put forward images that are untrue, he presents men and women with whose faults we sympathize, gods and goddesses whom we must judge as fallible. Literature, Plato says (and for Plato, Homer is its greatest literary craftsman), feeds that part in our soul that relishes 'contemplating the woes of others', praising and pitying someone who, though 'claiming to be a good man, abandons himself to excess in his grief'. This 'is the element in us that the poets satisfy and delight' and, to avoid it, we should 'disdain the poem altogether'; otherwise, 'after feeding fat the emotion of pity there, it is not easy to restrain it in our own suffering.'[2] ('That's the price we have to pay for stability,' says the Platonist Controller in Aldous Huxley's 1933 utopia, *Brave New World*. 'You've got to choose between happiness and what people used to call high art. We've sacrificed high art.')[3] Because, as Socrates tells his listeners, 'high art' especially corrupts us, whether we ourselves are good or bad, by pretending to offer spiritual enlightenment and a vicarious experience of the world, since in doing so it prevents us from seeking true self-knowledge and self-criticism. We think we know who we are by believing that we see our reflection in the characters of Achilles, Ulysses, Hecuba, Penelope. We stop defending Troy: we know that the walls will crumble. We stop searching for Ithaca: we know that, whatever we do, we will reach home at last.

According to Socrates, Homer was not an educator; he did

not know how to make men better and he possessed no real knowledge, only the art of imitation, which is why he was neglected by his contemporaries. Had Homer and the other great poets been able 'to help men achieve excellence', he asks, would his fellow men 'have suffered him and Hesiod to roam about rhapsodizing and would they not have clung to them far rather than to their gold, and constrained them to dwell with them in their homes, or failing to persuade them, would themselves have escorted them wheresoever they went until they should have sufficiently imbibed their culture?' Plato must have conceived these words tongue firmly planted in his cheek, thinking of the fate of poor Socrates, the greatest educator of all, condemned to death by the society he strove to make better. Obviously Plato knew (all artists know) that society, whatever pittance it may accord to grants, prizes and memorials, always fails to honour and reward adequately those who, through craftsmanship and imagination, strive to make us better, and that its citizens, wherever and whenever, will always cling to their gold rather than to their goldsmith. As in all his dialogues, Plato presents Socrates as pursuing an argument to whatever corner it might lead, making no absolute claims and reaching no unimpeachable conclusions. 'I cannot agree with you,' says Hippias to Socrates in another of the dialogues. Socrates answers: 'Nor can I agree with myself, Hippias, and yet that seems to be the conclusion which, as far as we can see at present, must follow from our argument.'[4] There speaks a man not afraid of allowing his thoughts absolute freedom to explore.

Whether convincing or not, Plato's argument against Homer has haunted our societies since he first put it forward. It is the great paradox: we build societies in order to become happier and wiser; art, even the greatest art, grants us only the vicarious impression of both. Homer, who first and best created for us the spectacle of human shadows in constant battle, longing, suffering and finally dying, is of all the most guilty, and must be held responsible for his progeny. When the Curate and the Barber decide to burn Don Quixote's library because, they believe, the books are responsible for the knight's madness, they come upon the *Amadís de Gaula*, the earliest of all novels of chivalry printed in Spain. 'As the dogmatizer of such an evil sect,' the Curate thunders, 'we must, without any excuse, condemn it to the flames.' But, counters the Barber, 'it is also the best of all the books written in this genre and thus, as unique of its kind, it must be pardoned.'⁵ The paradox is apparent in Plato: for all of art's supposedly noxious influence, Homer retains pride of place in Plato's library, surfacing at every occasion to illuminate a passage or provide a poignant reference: there are 331 references to Homer and his works in Plato's *Dialogues*. 'Do you yourself not feel [poetry's] magic and especially when Homer is her interpreter?' asks one of those who have listened to Socrates' arguments. 'Greatly,' Socrates answers. And at the end of Book IX, when one of the participants observes that such an ideal state as the Republic can be found in no place on earth, Plato lends Socrates an implicit reference to Homer that, by its very use, undermines the severity of the explicit ban. 'It makes no difference whether it exists or ever will come into being,' says Socrates. That is to say, it does not matter whether the Republic is built of stones and mortar or whether it remains an ideal, 'a pattern of it laid up in heaven for him who wishes to contemplate it and so beholding to constitute himself its citizen.' What matters to Plato is the truth of the model, just as in the *Iliad*, for example, what matters is not the tragic outcome itself, but the 'model' upon which the battle has been fought, as to us, its readers, the 'models' of life set out in the two poems. These ideas, via Plato, will be the Homeric inheritance of the justice-seeking Don Quixote, of Dostoevsky's idiot prince, even of Kafka's Josef K and of Melville's Ahab, each searching for the larger shape of his struggles and journeys within the little patch of universe he has been allotted. This then is Plato's (perhaps reluctant) reading of Homer: that our life must be lived to the best of our ethical abilities.

With Aristotle, the figure of the anecdotal man – the old, blind, wandering bard – faded into that of the literate, inspired poet. Homer came to mean his works, whether written by the poet himself or set down for posterity by others. For Aristotle too, Homer was the ultimate poetic reference, and not as an instance of the dangerous dream-life but as a craftsman's model, the example to be followed by those who aspired to high art, in tragedy as well as comedy. 'As in the serious style, Homer is pre-eminent among poets, for he alone combined dramatic form with excellence of imitation, so he too laid down the main lines of comedy, by dramatizing the ludicrous instead of writing personal satire.'[6] For Aristotle, Homer was not the ancient singer but the author of established texts, a master fully in control of his creation, and both the *Iliad* and the *Odyssey* (as well as a now lost mock-heroic poem called *Margites*) were exemplary solid works not subject to the fallible memory or the imperfect technique of the bards charged with performing them.

Though implicit references to Homer's books go back to the mid-seventh century BC, in the works of poets such as Alcman of Sardinia, Archilochus of Paros and Tyrtaeus of Attica, the earliest acknowledged readings date from two centuries after his books were supposedly composed. According to Cicero, Homer's books were given their definitive written form in Athens under the tyrant Pisistratus, in the sixth century BC.[7] The first known commentary on Homer (arguing that his books were allegorical, not historical accounts) is by a contemporary of Pisistratus, Theagenes of Rhegium, of whom we know nothing except that he wrote a priggish poem advising a youth called Cyrnus to stick with the aristocratic party and avoid the nasty democrats. In the fourth century BC, the Attic orator Lycurgus, says Milton in the *Areopagitica*, 'was so addicted to elegant learning as to have been the first that brought out of Ionia the scattered works of Homer',[8] presumably edited for the common reader. Four centuries later, commentaries on Homer were already so abundant and detailed, that sixty-two lines from the *Iliad* (the famous 'Catalogue of Ships') provided a certain scholar, Demetrius of Scepsis, with material for thirty volumes, now lost.[9]

Not only scholars knew their Homer. Greek colonists exported his books to their many outposts. In Italy, about the time of the foundation of Rome in the eighth century BC, Homer was deemed an essential part of a cultured person's world. The tomb of a twelve-year-old boy discovered in the Bay of Naples held, among various objects his parents had placed there to console the child in the afterlife, a cup inscribed with three lines of Greek. The first line is difficult to decipher, but the second and third read:

> I am the cup of Nestor, a joy to drink from,
> but anyone drinking from this cup will be struck at once
>   with desire for lovely-crowned Aphrodite.[10]

The reference is to the *Iliad*: Achilles, seeing that the Trojans have pushed the Greek army back to their camp, sends his friend Patroclus to find out what is happening. Old King Nestor receives him in his tent where drink and food has been set out, notably a splendid cup,

> studded with golden nails, fitted with handles,
> four all told and two doves perched on each,
> heads bending to drink and made of solid gold
> and twin supports ran down to form the base.
> An average man would strain to lift it off the table
> when it was full, but Nestor, old as he was,
> could hoist it up with ease.[11]

The cup placed in the tomb might have served at drinking parties where participants would demonstrate their 'heroic strength' by lifting it and perhaps quoting the appropriate Homeric lines. A moving comparison is implied between old Nestor, still able to lift the cup, and the boy who died before being able to demonstrate his manly strength.

CHAPTER 4

Virgil

> Virgil, it appears, was the first – in literature, at least –
> to apply the linear principle: his hero never returns; he
> always departs... Had I been writing *The Divine Comedy*,
> I would have placed this Roman in Paradise: for
> outstanding services to the linear principle, into its
> logical conclusion.
>
> Joseph Brodsky, 'Flight From Byzantium', 1985

By the third and second centuries BC, Homer's poems were being studied at the Library of Alexandria by remarkable scholars such as Zenodotus of Ephesus, Aristophanes of Byzantium and, perhaps the most erudite of all, the grammarian Aristarchus of Samothrace. The editing method they followed, by and large, was this: first, the authorship of a text was historically verified; the text was then meticulously edited and divided into books or chapters; finally, commentaries, exegeses and scholia were gathered and annotated to facilitate its interpretation. Zenodotus began work on Homer's poems by collating various copies of a presumed lost original. He deleted obviously 'foreign' elements, marked questionable verses with a horizontal stroke to the left of a particular line, and placed an asterisk next to those passages about which there might be some doubt, but which, in his learned opinion, had indeed been composed by Homer.[1] Aristarchus revised Zenodotus' work and added his own learned commentaries. For philological reasons, Aristarchus suggested that certain sections of the poems were later additions: among others, the story of the nocturnal expedition during which the Trojan spy Dolon is captured in the *Iliad*, Book X, and the 120-odd verses at the end of Book XXIII of the *Odyssey*, in which Ulysses and Penelope, lying in bed, tell each other their adventures. Contemporary research has tended to agree with him.[2] Aristarchus' painstaking erudition became legendary, so that, in his wake, any exacting critic became known as an *aristarchus*. Thanks to the efforts of all these scholars, the texts of Homer's poems were largely stabilized; later work done in Byzantium, during the early Middle Ages, completed the work of the Alexandrians.

Available now in authoritative editions, Homer became the inspiration for the first Greek novelists who, from the first century BC to the fifth century AD, produced a series of popular love stories (*'pathos erotikon'*) for which they adopted not only Homer's subjects and themes, but especially his story-telling techniques and stylistic choices. Chariton, Xenophon, Longus (author of the famous pastoral story *Daphnis and Chloë*) and Heliodorus made use of Homeric narrative devices such as the first-person account that Ulysses delivers at the Phaeacian court in Books IX to XII of the *Odyssey*, the shifting points of view from the particular to the general and vice versa in the *Iliad* and the beginning *in medias res*, in the middle of the story.[3] Thanks to them, these complex ways of creating character and plot, and of granting the reader emotion and conviction, became established as the primordial elements of fiction-telling.

In Rome, the *Iliad* and *Odyssey* were thought of as models to be copied or translated, to be then interpreted as allegories or taught as moral stories. 'What happened' became both history and fiction, fact and symbol. In the third century BC, Livius Andronicus, a Greek captive from Tarentum, produced a version of the *Odyssey* in Latin which Horace was to judge, 250 years later, as archaic, harsh and vulgar.[4] Nevertheless, the book became greatly successful and was used as a school text for the next three centuries. As if Greek history had been not only translated but transmigrated into the history of Rome, Roman children were introduced to Homer at the very start of their schooling. Commenting on the difficulty first-year law students experienced at the Roman court, Pliny the Younger wrote that 'boys begin their career at the bar with Chancery cases just as they start with Homer in school: in both places they place the hardest first.'[5] Children were taught that Ulysses ignored the Sirens in the same way the soul should ignore the senses (the image was so popular that it appeared on tombstones),[6] and that Achilles' anger showed how bad temper always turns against us. Horace, who learned Homer by heart at school, under his teacher's cane,[7] listed in one of his *Epistles* a number of these moral lessons and concluded, perhaps tongue-in-cheek, that through such stories 'The Greeks must expiate their rulers' folly'.[8]

Though Livius Andronicus introduced Homer to the Latin reader, it was Virgil who made Homer a Latin author by adoption. Virgil's *Aeneid*, perhaps the greatest Roman literary achievement, is explicitly modelled on Homer's poems, and if Virgil owes an immense debt to Homer, the reverse is also true, because after Virgil, Homer acquired a new identity, that of Rome's earliest myth-maker. During the first Roman centuries, three legendary figures competed for the position of founder of the city: Romulus who, with his twin brother Remus, was supposed to have been suckled by a she-wolf, Ulysses the traveller, and Aeneas, the survivor of Troy. It was Marcus Terentius Varro, 'the most learned of Romans',[9] according to the rhetorician Quintilian, who, in the first century BC, established Aeneas as the winner. Following the genealogy granted him by Homer ('Aeneas whom the radiant Aphrodite bore Anchises/down the folds of Ida, a goddess bedded with a man')[10] Varro established a detailed list of the ports of call on Aeneas's route from Troy (Ilion) to Italy and confirmed the claim of Julius Caesar that his family, the *gens Iulia*, were descended from the goddess of love via the Trojan refugee.[11] But it was Virgil who transformed the legend into something resembling history, lending the defeated Trojans a posthumous victory over their enemy. Thanks to Virgil, the works of Homer, which had seemed until that point to be merely stories (albeit masterly) of battling and travel, were read after Virgil as inspired premonitions of the world to come: first of Rome and its imperial power, and later of the advent of Christianity and beyond.

Virgil (Publius Virgilius Maro) was born in the Etruscan town of Andes, near Mantua, on 15 October 70 BC: his family name was probably Etruscan; his first name, a conventional Roman tag. Though his earliest biographies, written long after his death, made him out to be the son of a poor itinerant potter who married the daughter of one of his employers, Virgil was in fact a Roman citizen by birth, whose family held official posts of some importance in the Roman administration. During all of his childhood and youth, of which we know very little, Italy was ravaged by civil war, first in the struggles for power between Marius and Sula, then between Julius Caesar and Pompey. Only in the year 31 BC, did the victory of Augustus at Actium put an end to the upheavals. Perhaps due to poor health, Virgil never held an administrative or military position, nor did he aspire to become a lawyer or a senator. He never married.

At the age of seventeen, Virgil left the countryside for Rome. An early short poem, in an anthology which may not be entirely by his hand, reveals Virgil's intentions of abandoning youthful scribbles and dedicating himself to serious studies instead:

> Leave me Muses, you too, goodbye to you,
> Sweet Muses, because I will confess the truth,
> Sweet you have been, and yet you could sometimes
> Revisit my papers: decently: not often.[12]

In Rome, the young Octavius (who was to become the emperor Augustus) may have been Virgil's patron; in that case, it was probably for him that Virgil composed his *Eclogues* in the manner of the Greek poet Theocritus. The *Eclogues* made him famous. He was recognized and hailed in the streets, a painful experience for a shy man, who in such cases would seek refuge in the nearest house. Life in Rome became too exhausting and Virgil retired to Naples, where he spent most of his remaining years. In 19 BC, he set off with Augustus on a trip to Greece, but he soon became seriously ill and returned to die in Brindisi.

Virgil wrote slowly: the *Eclogues* took him three or four years; the *Georgics*, dedicated to Augustus' chief minister, the rich Maecenas, seven or eight. We know that Augustus read the *Georgics* around 29 BC, when Virgil was just over forty, and, whether through imperial encouragement or through a private sense of having acquired the necessary skills, Virgil now felt ready to undertake a more ambitious project. At about this time, he started work on a new poem which, like his two previous books, would carry a Greek name: the *Aeneid*.

At home, Virgil must have learned some Greek together with his Latin, since there were many Greek emigrés in Tuscany, but it was the poet Parthenius of Nicaea, author of a catalogue of erotic myths, who is said to have taught him in depth the language of Homer.[13] The Roman province of Greece, known as Achaea (a word that echoes Homer's designation), was for the Romans both a subservient colony and the ancient source of their own culture, with all the hierarchical implications of this dual identity. For the Romans of Virgil's time, Greece was attractive and exotic: the cultured Romans who travelled there visited the temples and palaces, studied the religious mysteries, brought back art objects to decorate their own households, and imitated the 'Greek manner' by growing beards and taking boyfriends. In all this, however, they ostentatiously remained the masters.[14] In the *Aeneid*, Aeneas's father warns his son never to forget that, however magnificent the art and culture of other civilizations (namely that of Greece), Romans are, and will remain, the rulers. Many an imperialistic credo is built on a similar distinction and has for today's readers a familiar ring:

> Let others fashion from bronze more lifelike, breathing images –
> For so they shall – and evoke living faces from marble;
> Others excel as orators, others track with their instruments
> The planets circling in heaven and predict when stars will appear.
> But, Romans, never forget that government is your medium!
> Be this your art: – to practise men in the habit of peace,
> Generosity to the conquered, and firmness against aggressors.[15]

Hearing that Virgil was hard at work, Augustus was eager to know exactly what the poem was about. He may have suggested to his favourite poet that an epic on the origins of Rome, glorifying of course his own rule, might be welcome.

We know that Augustus wrote to Virgil from Spain, asking to see even a fragment. Virgil declined. Years later, Virgil agreed to read out loud to the Emperor three books of the first half of the poem: the fall of Troy, the death of Dido, and Aeneas's visit to the Underworld. We know (because Virgil's secretary Eros tells us) that he wrote a page in the morning and then corrected it throughout the day until little was left of the original lines. He compared this method to a bear giving birth to her cubs and then licking them into shape. It isn't obvious that Augustus understood him: 'How could you ask that Caesar's pride admit the concept of metaphor, since Caesar never accepted the humility of perception?' asked Hermann Broch in his novel *The Death of Virgil*.[16]

Virgil was a keen, scholarly reader of Homer, not only of the poems but also of the ancient commentaries. Homer had told, first, of the siege of Troy, distilling the agonies of a ten-year-long war into forty days of fighting; and second, the return of one of the warriors, clever Ulysses, through a sea of troubles to his home in Ithaca. Virgil, accordingly, structured his poem in two parts: the first (Aeneas's flight and travels) based on the *Odyssey*; the second (his battles leading up to the foundation of Rome) on the *Iliad*. Legend has it that, before he died, Virgil asked his friends to burn the manuscript. Whether he was dissuaded or whether his friends chose to disobey, the book was soon after edited and widely distributed. Certain readers have felt that the second half of the *Aeneid* has something a little disappointing about it, less because Virgil did not have the time to polish it than, as Peter

Levi has perceptively pointed out, because Virgil 'did not understand the fundamental principle in Homer's world, that poetry belongs to the defeated and the dead'. In Virgil's poem, Aeneas the hero was necessarily a victor, founder of the dynasty whose present inheritor was Augustus himself. There are no true victors in Homer.

For a number of reasons, Aeneas was the obvious Homeric hero to choose as the protagonist of a Roman epic, someone who intuits that, as Virgil has it, 'An age shall come, as the years glide by,/When the children of Troy shall enslave the children of Agamemnon.'[17] Aeneas was the inheritor of the glory of Troy, a fate attributed to him implicitly in the *Iliad* where Achilles taunts 'the great-hearted fighter' and asks him whether his courage will really allow him to challenge Achilles 'In hopes of ruling your stallion-breaking friends/ and filling Priam's throne?'[18] Aeneas was a well-known hero: his escape from Troy, bearing his father Anchises on his back and leading away his infant son, was depicted in many frescoes, painted vases and mosaics, and was therefore constantly present in the popular imagination. Early writers[19] had continued his adventures all the way from Troy to the shores of Italy, and had suggested that he had conveniently settled in the neighbourhood of what was to become Rome. Already in the third century BC, the Latin poet Naevius had referred to Aeneas as 'the father of the Roman people'[20] and two centuries later, Lucretius began his lengthy poem *On the Nature of Things* by invoking the 'Mother of the Aeneadae, darling of men and gods, increase-giving Venus'.[21]

Homer's heroes have a pleasing complexity, a random-
ness of character that troubles the reader with endlessly rich
interpretations. Outside allegorical readings, the psychology
of Achilles, for instance, or of Ulysses, is rewardingly bewildering. Achilles – sulking, egotistical, brave, faithful in his
loves, lacking compassion towards his victims but capable of
magnanimity, 'a kill-ease' to use Lewis Carroll's pun[22] – has a
kaleidoscope personality that never quite resolves itself, not
even at the end of the book. Even his essential anger is mul-
tifaceted, impossible to define exactly. His anger at Agamemnon's military incompetence is not the same as his anger
at Agamemnon's insulting treatment, which is again quite
unlike his feelings after the death of Patroclus. 'Wrath',
'anger', even 'mania' have been chosen to define the passion
that triggers the narrative, each word qualified in turn to give
it a particular tone.

Different translators have rendered the first line of the
Iliad into English in different ways. In 1616, George
Chapman, whose translations so impressed John Keats, conceived it as: 'Achilles' baneful wrath resound, O Goddess,
that impos'd/Infinite sorrows on the Greeks.'[23] Thomas
Tickell, in 1715, suggested '*Achilles*' fatal Wrath, whence
Discord rose/That brought the Sons of *Greece* unnumber'd
Woes,/O Goddess sing.'[24] Alexander Pope published in
1715–20 a controversial *Iliad* that began like this: 'Achilles'
wrath, to Greece the direful spring/Of woes unnumber'd,
heavenly goddess, sing!'[25] In 1880, Henry Dunbar translated
it as: 'The baneful wrath of Peleus' son, Achilles, goddess

sing.'[26] Among the twentieth-century translations, A. T. Murray gave the line as 'The wrath sing, goddess, of Peleus' son Achilles.'[27] W. H. D. Rowse summed it up as 'An angry man – there is my story: the bitter rancour of Achilles, prince of the house of Peleus.'[28] H. D. F. Kitto's version was: 'Divine Muse, sing of the ruinous wrath of Achilles, Peleus' son.'[29] Richard Lattimore's read: 'Sing, goddess, the anger of Peleus' son Achilleus/and its devastation.'[30] Robert Lowell came up with: 'Sing for me, Muse, the mania of Achilles/ that cast a thousand sorrows on the Greeks.'[31] Robert Fagles, whose translations are used in this book, rendered it as 'Rage – Goddess, sing the rage of Peleus' son Achilles.'

A similar sampling of tempers (and equal problems of range) arise in every language into which Homer has been translated. Juan de Mena, in 1519, translating from a Latin version, was ploddingly explicit: *'Divinal musa, canta conmigo, Omero, la ira del sobervio hijo de Peleo – es dezir Archiles'*[32] ('Divine muse, sing with me, Homer, the ire of the haughty son of Peleus, that is to say, Achilles'). In 1793, the German Johann Heinrich Voss began his *Ilias* with the simplest rendition: *'Singe den Zorn, o Göttin, des Peleiaden Achilleus'*[33] ('Sing the wrath, O Goddess, of the Peleian Achilles'). Almost a hundred years later, Charles-Marie Leconte de Lisle attempted *le mot juste: 'Chante, Déesse, du Pèléide Akhilleus la colère désastreuse'*[34] ('Sing, Goddess, of the Peleian Akhilleus the disastrous wrath'). The twentieth-century Brazilian poet Haroldo do Campos was concise: *'A ira, Deusa, celebra do Peleio Aquiles'*[35] ('The anger, Goddess, celebrate, of Peleian

Achilles'). 'To call Achilles' anger "terrible",' wrote the nine-teenth-century scholar Juan Valera, commenting on a later Spanish version that spoke of 'terrible wrath', 'is to translate badly. [The word Homer uses] comes from the Greek verb "to lose, to destroy" and means "fatal, pernicious, unfortunate, harmful", all of which are not terrible but something more than terrible. There are terrible things in the world that lead to no harm whatsoever, but Achilles' anger was not one of them. (...) The sound Apollo's arrow makes when shot is terrible, the eyes of Minerva shine in a terrible manner, a ter-rible fire burns over the head of magnanimous Achilles. Finally Priam, when Helen comes to see him, seems in her eyes venerable and terrible, and yet Priam intends no harm to Helen, nor does he hurt her in any way; rather he treats her with fatherly kindness, even though he fills her with terror and shame. Who has been harmful is Helen, harmful to Priam, without for that reason having been terrible.'[36]

Why is anger, Achilles' anger, the subject of the *Iliad*? Because, in Homer's telling, it is the driving force of the war, without which there would be no story. And yet, Achilles' anger is neither constant nor clear. It covers a vast range of angers, and Homer carefully describes the circumstances under which they arise – fury at Agamemnon's insult, pique at the suggestion of giving up Briseis, spite when begged to join his comrades, sullenness when Patroclus asks to borrow his armour, frenzy at Patroclus' killing, rage against the assassin Hector. Even when dead, Achilles is not rid of his anger. In the Underworld, when Ulysses visits him, he bridles at the suggestion that death might be a good place.[37] The historian Nancy Sherman, discussing the make-up of the military mind, argues that, though anger is as much a part of war as weapons and armour, it is of military value only when held in control. The Stoics, though they believed that anger, like all emotions, is a voluntary state, denied that it is an acceptable warrior-like quality, since it distorts our view of the world. Sherman notes that, to temper the feeling of anger, the Stoics proposed an *apatheia*, 'a freedom from passions in which there is no frenzy or rage, no annoyance or bitterness, no moral outrage.'[38] In the nineteenth century, Stendhal associated this steadfast state with the heroes of Greece and Rome. 'I've forgotten to be angry!' says Fabrice in *The Charterhouse of Parma*. 'Am I perhaps one of those great courageous beings of which antiquity has given the world a few examples? Am I a hero without knowing it?'[39] If Fabrice is an ancient hero, he is certainly not a Homeric one. There is no *apatheia* among Homer's heroic characters.

In Virgil, this variety of emotional traits is much simplified. Not that the psychology of the characters is less believable; it is only less ambiguous, with the exception perhaps of Queen Dido who casts her abused, mournful shadow well into our time. Aeneas, however, has appeared to some readers as too single-minded, too word-perfect. 'We will always admire more the Achilles described by Homer, with all his defects, than the perfect hero incarnated by the Aeneas of Virgil, because of the illusion and persuasion that render the former more believable,' observed the nineteenth-century poet Giacomo Leopardi,[40] careful reader of both.

In the *Iliad* and the *Odyssey*, the heroes are in the hands of gods who, if not mad, at least behave in an erratic manner. In the *Aeneid*, because their designs, however whimsical, have already been laid out by Homer, the gods seem to have a clearer purpose, so that the misfortunes that befall Aeneas or the difficult decisions he must make (to leave Dido, for example) acquire a specific meaning in the fateful story. In Homer, the funeral of Hector and the arrival in Ithaca are powerful moments in the dramas, and the last ones, but they are not conclusions. The implicitly announced foundation of Rome is not only the conclusion of the *Aeneid*; it is its *raison d'être*. 'How shall it end now?' asks Jupiter to Juno in the final lines. And then, following Juno's answer, the god commands:

> 'All will be Latins, speaking
> One tongue. From this blend of Italian and Trojan blood shall arise
> A people surpassing all men, nay even the gods, in godliness.'[41]

Augustus could not have wished for a better ending.

CHAPTER 5

Christian Homer

I believe in Michael Angelo, Velasquez, and Rembrandt;
in the might of design, the mystery of colour, the
redemption of all things by Beauty everlasting, and the
message of Art that has made these hands blessed.

George Bernard Shaw, *The Doctor's Dilemma*, 1906

After Virgil, and from the very first centuries of the Christian
era, the Church fathers attempted, not so much to reconcile
Homer with the godliness of the authority of the *vera religio*,
but to find in the tenets of that religion gaps into which
Homer might fit. God had created the book of the world in
which we are all written, and His Son had corrected in his
blood our errors; now the new stories were forced to share
the shelf which until then had been allotted exclusively to
Homer.

For the great scholars and readers of the early Church, the
apparent conflict between the old pagan literature and the
dogma of the new faith presented a difficult intellectual problem. One of the most learned of these Christian scholars, St
Jerome, attempted throughout his long life to reconcile the

two. Jerome realized that he could never honestly disclaim Homer as his own beginning, nor could he ignore the intellectual and aesthetic pleasure Homer's books had given him. Instead, he could create a hierarchy, a *gradus ad Parnassum* of which Homer and the ancients were the necessary grounding, and the Bible the highest peak.

Jerome was born in Dalmatia around 342. Though his parents were Christian, he wasn't baptized until his eighteenth birthday. He studied Latin in Rome under the guidance of the celebrated scholar Aelius Donatus, author of the most popular of medieval grammar books, the *Ars grammatica*. Thanks to Donatus, Jerome became thoroughly familiar with the great names of antiquity, names which he later quoted copiously in his writings. In his thirties, he travelled to Syria where he learned Hebrew from a distinguished rabbi and lived among the hermits in the deserts near Antioch. He was ordained priest but did not exercise his office; instead, he became secretary to Pope Damasus I who ordered him to revise the Latin translation of the New Testament, from the Hebrew and Greek.[1] Jerome did more than revise it: he rewrote most of it, as well as translating afresh a large part of the Old Testament. The colossal achievement, the Latin Bible known as the Vulgate, ensured his intellectual fame, and became the standard version of Scripture for the next fifteen centuries. The long hours he toiled on this commission, urged on by his impatient patron, the meticulous research he undertook to overcome the obstacles presented by the original, and the pittance he received for all his work, inspired the Catholic Church to name him the patron saint of translators.

In an autobiographical letter to a friend, Jerome recounts a dream which soon became famous. To follow his religious vocation and in compliance with the precepts of the Church, Jerome had cut himself off from his family and renounced the luxuries (especially 'dainty food') to which he was accustomed. What he could not bring himself to do was to abandon the library that, 'with great care and toil', he had put together in Rome; racked by guilt, he would mortify himself and fast but 'only that I might afterwards read Cicero'. A short time later, Jerome fell deathly ill. Fever caused him to dream and he dreamt that his soul was suddenly caught and hauled before God's judgement-seat. A voice asked him who he was, and he replied: 'I am a Christian.' 'Thou liest,' said the voice, 'thou art a follower of Cicero, not of Christ. "For where your treasure is, there will your heart be also".'² Overcome with dread, Jerome promised God that 'if ever again I possess worldly books, or if ever again I read such, I have denied thee'. But the great oath was too onerous and impossible to keep: every reader's memory furnishes him with remembered books, whether he desires it or not, and even if Jerome had firmly resolved never to read worldly books again, the ones read in his youth would open their pages for him, calling up line after line in front of his mind's eye, and he would have broken his oath through powers beyond him. Jerome then changed his promise to one that seemed more reasonable: 'to read the books of God with a zeal greater than

I had previously given to the books of men'.[3] Jerome promised God to make use of the ancient authors in order to better read His word.

In his childhood, Jerome had befriended a boy called Rufinus who, in later years, became his strongest intellectual opponent. Rufinus, intent on persecuting his one-time friend, prompted a Roman orator called Magnus, to raise once more the question of pagan versus Christian culture, and ask Jerome why he so often made use of the writings of the ancients in his ecclesiastical work, 'contaminating the sacred with the profane'. Jerome answered with an impassioned defence of the classics, giving arguments that were used for centuries afterwards. Jerome suggested that every reader, by culling and interpreting, transforms an old text into a new one, one capable of shedding light upon problems ignored by the original author. 'My efforts,' wrote Jerome of his readings, 'promote the advantage of Christ's family, my so-called defilement with an alien increases the number of my fellow servants.'[4] Above all, were not the words of Christ to be treated with the uttermost respect, and therefore translated into the best and purest words available? And was not the best and purest tongue that of the old masters, whose devices and styles needed therefore to be studied? Erasmus, who annotated Jerome's letters, pointedly asked: 'Is the profession of Christ at odds with eloquence? If Cicero speaks eloquently about his gods, what prevents a Christian from also speaking eloquently about holiness and true religion?'[5]

A contemporary of St Jerome, St Augustine, was also, in

his youth, a great reader of the classics, but when the problem of conflicting cultures presented itself to him, his answer was not that of Jerome's. Augustine was born in Thagaste, in what is now Algeria, in 354. His mother was a Christian, and though she tried to teach her son the faith of her Church, he was clearly more drawn to the old stories of Greece and Rome – more Rome than Greece since, as he tells us, Greek held little charm for him as a child, and even as an adult he was not able to understand the language fully.[6] Perhaps because he could not read it properly, he disliked Greek literature. 'Homer,' he says, 'as well as Virgil, was a skilful spinner of yarns and he is most delightfully imaginative. Nevertheless, I found him little to my taste. I suppose,' he adds apologetically, 'Greek boys think the same about Virgil when they are forced to study him as I was forced to study Homer.'[7]

In Carthage, where he was sent to complete his education, Augustine set up house with a young woman with whom he had a son; following his parents' orders, he left her to marry another woman whom his mother had picked for him, but the second marriage did not take place. Augustine became a teacher, worked in Rome and then in Milan, where he was instructed by the aged Ambrose, an old friend of his mother's. In his youth, Augustine had been seduced by the Manichaeans, whose doctrine proclaimed that the universe was the fruit of two independent principles, Good and Evil, permanently in conflict. Now, under the influence of Ambrose and of the writings of Plotinus and the Neoplatonists, he abjured the Manichaeans (he was to become one of their fiercest enemies), accepted the religion of his mother, and decided to devote his life to God. He returned to Africa, where he founded a religious community. In 396 he was made bishop of Hippo. The Vandals invaded North Africa in 428 and two years later besieged Augustine's city. Augustine was then seventy-six years old. He died in the fourth month of the siege, on 29 August 430.

All his adult life, Augustine was conscious of the haunting shadow cast by the books he'd read in his past; he knew that his old love for Virgil coloured all his reading and writing, and the alluring influence of the pagan classics troubled him deeply. Horace (whom Augustine had also read in his youth and much admired) had written an epistle to a young student of rhetoric, Lollius Maximus, telling him that he was re-reading Homer, and that, in his opinion, Homer, better than any rhetorician, could show us 'what is honest and what dishonest, what is useful and what is noxious'. 'Even now that you are still young and your heart pure,' Horace urged, 'take my advice, trust him who is wiser than you. The new cask preserves long afterwards the scent of the wine poured into it.'[8] Augustine turned Horace's words around and used them as a warning against allowing young children to read Virgil: 'they take great draughts of his poetry into their unformed minds,' he wrote, 'so that they may not easily forget him.'[9] Horace, Augustine agreed, was right: the books we loved best in our youth keep haunting us throughout our life. Therefore, since he could not uproot them from his soul, he needed to find a method to convert these ancient stories into cautionary tales in spite of themselves, thereby satisfying both Augustine's taste for good literature and his demand for higher morals – in effect, having his classical cake and eating it too. 'Can any schoolmaster in his gown,' Augustine asked, 'listen unperturbed to a man who challenges him on his own ground and says "Homer invented these stories and attributed human sins to the gods. He would have done better to provide men with examples of divine goodness"? It would be nearer the truth to say that Homer certainly invented the tales but peopled them with wicked human characters in the guise of gods. In this way their wickedness would not be reckoned a crime, and all who did as they did could be shown to follow the example of the heavenly gods, not that of sinful mortals.'[10]

Augustine put his own advice into practice. *The City of God*, for example, begins with a long analysis of the various ways in which the ancient authors described and commented on the fall of Troy – authors other than Homer, since the *Iliad* ends before the destruction of the city. This classic example allowed Augustine better to praise the building of a heavenly city, and to cite the heroes of Greece and Rome in order to enhance the greater example of the Christian martyrs. The arguments are mostly convincing because Augustine is an extraordinary rhetorician well versed in the methods of Cicero and yet, at the same time, the reader feels that the scent of the early wine has not vanished entirely, and that the boy who wept for Dido, and 'was sad not to be able to read the very things that made me sad', is still there, lusting for his beloved books. In his attempt to reconcile past and present cultures, it wasn't clear whether Augustine eventually came to understand that it wasn't necessary to forgo either. For Christianity, the reading of the ancient authors lent the new faith a prehistory and a universality. For the ancient world, it meant continuity and transmission of intellectual experience.

Fifteen hundred years after Augustine, one of his distant readers, the German poet Heinrich Heine, gave the division between pagans and Christians yet another twist, forcing a choice between that which Homer and the Greeks represented – an archetypal conception of Beauty – and that which the Judaeo-Christian world sought to impose: a dogmatic and divinely revealed Truth. In the last poem he wrote, 'For Mouche', a fortnight before his death in Paris in 1856, Heine described a disturbing dream. Heine sees a dead man (Heine himself is that man) lying in an open sarcophagus, surrounded by bits of broken sculpture. The sarcophagus is decorated with scenes taken both from classical mythology and from the Old Testament. Suddenly, quarrelling voices break into the quiet of the place.

Oh, the argument will never end.
Always will Truth quarrel with Beauty.
The human host will always split
In two halves: Greeks and the Barbarians.[11]

CHAPTER 6

Other Homers

Achilles only exists because of Homer.

François-René de Chateaubriand,
Preface to *Les Natchez*, 1826

Almost a century and a half after Augustine's death, a quaestor of the Ostrogoth king Theodoric and minister to three of his successors, Flavius Magnus Aurelius Cassiodorus Senator, wrote a treatise on religious and civil education called *Institutiones Divinarum et Saecularium Litterarum* in which, for the first time, instructions were given on how to study the liberal arts in the context of the Christian doctrine. Time abbreviated both the author's name and that of his book, which became known as Cassiodorus' *Institutiones* and was considered an essential learning tool well into the Renaissance. The *Institutiones* is divided into two parts. The first is a guide to scriptural study and to the art of collecting and copying manuscripts; the second is an encyclopaedic treatment of the seven liberal arts. According to Cassiodorus, all the arts, ancient and modern, are to be found 'in essence' in the Holy Scriptures: all wisdom and all art comes from them, and even the pagan writers (such as Homer) received their illumination from the eternal Word of God, not yet revealed but ever-present. One of Cassiodorus' early works is the *Expositio Palmorum*, a detailed and methodical examination of the Psalms. Here Cassiodorus analysed the text that would sustain the argument of the *Institutiones*. Did not Psalm 19 clearly say that 'The heavens declare the glory of God' everywhere and in all time? Did it not declare that 'There is no speech nor language, where their voice is not heard'? For Cassiodorus, anyone in any age was therefore capable of learning from that all-embracing voice.[1]

But which was the best language to learn this heavenly wisdom? In 324 AD, shortly before the birth of Augustine, the Emperor Constantine had transferred the seat of government to Byzantium, renamed Constantinople, a city which was to become the centre of all political and cultural activities. By the eighth century, even though the laws of Byzantium, in order to satisfy both halves of the Empire, were being translated into Latin and Greek, only Greek was held to be the natural language of literature and philosophy, and therefore the business of monasteries and colleges. Children, from the age of eight on, were taught elements of Greek grammar not only through pious works but also by means of anthologies of the classics, including selections of Homer. After learning the rules of the language by heart, the student was supposed to compose poems and speeches imitating the ancient models. These formal tasks reached their absurd peak with a teaching exercise called the schedograph. This consisted of the dictation of a text with as many homonyms and rare words as possible, so that the student would have to learn the spelling of the first by context and of the second by memorizing an abstruse vocabulary. Memory played an important part in Byzantine education: after several years of schooling, students were expected to know the *Iliad* by heart.

Principal among the schools of higher learning was the Royal College of Constantinople whose president was pompously called the Sun of Science, while his twelve assistants, the twelve professors of the various faculties, were known as the Twelve Signs of the Zodiac. The College possessed a library of over 35,000 volumes, including many Greek works, among them a manuscript of Homer written on a roll of parchment 120 feet long, said to be the intestines of a fabulous serpent.

In the seventh century AD, Egypt had ceased to be part of the empire, and parchment began to replace the Egyptian papyrus, just as papyrus had, in the seventh century BC, as mentioned earlier, replaced parchment among the Greeks. The invention of lower case cursive allowed scribes to produce more copies at a lower cost, since fewer pages were needed to hold a given text. More readers were therefore able to become familiar with the whole of an original work, rather than with a selection compiled in an anthology, in order to transcribe or annotate it. For the Byzantines, the craft of literature was above all copy and gloss, and originality was deemed a worthless endeavour, except when displaying one's knowledge of arcane words and phrases. A deliberate preciousness clung to the Byzantine appreciation of the classics, and the Greek writers of Constantinople imitated the ancient models without aspiring to either their charm or their power. 'Their prose,' wrote Edward Gibbon, 'is soaring to the vicious affectation of poetry: their poetry is sinking below the flatness and insipidity of prose. The tragic, epic and lyric muses were silent and inglorious: the bards of Constantinople seldom rose above a riddle or epigram, a panegyric or tale; they forgot even the rules of prosody; and with the melody of Homer yet resounding in their ears, they confound all measure of feet and syllables in the impotent strains which have received the name of *political* or city verses.'[2]

Gibbon's judgement is perhaps too harsh. If the wordsmiths of Constantinople were not as admirable as their ancestors, they nevertheless produced some remarkable work, especially in the realms of history and biography, in which Homer's influence was heard as a distant beat. For any educated person at the court, familiarity with some of Homer's work was a mark of distinction. An anecdote recorded in the eleventh-century chronicle of Michel Psellus illustrates the point. During a court procession, an onlooker, seeing the beautiful imperial consort Sclerena go by, softly quoted the first part of a line from the *Iliad*, in which the Trojans, speaking of the beautiful Helen, say: 'It were no shame that Trojans and well-greaved Achaeans should suffer long for a woman such as she.' At the time, Sclerena 'gave no sign of having heard the words, but when the ceremony was over, she sought out the man who had uttered them and asked him what they meant. She repeated his quotation without a single mistake, pronouncing the words exactly as he had whispered them. As soon as he told her the story in detail, and the crowd showed its approval of his interpretation of the anecdote, as well as of the Homeric reference, she was filled with pride, and her flatterer was rewarded for his compliment.'[3] Sclerena hadn't read the *Iliad*, and yet, in her eyes, apposite knowledge of Homer granted the courtier a certain prestige.

By the end of the fourth century, the division between the Greek east and the Latin west half of the Empire became more evident. In the east, Church and state lent its citizens the sense of living in a divinely appointed Christian realm, while in the west, service to the emperor and service to the Christian authorities were seen as two separate duties. Intellectually, the east held as essential the traditional study of the classics, both Greek and Latin; in the west, classical scholarship was judged part and parcel of pagan beliefs. Therefore, while Homer continued to be edited, studied and read in Constantinople, in Rome he all but faded from the memory of readers. Many Roman Christians now believed that their intellectual duty was exclusively to the revealed New Word and felt no deep attachment to the old written culture; consequently, they may have experienced no compunction in throwing away the old papyrus scrolls in which the classical texts were preserved.[4] While in the east, Bishop Athanasius told holy virgins 'to have books in their hands at dawn', in the west, Christians quoted Augustine who had written approvingly of holy men who lived through 'faith, hope and charity – without books'.[5]

The dispute that had preoccupied Jerome and Augustine, between Roman Christianity and ancient Rome, was largely to blame for the neglect of classical culture. In 382, the statue of the goddess Victory, symbol of Rome's glory since the times of Augustus, was removed from the altar of the senate house by imperial orders, to placate the Christians among the senators. The spokesman for the pagan majority was Quintus Aurelius Symmachus, father-in-law of the philosopher Boethius (both of whom, years later, under Ostrogothic rule, would be accused of treasonable dealings with Constantinople and tortured to death). Symmachus argued eloquently not for the suppression of Christianity but for Christian tolerance 'of the age-old cult of his class', noting that surely the emperor had nothing to gain by outlawing the rites of his own ancestors. 'Was not Roman religion (and here is the heart of the matter) inextricably tied to Roman law? If one part of the heritage went, must not the others follow?'[6] Symmachus' quiet argument was answered by the bishop of Milan, Augustine's instructor, St Ambrose. He accepted the points made by his opponent, and yet the question, he said, was not an intellectual but a political one. If the emperor agreed with the pagans, the bishops would withdraw their support of the government. The Christian threat won the battle.

When the Gothic king Alaric, who had invaded the Italian peninsula in 401, besieged and entered Rome nine years later, the fall of the city was perceived as a punishment willed by the ancient gods on the followers of the new one. The Goths too were Christians: they had been converted in the mid-fourth century by a Greek preacher called Ulfilas who, being a follower of the Arian heresy, taught that while God the Father was divine, Jesus his Son was not. For the Roman Christians, the fact that the invaders were heretics compounded the humiliation. It no longer seemed important even to attempt reconciliation with the pagan past. For a time, the ancient texts were still preserved and studied in monasteries and abbeys, and copied in both secular and religious workshops. But with the fall of the Gothic kingdom, after the sack of Rome by the Vandals in 455 and the beginning of the long wars that devastated the Italian peninsula, the culture of books, in which libraries were the traditional vessels for preserving the memory of a society, all but disappeared from everyday life.[7] For a people who had undergone two sieges in the space of four decades, books became objects and relics rather than vessels for stories, and even the tale of the archetypal siege vanished into the obscure past. Homer became a monument, known by hearsay to exist somewhere and dutifully respected from afar.

In the east, however, Homer continued to be read and was recognized as part of the social imagination. Though only certain sections of the poems were quoted or glossed, and knowledge of his work was, by and large, reduced to a few set-pieces, Homer's presence was felt across the whole cultural landscape. Perhaps a sense of this ghostly influence can be had by considering the many attempts to contradict, undermine and even deny his stories. Though Homer's poems were, for the Byzantine scholars, exalted literature worthy of imitation, several other texts competed with them for pre-eminence, and these in turn gave rise to a vast secondary literature. According to the literary historian Proclus, probably writing in the second or fifth century AD, there existed a group of epic poems known as the Epic Cycle and composed in Homer's time or earlier, from which Homer himself might have drawn his material. Of the six epics dealing with the Trojan War only a few quotations survive, but their titles and contents were preserved in a manuscript of the *Iliad* now in Venice.[8] The longest is the *Cypria*, a sort of prequel to the *Iliad*, which begins with the Judgement of Paris, when Aphrodite promises the Trojan prince the love of Helen as a reward for declaring her the most beautiful of the goddesses. The *Aithiopis* follows on from the funeral of Hector at the end of the *Iliad* up to the death of Achilles and the dispute of Ajax and Ulysses over his armour. The *Little Iliad* (once attributed to Homer himself) continues the story from the adjudging of the armour to Ulysses to the entry of the Wooden Horse into Troy. The narrative is then picked up by the *Ilion Persis (The Sack of Ilion)* which chronicles the fall of the city and ends with two sacrifices and a departure: Polyxena slaughtered at the tomb of Achilles and Hector's son killed by Ulysses, while the Greeks sail home threatened by an angry Athena. Finally, the five books of the *Nostoi (The Returns)* follow the fate of the victors: Menelaus' voyage to

Egypt and his successful homecoming, Agamemnon warned by the ghost of Achilles that he will be murdered by his wife Clytemnestra, the shipwreck and death of Ajax, the long journey home of Achilles' son Neoptolemos. Ulysses' further adventures are told in the *Telegony*, a sequel to the *Odyssey*: after Penelope's suitors are buried, Ulysses sails off to Thesprotia (a last adventure forecast by Tiresias[9]) where he marries the queen, fights a war, returns to Ithaca, and is killed there by his son Telegonos, born from the enchantress Circe. Upon discovering his mistake, Telegonos, accompanied by Penelope and Telemachus, takes the body back to his mother, who makes them all immortal.[10]

The Epic Cycle was at the origin of what has been called 'the Trojan genre', and served as source material for innumerable writers. Notable among these was Quintus of Smyrna, an educated Greek living in Asia Minor in the third century AD who wrote a 'complete' (and grisly) history of the Trojan War known as the *Posthomerica*, in a style imitating Homer's.[11] But the most famous of all the Trojan stories were two firsthand accounts supposedly written by a couple of soldiers who had taken part in the war, Dictys of Crete and Dares the Phrygian, and who were thought to antedate Homer by several centuries. A number of Byzantine writers based their stories on Dictys' account, *A Journal of the Trojan War*; fewer on that of Dares, *The History of the Fall of Troy*, perhaps because Dictys had offered the Greek version of the facts, while Dares had told that of the Trojans.[12] Furthermore, Dictys' narrative went on to tell the story of how the Greek victors returned to their homelands, thereby providing a useful bridge from the *Iliad* to the *Odyssey*. Far from being authentic records of the events, both accounts were probably composed in Greek in the first century AD. These original versions have not survived, with the exception of a small fragment of Dictys' text, discovered in 1899 on the back of an income tax return for the year 206 AD.

Both stories were translated into Latin and, in this new version, Dares' account, since it narrated the events from the point of view of Aeneas' people, now became more popular than his Greek colleague's among the inheritors of the Roman Empire. Dares' text was quoted as the primary source by all those who retold the history of Troy, overtaking the popularity of the *Iliad*. As mentioned, Homer had been criticized for depicting the gods as prone to all the human foibles and interfering with the affairs of mortals. Dares (and Dictys) referred to the gods only as figures of reverence and placed the responsibility for the fighting on the shoulders of human beings alone. For many centuries, the chronicles of Dictys and Dares were considered to be authentic documents, written, as it were, one against the other. Not until the beginning of the eighteenth century did confidence in their veracity diminish, when the scholar Jacob Perizonius proved beyond doubt that both men were consummate forgers[13].

Towards 1165, a clerk from Normandy, Benoît de Sainte-Maure, serving in the entourage of King Henry II, based his account of the Trojan War, *Le Roman de Troie*, on the chronicle of Dares. One day, says Sainte-Maure, in Athens, a scholar named Cornelius 'was searching all over in a library for learned books, when he came across the history that Dares had composed in the Greek tongue'. Cornelius translated it into Latin, and it was this translation that Sainte-Maure says he followed 'word by word' in his own book. Though Sainte-Maure acknowledged Homer as 'a clerk of extraordinary talent and full of wisdom', Dares' chronicle was, in his opinion, even better, since the Trojan soldier had taken part in the events he described, while Homer had obtained his facts by hearsay. Sainte-Maure acknowledges that he hasn't read Homer himself, but that he obtained his information on the poet 'from the source' (i.e. Dares). Sainte-Maure presents himself simply as a translator for the benefit of those who can't read Latin script (the '*illitterati*'), explaining that he intends 'to translate it into Romance from the Latin in which I found it, if I have the intelligence and the skill, so that those who don't understand [Latin] letters can nevertheless delight in the story'.[14]

Of the lengthy poem, one episode in particular – not in Dares but invented by Sainte-Maure – caught the imagination of those who 'delighted in the story': the tragic love of the Trojans Troilus and Cressida (named Briseida in the *Roman de Troie*). Briseida, beloved of Troilus, is forced to leave the city when her father Calchas defects to the Greek side. The Greek Diomedes sees her and falls in love with her, and, after some hesitation, Briseida accepts Diomedes' proposal. She gives him, as a token of her love, the right sleeve of her dress, and the forlorn Troilus is killed in battle by Achilles.

Two centuries later, the Sicilian writer Guido delle Colonne wrote (without acknowledging the source) a Latin prose version of *Le Roman de Troie* which was later translated into English by John Lydgate,[15] but it was Geoffrey Chaucer who first rendered Sainte-Maure's story into English. His *Troilus and Criseyde*[16] inspired the Scottish poet Robert Henryson to produce a sequel, *The Testament of Cresseid*, in which the unfaithful young woman is punished by the gods with leprosy and dies after receiving alms from Troilus who fails to recognize her in her pitiful state.[17] In 1474, William Caxton included the story (by then extremely popular) in his *Recuyell of the Historyes of Troye*.[18] Finally William Shakespeare, who famously had 'small Latin, and less Greek',[19] and therefore almost certainly had not read Homer in the original, made use of these various English versions as sources for his *Troilus and Cressida*.[20]

CHAPTER 7

Homer in Islam

> There is not only Arab poetry: foreign nations also have
> their own. There have been Persian poets and Greek
> poets. For instance, Aristotle, in his *Logic*, praises the
> poet Umatîrash (Homer).
>
> Ibn Khaldun, *Al-Muqaddima*, 1377

While in Byzantium the study of Greek was, by and large, the
study of antique models, in the centres of Arab culture (first
Baghdad, and later Cairo, Damascus, Cordoba and Toledo)
the study of Greek literature was perceived as a dialogue
between contemporaries. Aristotle and Plato were not figures
from a misty past: they were active voices in constant dialogue with their readers, readers who were also their prom-
ulgators and conveyors through translation and commentary.
In the ninth century, the great Abu Uthman 'Amr ibn Bahr al-
Jahiz, known simply as Jahiz, accused scholars of preferring
Aristotle to the Koran, without acknowledging that he himself had followed the philosopher in several of his books.[1]

Although translation of foreign literature into Arabic can
be said to have begun in the mid-eighth century during the

rule of the celebrated Abassid caliph al-Mansur, with the Indian story collection *Kalila and Dimna*, Ptolemy's *Almagest* and Euclid's *Geometry*, among others,[2] the great tradition of translation from the ancient Greek was firmly established a century later, starting with a dream. One night in Baghdad, the Caliph al-Ma'mun, known as 'Lover of Knowledge' and son of the famous Harun al-Rashid (who, as a character in the *Arabian Nights* would delight the European imagination in later centuries), saw a pale, blue-eyed man with a broad forehead and frowning eyebrows. With the assurance of dreamers, the caliph understood that the stranger was Aristotle.[3] Al-Ma'mun and Aristotle talked all night. In the morning, and as a result of the encounter, the caliph ordered that a library should be founded in Baghdad that would house a translation centre devoted mainly to the works of the philosopher. The centre was placed under the direction of the scholar Hunayn ibn Ishaq al-'Ibadi who, assisted by a school of disciples, translated into Syriac and Arabic almost the entire corpus of Greek and Hellenistic philosophy and science.

Hunayn often made use of his knowledge of Homer to help clarify certain obscure images, unknown names and difficult analogies in the classical Greek texts. Because Hunayn knew his Homer, he was able to explain to his readers that, for example, the Cyclops mentioned in a certain book was 'a giant whose name was Cyclops' and that when the monster Scylla received the epithet 'Hound of the Sea', it was because Homer had compared her cries to the yelping of a pup.[4] According to his contemporary, the scholar Yusuf ibn

Ibrahim, Hunayn had begun his scholarly career as a brilliant though over-inquisitive student in Baghdad. He had shown such a passionate curiosity in class, that his teacher, exasperated by the constant flow of questions, had ordered him out of the lecture hall, and the young man, taking the dismissal to heart, had left Baghdad without letting anyone know where he was going. Two years later, Ibrahim found himself called to the bed of a patient of Greek ancestry, whose aunt had been a Greek slave of Harun al-Rashid. There he noticed a strange man, his hair falling over his face in the fashion of Byzantium, who was reciting Homer in the original to his ailing host. The stranger was Hunayn, returned to Baghdad with a word-perfect knowledge of Homeric Greek.[5]

Beyond the fame acquired for the excellency of its translations, the centre's prosperity was largely due to monetary incentive: sponsors paid generously for translated works that lent them intellectual and social prestige among the Baghdad aristocracy. Translators were highly specialized; they had no overall knowledge of Greek but acknowledged being familiar with the style and vocabulary of only certain authors. For instance, translating a medical text by the second-century physician Galen, Hunyan comes upon a quotation from a play by Aristophanes and confesses to the reader: 'But I am not familiar with the language of Aristophanes, nor am I accustomed to it. Hence, it was not easy for me to understand the quotation, and I have therefore omitted it.' Not all translators displayed (or display today) such disarming honesty.

Although poetry was not part of the centre's mission, a

few fragments of Homer were translated as well, as attested in several collections of philosophical sayings, some reliable and some apocryphal, and in Arab versions of Greek authors who had quoted Homer, such as Aristotle himself. So great was the thirst for these ancient texts that to the recognized works of acclaimed writers were added pure inventions, as for instance the *Kitab al-Tuffaha ('Book of the Apple')*, a gloss of Plato's *Phaedrus* accompanied by a series of meditations supposedly jotted down by Aristotle on his death-bed.[7] Biographies of Homer, 'the wandering poet' as he was known, were included in dictionaries and encyclopaedias.[8]

Just as the pagan authors had served in Christian Europe as a source of analogies to prove the superiority of the religion of Christ, so the Islamic writers made use of the Greek corpus (and to a lesser extent of the Latin one) to prove the truth of the Koran. Examples drawn from the Greek authors served to illustrate the laws that rule the soul, according to the words of the Prophet Muhammad. The tenth-century scholar al-Farabi, the foremost logician of his time, was one of the most important and influential of these commentators. After studying in Baghdad with the disciples of Christian scholars from Alexandria, al-Farabi settled in Damascus where, in relative seclusion, he wrote the critical treatises on Aristotle, Plato and Galen that earned him his fame. In these, al-Farabi set out his belief that philosophy, like religion, can help us attain the truth, following a different path and beckoning to all kinds of travellers. Each of these paths, the religious and the philosophical one, offered two levels of pursuit. The highest, that of metaphysical enquiry, was meant for the few whose intelligence or gifted spirit allowed them to comprehend complex abstract formulations; the other, available to the common majority, was followed through stories, myths, riddles and parables. In an ideal society, both paths, and both levels in each path, coexisted with more or less ease, though there were scholars who thought that the exponents of the lower level (poets and mythographers such as Homer, and 'everyday prophets', as the philosopher al-Saraksi called ambulant preachers) were charlatans. Plato had put it more sternly when he called them 'falsifiers of the truth' and, as mentioned, banned them from his Republic. Al-Farabi was less severe. Muhammad had declared that the ideal community of the faithful constituted an *umma*, a perfect city-state; for al-Farabi, Plato's ideal republic and Muhammad's *umma* were two incarnations of the same idea, and though one disallowed poets and the other did not, both spoke of the same holy place.[9] In this context, Homer's poems, though not as exalted as the works of Aristotle and Plato, deserved to be read because, albeit their watered-down, vulgar idiom, they too held inklings of the truth.

As far as we know, no version of Homer's work was produced during the golden period of Arabic translation. A few Abassid scholars were aware of the contents of the two poems, and fragments of the *Iliad* and the *Odyssey* appeared in popular narratives: for instance, several of Ulysses' adventures surface in the stories of Sindbad the Sailor.[10] A late-thirteenth- or early-fourteenth-century anthology of military exploits, the *Raqa'iq al-hilal fi Daqaiq al-hiyal* ('Cloaks of Fine Fabric in Subtle Ruses'), includes a potted version of Achilles' wrath and the killing of Hector. The source, of course, may not be Homer but one of the many other retellings of the story of Troy.

We are told how the King of the Greeks of Byzantium used cunning when he invaded Ifriqiya [Phrygia] and the population learned of this well enough in advance for them to organize resistance and entrench themselves in a city [Troy] that he besieged for a long time to no avail. The city gate withstood all his attacks. Among the citizens there was a man called Aqtar [Hector] who was very daring and courageous. Anyone who fought him was invariably killed. The King of the Greeks [Agamemnon] was told of this.

He had a commander named Arsilaous [Achilles], unsurpassed for his bravery throughout the world. Following an outburst of anger from the King, he had refused to take any part in the war. The King had asked him to, but he did not obey. The King then said: 'Spread the rumour that our enemy Aqtar has captured the brother of Arsilaous.'

The latter was distressed when he heard the news. He looked everywhere for his brother, but could not find him. Then he asked for his weapons and went out against Aqtar. He fought against him and took him prisoner, and led him before the King of the Greeks. The latter put Aqtar to death. The people of Ifriqiya and all their supporters were terror-stricken when they found out that their hero was gone. The

King of the Greeks, with Arsilaous, attacked the city, inflicting heavy losses on the enemy and conquering the region.[11]

Two important changes are introduced in this version of Homer's story. Hector hasn't killed Achilles' 'brother' – it is only a rumour spread by Agamemnon. Achilles does not kill Hector; he only captures him, and it is Agamemnon who orders the execution. In the Arabic telling, Agamemnon is the secret protagonist of the story.

The great Arabic translation schools began to decline towards the end of the tenth century, but the impulse to bring into one's own language the wisdom expressed in that of another continued long afterwards. The Arab scholars who had rendered the Greek works into their tongue and enlivened them with their own comments, had done so less out of a will to preserve the Greek culture (the Persian heritage was for them as important as the Greek) than for the sake of what has been called 'appropriation and naturalization',[12] absorbing another culture into their own. Now, from the eleventh to the thirteenth centuries, many of these Arab versions of the Greek classics were in turn translated into other languages, particularly Latin and Hebrew. In Sicily, but especially in Spain, the works of Aristotle annotated by al-Farabi, Avicenna and Averroes acquired a new life through fresh glosses and interpretations. Some fiction and poetry, too, entered Europe in Arabic versions and was then rendered into local tongues, so that the handful of Homeric episodes that had metamorphosed into an Arabic setting underwent a further transformation and became Spanish *romances*, Provençal *canzones*, French *fabliaux* and German *Märchen*.

Centuries later, in 1857, Wilhelm Grimm, one of the brothers of fairy-tale fame, suggested that Homer's stories, which in the original were told as legends, with a historical basis, that happened in a specific time and place, had been carried throughout the world and had changed over the centuries in the telling. They became folktales set in the indefinite past ('Once upon a time') and featured generic heroes with names such as Hans, Elsie or Jack.[13] How far Homer's poems travelled is a matter of conjecture but, for instance, scholars have recognized in an Icelandic saga composed about 1300, *The Story of Egill One-hand and Asmundr the Berserks' Killer*, the influence of the *Odyssey*, in particular the story of the encounter between Ulysses and the Cyclops,[14] which later, in English folklore, became 'Jack and the Beanstalk'.

It must be said that Arab translators were not solely responsible for the renewed European awareness of its Greek heritage.[15] Far from it; most of the great poetry and theatre arrived much later and through different byways. And yet, either as translated text or read in the original Greek, through commentaries and glosses or as literary hearsay, broken up into stories and specific characters, whether as historical facts or as allegories and symbols, the poems of Homer gradually filtered back into the imagination of medieval Europe. Writing in the early sixteenth century, Juan de Mena, in the Preface to his *Iliad*, attempted to explain the mechanics of this late transmission to King Juan II. Authors such as Avicenna, he said, were like silkworms who wove their own books out of their entrails, while he worked like the bees 'who steal the substance from mellifluous blossoms in other men's orchards'. 'A great gift I bear,' Mena assured his king, 'if my thieving and looting does not corrupt it, nor my bold and fearless daring, and that is to translate and interpret such a seraphic work as Homer's *Iliad*, from Greek carried into Latin and from Latin into our vulgar Castilian mother tongue.'[16]

A book's influence is never straightforward. Common readers, unrestricted by the rigours of academe, allow their books to dialogue with one another, to exchange meanings and metaphors, to enrich and annotate each other. In the reader's mind, books become entwined and intermingled, so that we no longer know whether a certain adventure belongs to Arsilaous or to Aquiles, or where Homer ends Ulysses' adventures and the author of Sindbad takes them up again.

CHAPTER 8

Dante

Dante – known to that gentleman as an eccentric man in
the nature of an Old File, who used to put leaves round
his head, and sit upon a stool for some unaccountable
purpose, outside the cathedral at Florence.

Charles Dickens, *Little Dorrit*, 1855–7

Towards the end of the Middle Ages, scholars and poets
returned, once again, to the questions that had preoccupied
Jerome and Augustine regarding the relationship between
Homer's stories and the stories of the Bible. Allegorical interpretations continued, but these were accompanied by a
search for correspondences between what the ancients had
told and what the Church had revealed, establishing a
sequence of parallel readings that honoured one without dis-
honouring the other. A tradition of typological commentaries
on the Old and New Testaments was already common in art
and literature, setting side by side episodes of the former
with those of the latter: for instance, the tree from which
Adam ate the forbidden fruit next to the Cross on which
Christ died for our salvation. Accordingly, a similar typology

was established between Homer and the Bible: between, for example, Achilles in the *Iliad* and David in the Old Testament, or between the stages of Ulysses' return and the troubled exodus of the Hebrews from Egypt. In the early fourteenth century, Albertino Mussato, the most celebrated of the members of the *cenacolo padovano* or Paduan Circle of Latin poets, argued that the pagan writers had expressed the same ideas as those found in Scripture, but in the form of enigmas or riddles in which they had secretly announced the coming of the True Messiah. Their poetry, Mussato boldly declared, was 'a second theology',[1] a notion that Petrarch was later to invert as 'theology is poetry that comes from God'.[2]

When Mussato spoke of pagan poetry, he meant, first and foremost, Homer. Even though the Latin classics had pride of place in the libraries of the Renaissance, Homer was considered the fountainhead, the primordial spring without which there would have been no culture. For that reason, when Dante meets the great writers of antiquity in the first circle of his Hell, he has Homer, brandishing a sword to indicate the supremacy of epic poetry, appear at the head of the delegation of writers. Homer and his colleagues come forward to greet, first Virgil – 'Honour the highest of poets, his shadow which had left, returns' – and then, to Virgil's amusement, Dante;[3] that is to say, first the master poet who sang of the triumph of Rome, and secondly (but this is in the future) the master poet who sang of the triumph of Christianity.

Homer exercised on Dante and his contemporaries an influence in some ways similar to that which the gods effected on the ancients. As depicted in the *Iliad* and the *Odyssey* (but in much of the later literature as well), Zeus and his fellow divinities walked among the mortals, inspiring them, haunting them, seeking their glory or their death, or just being a nuisance (as when, in the *Iliad*, Athena pulls Achilles' hair).[4] They were phantom presences in heaven and material representations in marble and bronze in the temples, but they were also alive in bedrooms and markets and battle-fields, sitting by mortals in their studies or accompanying them on their voyages. After Plato's death, his disciples defended Homer's notion of the gods as 'spies in disguise', which Plato himself had ridiculed; in his gossipy books, Plutarch spoke again and again of the appearance of the gods among men; and the Emperor Marcus Aurelius meditated on the divine presences 'visible as the stars in the sky but also present as friends and instructors in dreams'.[5] For Augustine, however, only one God filled the world with His presence. The philosopher and dramatist Seneca, writing in the first century AD, offered a middle way. For him, not the gods but the great writers and thinkers of antiquity lived among us. 'Only men who make Zeno and Pythagoras and Democritus and the other high priests of liberal studies their daily famil-iars, who cultivate Aristotle and Theophrastus, can properly be said to be engaged in the duties of life,' he wrote. 'It is a common saying that a man's parents are not of his own choosing but allotted to him by chance. But we can choose our own genealogy.' Pointing at his library, Seneca argued that these great men could share with us their experience.

'Here are families with noble endowments: choose whichever you wish to belong to. Your adoption will give you not only the name but actually the property, and this you need not guard in a mean or niggardly spirit: the more people you share it with, the greater will it become. These will open the path to eternity for you and will raise you to a height from which none can be cast down. This is the sole means of prolonging your mortality, or rather, of transforming it into immortality.'[6]

For Mussato, Dante, and their contemporaries, Seneca's argument was commonplace. To the company of the poets of Greece and Rome were assimilated the Fathers of the Catholic Church, so that, in the same way that Mussato could address Livy as his master in his *Historia Augusta*,[7] Petrarch could later engage in a dream dialogue with St Augustine.[8] These relationships were devotional, similar to those that readers have with their favourite books.

Only Dante's case is different. Dante was the first non-classical writer to be treated by his contemporaries as equal to the great Greek and Latin authors, a position that he himself did not find surprising:

> The sea I travel is no longer travelled.
> Minerva fills my sails, Apollo leads me,
> And the Nine Muses point me towards the Polar Star.[9]

Even then, Dante knew that he couldn't tell his story all by himself: he required divine guidance. Homer had started the tradition by which the poet establishes his authority not as the inventor but as the performer of tales that a divine voice has dictated. Both the *Iliad* and the *Odyssey* begin by asking the Muse to sing the chosen subjects: the rage of one man, the cunning of another. There is, however, a difference between the two beginnings. In the *Iliad*, the earlier poem, Homer humbly leaves the stage to the Muse alone: 'Goddess, sing the rage...' But in the *Odyssey*, the poet allows himself to appear as the receiver of the song: 'Sing to me of the man, Muse...' Virgil and Dante profit from the daring intrusion of that 'to me'. Virgil, in the *Aeneid*, asks the Muse to recall *for him* the cause of the war that set Aeneas on his journeys.[10] Dante too, in his *Commedia*, invokes the Muses for help, but so that his memory, capable of 'setting down' what he saw on his marvellous journey, might now reveal *to him* its excellence in the telling.[11]

G. K. Chesterton remarked that it isn't necessary to have read the classics in order to accept the fact that they are classics;[12] in other words, we can take it as read that Cervantes, Shakespeare and Dostoevsky are 'important' writers, in the sense that they have carried import for successive generations of readers. When we finally come to them (if we finally come to them) singly and on our own terms, we rescue from the blanketing notion of classic a primary judgement and a personal meaning: 'I like – or I don't like – Homer's books, and this is what they say to me.' Dante's own knowledge of the classics was limited to what was available in the Latin original, especially Horace, Seneca and, of course, Virgil. Of the great Greek tragic poets that Dante has Virgil introduce as his fellow residents – Euripides, Antiphon, Simonides, Agathon 'and several other Greeks with laurel wreaths' – Dante had no knowledge except by hearsay; neither Sophocles nor Aeschylus are mentioned because, in the fourteenth century, their names had fallen into oblivion and Dante had never heard of them. Even Euripides was known only by name since none of his works was available.[13]

Dante and his contemporaries accepted the time-honoured glorification of Homer as an undisputed fact, and read him, if at all, in Latin translations such as the popular anonymous paraphrase of the *Iliad* known as the *Ilias latina*, probably written in the first century AD. Petrarch kept, with devotional care, a Greek manuscript of Homer which he didn't know how to read. To the friend who sent it to him from Constantinople, he wrote: 'Your Homer lies mute by my side, while I am deaf by his, and often I have kissed him saying: "Great man, how I wish I could hear your words!"'[14] At Petrarch's suggestion, and with the help of Boccaccio, their friend Leonzio Pilato, a Calabrian monk of Greek origin, translated the *Odyssey* and the *Iliad* into Latin, both very badly.[15]

Dante acquired his Homer through Virgil. 'If indeed he knew nothing of the Greek original,' George Steiner remarked, 'Dante's clairvoyant genius intuited, discerned the Homeric presence in the *Aeneid*.'[16] In this sense, Virgil was not only Dante's guide through Hell, he was also his source and inspiration, and through him Dante was able to enjoy the experience of Homer's work. Virgil was for Dante, among other things, a poet who had clearly identified the Roman Empire as a unified cultural world, a world that, in Dante's time, aspired to that same unification: spiritual, under the sceptre of a God-chosen pope, and material, under that of a God-chosen emperor. Those who obeyed the laws of God as dictated by His two servants were rewarded; those who broke them had either to undergo a redemptive purge or, if the fault was too serious, suffer a dreadful and eternal punishment. Dante's *Commedia*, the account of his cautionary excursion to the Kingdom of the Dead, is therefore divided into three parts. The first, Hell, is the dwelling-place of those condemned absolutely, a funnel-shaped pit that runs from the northern hemisphere to the centre of the earth; the second, Purgatory, where souls are redeemed after death, is a high mountain that rises on an island in the southern hemisphere; the third and last, Paradise, is a place beneath the ten heavens of medieval astronomy which form all one single heaven.

The model for Dante's *Commedia* is a composite of many sources, from Homer (via Virgil) to Arabic accounts of Muhammad's journey to the other world, the *Mi'raj*; one version of the latter was translated into Castilian by order of Alfonso X, and then into Latin, French and Italian, the last of which Dante probably read. Even though the complex architecture of the afterlife realm is, to a large degree, Dante's own, the foundation-stone is Homer's.

CHAPTER 9

Homer in Hell

The noise, my dear! And the people!

Ernest Thesiger, on being asked about serving in the
First World War, 1950

Homer's Hell has no remarkable physical features. According to the *Odyssey*, it is a simple, schematic dwelling-place for the souls of the dead, ruled unobtrusively by the god Hades. There, according to the witch Circe, Ulysses must travel in search of instructions for his voyage home when, after keeping him for a year as her lover, Circe at last consents to let him go. But first, she tells him that he must 'travel down/to the House of Death and the awesome one, Persephone,/there to consult the ghost of Tiresias, seer of Thebes'. Ulysses is terrified. 'Circe, Circe,' he cries, 'who can pilot us on that journey? Who has ever/reached the House of Death in a black ship?'[1]

Circe gives Ulysses precise instructions. Driven by the North Wind, his ship will cut across the River Ocean and reach the dark, desolate coast of Persephone's Grove. From there he must descend to the Kingdom of Hades and to the waters of the Acheron into which flow two smaller rivers, that of Fire and that of Tears (the latter a branch of the Styx or Stream of Hate). Here Ulysses must make offerings to the dead and wait for them to appear, and eventually the ghost of Tiresias will tell him by what means he may return to Ithaca.[2] Ulysses follows Circe's instructions to the letter.[3] (Later on, in Book XXIV, there will be a second excursion to the Underworld, when Hermes leads the ghosts of the slaughtered suitors 'past the White Rock and the Sun's Western Gates and past/the Land of Dreams', into the 'fields of asphodel'.[4] No doubt there are several routes to Hell.)

Homer had described a place without graded categories, an Underworld in which souls wander about, incorporeal and listless, like the inmates of a retirement home, some still suffering from regret for what they have done or left undone on earth, others undergoing hideous tortures decreed for them by the gods: Tityus devoured by vultures, Tantalus condemned to eternal hunger and thirst, Sisyphus ineffectually rolling his boulder up the hill. Though Pindar, in the sixth century BC, located specific areas in the Underworld for the 'happy shades',[5] Homer's dead are never pleased to be where they are. 'No winning words about death to *me*, shining Odysseus!' says the ghost of Achilles when he sees him. 'By god, I'd rather slave on earth for another man... than rule down here over all the breathless dead'[6] (a sentiment echoed in Ecclesiastes 9:4, where it is written that 'a living dog is better than a dead lion').

Homer's account proved not vivid enough for Virgil. In

the *Odyssey*, since Circe has described in detail the route to the realm of Hades, there is little for Ulysses to do in the next episode but follow her instructions. Twelve lines suffice to chronicle his journey, a further sixteen to narrate the sacrificial offerings to the dead. Then, as Circe had predicted, the ghosts arrive in awful droves:

> Brides and unwed youths and old men who had suffered
> much
> and girls with their tender hearts freshly scarred by sorrow
> and great armies of battle dead, stabbed by bronze spears,
> men of war still wrapped in bloody armour – thousands
> swarming around the trench from every side –
> unearthly cries – blanching terror gripped me![7]

The arrival of the dead is horrible; compared to the overwhelming menace of the moaning crowd, the individual spirits who thereafter dialogue with Ulysses are tame in their demeanour. It is the swarm of souls that haunts the reader, as Homer knew it would, since he repeats it at the end of the section, with almost identical words:

> … the dead came surging round me,
> hordes of them, thousands raising unearthly cries,
> and blanching terror gripped me…[8]

Homer's ghastly picture of the dead as a confused mingling of sexes and ages, occupations and social classes, extends across many hundreds of future years and will eventually take on its most recognizable shape towards the middle of the fourteenth century in the *danse macabre*,[9] a human chain in which Death leads by the hand all men and women on earth, from pope to humble peasant. The earliest depictions of the *danse macabre* appeared in Europe in the early fifteenth century: on the walls of the Cimetière des Innocents in Paris; in the cloister of old St Paul's in London; in the Marienkirche of Lübeck.[10] A century later, Hans Holbein the Younger produced a series of woodcuts illustrating the Dance of Death that became the subject's standard iconography, translated in the twentieth century as the Triumph of Death in Ingmar Bergman's film *The Seventh Seal* and as its mirror image, the Triumph of Life, at the end of Federico Fellini's *8 1/2*.

The sight that confronts Ulysses is one of wretched things rising in the air, a storm of howling ghosts conjured up by the sacrificial offerings, all generations mingled. But not only death is common to us all: in order to round the circle of human life, Homer broadens the image to include the newly born. In Book VI of the *Iliad*, on the bloodied battlefield, the Lycian Glaucus, fighting on the side of the Trojans, is taunted by the Greek Diomedes, who will reveal himself to be Glaucus' friend. Glaucus says:

> Like the generations of leaves, the lives of mortal men.
> Now the wind scatters the old leaves across the earth,
> now the living timber bursts with the new buds

and spring comes round again. And so with men:
as one generation comes to life, another dies away.[11]

The souls that meet Ulysses are like an autumn whirl-wind. Glaucus describes the dead as 'old leaves' but recalls their counterpart, left unmentioned in the *Odyssey*, the promised new budding in the spring.

A similar throng of souls confronts Virgil's Aeneas in the Underworld. In Homer, the ghosts descend upon Ulysses; in Virgil, the ghosts crowd the shore in front of him, forced to wait one hundred years before they are allowed to cross over (like a throng of refugees, the twenty-first-century reader will say). The frightening description ends with one of Virgil's most famous, most beautiful lines: '*tendebantque manus ripae ulterioris amore*'.

> Matrons and men were there, and there were great-hearted
>   heroes
> Finished with earthly life, boys and unmarried maidens,
> Young men laid on the pyre before their parents' eyes;
> Multitudinous as the leaves that fall in a forest
> At the first frost of autumn. (…)
> So they stood, each begging to be ferried across first,
> Their hands stretched out in longing for the shore beyond the
>   river.[12]

Virgil, remembering his Homer, uses in the *Aeneid* the leaf metaphor in the *Iliad* to illustrate the phantom hordes of the

Odyssey and, with that overlapping of images, the dead become innumerable, including all generations of men and women, falling to the ground autumn after autumn. Suddenly the reader realizes: I too shall be one of them.

Dante has this reading firmly in mind when he describes the corresponding scene in his *Commedia*. Led by Virgil, Dante has crossed the Gate of Hell and reached, like Ulysses and Aeneas before him, the shores of Acheron and the legions of dead.

> As in Autumn the leaves detach and fly
> One after the other, until the branch
> Sees on the ground all of its mortal coils (…)[13]

In Homer, the dead surge up in crowds, and men come and go like leaves: the accent is on the cyclical nature of succeeding generations. In Virgil, the dead are as many as the leaves that must fall when autumn comes: the accent is on the number. And now, to the notions of perpetual movement and infinite quantity, Dante adds that of individual fate, of each leaf coming to its own singular end, 'one after the other'. André Malraux, describing the death of his protagonist in the 1930 novel *La Voie royale*, has him say this: 'There is no… death… There's only… me… me… who's dying…'[14] Equally, Dante insists that the verb 'to die' must always be conjugated in the first person singular. Where Virgil has used *cadunt* ('fall') to describe the action of the leaves, Dante uses *si levan* ('they fly off', 'they detach themselves'), granting each leaf and, by implication, each soul, a voluntary movement.[15] Death is our allotted end, Dante seems to say, but it is also an act for whose quality we ourselves are responsible. That each of us dies is decreed; the act of dying is ours, individually. (In the Second Circle, the souls of the lustful are tossed about like leaves in a howling wind, but each separate soul has its own story.)

Dante's inheritors took advantage of his reading of Homer through Virgil. Milton, in *Paradise Lost*, placed the composite image in a Virgilian landscape to describe Satan's legions at the edge of the Sea of Fire.

> Thick as autumnal leaves that strow the brooks
> In Vallombrosa, where th'Etrurian shades
> High over-arch'd embow'r.[16]

Two centuries after *Paradise Lost* was published, Paul Verlaine, with Dante in mind, reverted to Glaucus' image, not as depicting the numerous dead but just the poet himself.

> And I depart
> on an evil wind
> That carries me off
> This way and that
> Exactly like
> A leaf that's dead.[17]

Verlaine employed the plural image in the singular; Gerard Manley Hopkins, contemporary of Verlaine, held it up as a mirror to a child, addressing her in the second person:

> Margaret, are you grieving
> Over Goldengrove unleaving?
> Leaves like the things of man, you
> With your fresh thoughts care for, can you?
> …
> It is the blight man was born for,
> It is Margaret you mourn for.[18]

In a famous letter to the imperial vicar Can Grande della Scala, Dante explained that every image in the vast pageant of the *Commedia* is to be read in four senses: literal, allegorical, anagogical (spiritual) and analogical (by analogy).[19] That is to say: one, the dead are as 'thick as autumnal leaves'; two, all men will suffer 'the blight man was born for'; three, we must accept death as the 'evil wind' God has willed for us, but we must attempt to depart gracefully, carried 'this way and that'; four, as we are told in Ecclesiastes, 'One generation passeth away, and another generation cometh: but the earth abideth forever.'[20]

Percy Bysshe Shelley, describing the ruins of Pompeii in the autumn of 1820, gave the image a further twist. He inverted the sense of the comparison and lent the falling leaves the quality of wandering ghosts.

I stood within the City disinterred;
And heard the autumnal leaves like light footfalls
Of spirits passing through the streets;[21]

Like several of Dante's images, the autumnal dead illustrate the Thomist tenet in which Dante believed: that man can
only attain perfection in the afterlife by reaching his end in
the correct manner – though he may have been unable to
make explicit the exact meaning of 'correct'. At the same
time, by association with terrestrial things (trees, wind, earth)
Dante's images ground in our everyday experience the higher metaphysical realities.[22] This latter point is important: what
happens on the Otherworld journey only attracts Dante's
attention if it relates to the spiritual outcome of the subject;[23]
in the case of the ghostly crowd, numerous as leaves, what
matters to him is the fact that the dead risen in the *Odyssey*
were once the seasonal flesh and blood described in the *Iliad*.
Homer made the observation, Virgil saw the association,
Dante drew the conclusion.

CHAPTER 10

Greek versus Latin

When a Prince lacks a Homer, it means that he is not
worthy of having one.

Fénelon, *Dialogues des morts: Homère*, 1692–6

Given Homer's role as founding father of these narratives, why
does Dante place Homer in Hell? Dante's Hell is not absolute:
it is a cautionary place that Dante the poet is given the grace to
see while he (the man Dante) still has the opportunity to repent
of his sins. In this vision of the afterlife, Dante lodges Homer,
together with the other pagan poets, in a suburb of that Hell, as
a charitable alternative that is Dante's own invention.

In Dante's Hell, souls descend by their own choice, as a
result of the life they have led; the greater the error of a soul's
conduct on earth, the deeper its place. The divisions are strict
and many. After Hell's entrance gate comes the vestibule of
intellectual cowards, where dwell the souls of those who
remained undecided in their choice between good and evil.
Next, on the edge of the pit of Hell, begins the First Circle or
Limbo. Here dwell the souls of infants who have died unbap-
tized, and of those who, having practised a moral life, chose

not to enter the Christian fold, such as Avicenna and Averroes.[1] This is the home of the virtuous pagans such as Homer whose 'honoured names echo in your life and won them grace in heaven',[2] but who, having lived before the coming of Christ, 'were not able to adore God properly'. Movingly, Virgil adds: 'Of that lot am I.'[3] To Homer and his friends, Dante grants a moated castle surrounded by seven walls and a green meadow. Allegorically, the moat represents earthly possessions or the art of rhetoric; the walls, the seven liberal arts or the intellectual and moral virtues. Homer remains exalted.

The artists of the Renaissance adopted this notion of Homer as first among these ancient 'virtuous pagans'. In about 1470, in his Palace of Urbino, the Duke Federigo de Montefeltro, said to be 'the most learned man of his learned court', placed in his study twenty-eight portraits of celebrated historical figures: Ptolemy next to King Solomon, Virgil next to St Ambrose, Seneca next to Thomas Aquinas and, of course, Homer leading the lot. Though Federigo preferred the philosophers to the poets, Homer could not be absent in a cultured man's workshop.[4]

When, three decades later, in 1508, Raphael was asked by Pope Julius II to decorate his chambers in the Vatican, the twenty-three-year-old painter chose for the room overlooking the Belvedere Gardens the theme of Mount Olympus, home of the pagan gods, and gave Homer pride of place. In the days of ancient Rome, the Vatican Hill had been consecrated to Apollo, and it was Apollo that Raphael decided to depict, playing, instead of the classical lyre, the Italian *lira da braccio*, a sort of lute of nine strings popular in the Renaissance, to symbolize the contemporary presence of the god. Around Apollo are grouped eighteen poets, ancient and modern, with blind Homer presiding, stage right, a sort of secular Trinity, over Dante on his right hand and Virgil on his left.[5]

Greek scholarship flourished some time after Boccaccio and Petrarch's incipient efforts, thanks largely to the Greek exiles fleeing from the Turkish invasions. After the conquest of Constantinople by Mehemet II, on 29 May 1453, a number of accomplished Hellenists migrated to Florence, Rome, Padua and Venice, setting up schools of Greek and working on editions of Greek manuscripts. In Venice, thanks to their erudition, the printer Aldus Manutius was able to produce some of the most exquisite versions of the classics, notably, around 1504, several editions of the *Iliad* and the *Odyssey*.[6] Familiarity with the classics became essential for a person of social standing. The sophisticated scholar Tommaso Parentucelli, who in 1447 was elected pope under the name of Nicholas V, was said to be 'as fond of books as the Borgias were of women' and to have paid ten thousand gold pieces for a translation of Homer.[7]

The educational treatises of the time underline the importance of teaching Homer and Virgil to young children, because 'this is a knowledge which all great men have possessed'.[8] 'Homer, the prince of poets,' wrote the philosopher Battista Guarino, 'is not difficult to learn, as he seems to have been a source for all our [Latin] writers. Their minds will delight in Virgil's imitation of him, for the *Aeneid* is like a mirror of Homer's works, and there is almost nothing in Virgil that does not have an analogue in Homer.'[9] Aeneas Silvius Piccolomini, who became Pope Pius II, found an exquisite reason for studying the ancient authors: 'The commerce of language,' he wrote, 'is the intermediary of love.'[10]

Like Piccolomini, Popes Paul II and Paul III had a good knowledge of Greek, but not his firm belief in the importance of the survival of the ancient cultures. Paul II, an eclectic collector, a lover of sports and lavish parties, and the founder of Rome's first printing-press, issued a ban forbidding schools to teach children the pagan poets. Paul III, a patron of artists such as Titian and Michelangelo, established in 1542 the Congregation of the Roman Inquisition or Holy Office whose mission, among many others, was the banning of heretical and pagan works.[11] Between 1468, when Paul II ordered the suppression of the prestigious Roman Academy, which he suspected of performing pagan rituals under cover of studying the classics, and Paul III's death in 1549, interest in Greek studies on the Italian peninsula began an irreversible decline.[12] There were, however, a few enlightened interludes. Shortly after his election to the Holy See in 1513, Leon X, second son of Lorenzo the Magnificent, ordered that the Roman Academy be reopened and that a college for young Greek students be founded under the direction of the eminent scholar Giovanni Lascaris. The Quirinal College was active for approximately seven years, during which it educated a select number of young boys of Greek ancestry in Greek language, literature and thought. A letter has been preserved from a Greek notary established in Venice which gives a detailed account of the ceremony during which the children welcomed the pope with elaborate salutations in ancient Greek, using terms borrowed from the classic authors, notably from Homer.[13]

Greek scholars started to emigrate to the northern countries, and humanists such as Erasmus, Thomas More and Guillaume Budé, benefiting from their knowledge, carried on the work of commentary and editing. Peter Schade, a twenty-four-year-old friend of Erasmus and professor of Greek at Leipzig University, published in 1518 a book entitled *Discourse on the Need to Learn Different Languages* in which he ardently defended a multilingual culture. To the opposition's argument that God had punished humankind with the plurality of tongues after Babel (according to Genesis 11:1–9), Schade answered with the notion that God is a polyglot ('God understands the tongues of all people') and that angels and saints, being our intercessors, are also polyglots by necessity. 'Indeed, if they did not understand prayers conceived in any language, it would be useless for a German or a Frenchman to murmur a prayer in their mother tongue addressed to saints of other nationalities. Certainly, they would be thus no less ridiculous than if they attempted to speak to the dead.'[14]

But after the Reformation, Latin was confirmed as the language of the Catholic Church, and Greek that of Protestant culture (not counting, of course, the endemic languages into which the Protestant Bible was translated). The Council of Trent (1545 to 1563) forbade Catholics the reading of the Greek and Hebrew Bible except in the case of appointed scholars, and in the eyes of the Church of Rome students of Greek became synonymous with heretics. As a consequence, several Greek scholars were burnt at the stake in 1546 as 'offenders of the faith', by the Catholic king of France, François I, in spite of the royal devotion to the arts and letters. In the Protestant countries instead, the study of Greek was assiduously encouraged and, even in the Protestant colonies, Greek became part of the ordinary school curriculum. In 1788, for instance, in the Danish Virgin Islands, the Rector Hans West opened in Christiansted a school to teach the children of planters the works of Homer and other classical poets.[15] Not knowing Greek became, in Protestant countries, a mark of ignorance. In Oliver Goldsmith's 1766 novel *The Vicar of Wakefield*, the foolish principal of the University of Louvain in Belgium makes this boast: 'You see me, young man, I never learned Greek, and I don't find that I have ever missed it. I have had a doctor's cap and gown without Greek; I have ten thousand florins a year without Greek; I eat heartily without Greek; and, in short,… as I don't know Greek, I do not believe there is any good in it.'[16]

This division had far-reaching consequences: from the seventeenth century onwards, Homer was being rigorously studied in English, German and Scandinavian universities, while in Italy, Spain, France, Portugal and Italy he was being neglected for the sake of Virgil and Dante. The first Spanish translation of the *Odyssey* made directly from the Greek, by Gonzalo Pérez, was published in Amberes in 1556, and hardly distributed; the *Iliad*, in a version by García Malo, also from the Greek, had to wait until 1788 and met with as little success. For centuries, Spanish-language readers learned their Homer through quotations in classical texts or through a handful of Latin translations. This remained the norm long into the nineteenth century. When Miguel de Unamuno was given the chair of Greek at the University of Salamanca in 1891, it was pointed out that the celebrated intellectual had no Greek. Juan Valera, chairman of the committee that had selected him, explained: 'None of the other candidates knows Greek, so we selected the one most likely to know it.'[17] The first encyclopaedia written in Spanish, the *Silva de varia lección* by Pedro Mexía, was published to great acclaim in 1540 in Seville.[18] Though it purports to be a compendium of 'books of great authority', its references to Homer, since the author knew no Greek, are few and most likely taken from either a Latin translation of the *Iliad* that appeared in Basel in 1531,[19] or from quotations of Homer by other authors. When Mexía does mention Homer's works, he chooses only the best-known episodes, such as Hector addressing his horses in Book VIII of the *Iliad* or Aeolus giving the number of winds in Book X of the *Odyssey*.

Only a handful of Spanish writers defended Homer against his disparagers. The poet Francisco de Quevedo, for instance, mocked the ignorance of those who invented 'shameless lies against Homer and false testimonies in order to raise altars to Virgil'[20] and, in a somewhat convoluted prose, accused these pseudo-scholars of perjury: 'In all ages there have been infamous men who have preferred to lend infamy to those who are famous rather than become famous themselves, being as they are, infamous.'[21]

A learned writer, the Mexican Sor Juana Inés de la Cruz, published in 1689 a curious imitation of the Spanish poet Luis de Góngora under the title 'The Dream', in which she mentioned Homer as the 'sweetest of poets' who wrote of 'Achillean feats and Ulysses' martial subtleties'. Though she had only read him in the works of other contemporary writers, such as the German scholar Athanasius Kircher,[22] this did not prevent her from exalting his perfection: 'It would be easier,' she said, 'to remove from the fearful Thunderer his lightning… than half a line of verse dictated to [Homer] by propitious Apollo.'[23]

For Francis Bacon, instead, writing in 1609, Homer was a familiar instrument of poetical instruction, to be consulted carefully and constantly. To dismiss the poets of old because of their 'casual licentiousness' (as the Council of Trent had decreed) 'would be rash, and almost profane; for, since religion delights in such shadows and disguises, to abolish them were, in a manner, to prohibit all intercourse betwixt things divine and human.'[24]

For Sor Juana, Homer was an uncontested, unread reference; for Bacon, he was a sourcebook to be studied and analysed. This divided inheritance was passed on to the Americas and was reflected in their lifestyle and in their libraries. In the United States, the elite chose to model its architecture after the tenets of the Greek Revival, while in Latin America the bourgeoisie chose to fashion its houses after the French and Italian baroque. In the north, Emerson and Whitman and Thoreau read Homer; south of the Rio Grande, José Martí, Rubén Darío and Machado de Assis read Virgil.

CHAPTER 11

Ancients versus Moderns

How unlike the home life of our own dear Queen!

A Victorian lady upon seeing *Antony and Cleopatra*
played by Sarah Bernhardt in 1899

Michel de Montaigne, writing in the last decades of the sixteenth century, chose Homer as one of the three 'most excellent of men' of all time (the other two were soldiers, Alexander the Great and the Theban commander Epaminondas). Confessing that his Greek was not up to truly appreciating Homer, whom he knew mainly through Virgil, Montaigne granted the blind bard primacy because of the far-reaching power of his invention. 'Nothing lives on the lips of men,' wrote Montaigne, 'like his name and his work: nothing is as known or accepted as Troy, Helen and his wars – that may never have taken place on real ground. Our children are still given names which he forged over three hundred years ago. Who does not know of Hector and Achilles? Not only individual lineages but most nations seek their origins in Homer's inventions. Mehemet II, Emperor of the Turks, wrote thus to our Pope Pius II: "I am amazed that the Italians should band against me, since we both have a common Trojan origin and, like the Italians, I have an interest in avenging the blood of Hector on the Greeks whom they however favour against me." Isn't all this a noble farce in which Kings, Republics and Emperors, all play their parts over many centuries, and for which this vast universe serves as a stage?"[1]

To his cast of farce-players, Montaigne could have added writers and scholars. From the mid-seventeenth to the mid-eighteenth century, the study of Homer in France became embroiled in what came to be called 'the Battle of the Ancients and Moderns', a hundred-year-long quarrel in which both sides held confused and contradictory opinions. According to the *anciens*, the classics were the admired model to be imitated and continued; according to the *modernes*, traditional literature was a creative millstone and writers and artists ought to be able to invent something distinctively new. The *modernes* defended Christianity over paganism; the *anciens*, the official power of the king at Versailles against the mundane intellectuals of the Paris salons. The debate covered many subjects: the use of Olympic gods or angels and demons in epic poetry, the language (Latin or French) in which public inscriptions should be written, the inclusion of colloquialisms and common actions in literary compositions. With aristocratic haughtiness, *modernes* such as Charles Perrault, author of the famous fairy-tales, admitted Homer's importance but scoffed at him for being vulgar:[2] for comparing the retreating Ajax to a stubborn ass beaten by children,[3] or for presenting a princess who declares that she must go down to the river to do her brothers' laundry.[4] Perrault's attitude towards Homer, wishing that he were purged of vulgarity, was compared by the critic Sainte-Beuve to that of the child who wants his mother to read him a story, saying 'I know it isn't true, but tell me the story anyway.'[5] The *anciens* said that they admired Homer in spite of all his coarseness and incivility.

One of the *anciens*, the twenty-three-year-old Jean Racine, whose mastery of Greek, even at that age, was remarkable, responded by praising Homer's sense of 'what is true'. Racine had little patience with what he considered pretentious niceties. 'Those husbandry terms,' he wrote, 'are not as shocking in Greek as they are in our tongue, which has little tolerance for anything, and which will not approve of composing eclogues about farmers, like Theocritus did, nor that one speak of Ulysses' swineherd in heroic terms. Such delicate sentiments are nothing but weakness of character.'[6]

Racine had the knowledge, memory and literary acumen to back his opinions. Born in 1639 and orphaned at a very young age, Racine was educated at the Cistercian School of Port-Royal. He completed his education in Paris and, after considering and rejecting an ecclesiastical career, settled in Paris in 1663 to become a writer. Once, when he was still an adolescent at Port-Royal, he had discovered Heliodorus' novel, written in the late second century AD, *Aethiopica* or *The Loves of Theogonis and Charicles*, inspired by the stories of Homer. The *Aethiopica* was an example of the kind of literature frowned upon by the Cistercian monks. Therefore, the sexton, finding the boy reading it in the Abbey forest, pulled it out of his hands and threw it into a bonfire. Racine managed to secure a second copy which was also discovered and condemned to the flames. He then bought a third copy and learned the text by heart. Then he handed it over to the sexton, saying: 'Now you can burn this one too.' We are told that, likewise, Racine had also been able to memorize much of the *Iliad* and the *Odyssey*.[7]

At Port-Royal, the adolescent Racine became familiar not only with the classics of Greek literature but with the strict tenets of Jansenism. The doctrine of Jansenism took its name from the theologian Jansenius who, in the early seventeenth century and under the influence of St Augustine, taught the doctrine of predestination, according to which it is not good deeds that can save men from the eternal fire but the 'gratuitous gift' of God's grace alone. Augustine had suggested a similar argument against the Pelagian heretics (who believed that good actions on earth led to salvation in heaven) but had defended the notion of man's free will in his debate against the Manichaeans. For twenty-two years, Jansenius worked on his thesis which he ambitiously called *The Augustine of Cornelius Jansen, Bishop, or On the Doctrines of St Augustine Concerning Human Nature, Health, Grief, and Cure Against the Pelagians*, but he died of the plague in 1638, before he was able to deliver it for publication. Two years later, his friends had it published under the abridged title of *Augustinus*. Outraged by its assurance, Pope Urban VIII declared several of its propositions heretical and the book was condemned by the Inquisition in 1641.[8] Blaise Pascal, defending Jansen's argument, wrote in his *Pensées* that 'We understand nothing of the works of God, if we do not start from the principle that He blinds some and enlightens others.'[9]

At least two of these heretical propositions run through most of Racine's work. First, that because of the lack of powers granted to us, some of us are unable to obey God's commands; second, that since we are all victims of Adam's sin, in order to merit or deserve punishment we need not be free from interior necessity but only from exterior constraint. According to Racine, both these notions are evident in Homer's depiction of the relationship between mortals and gods; for this reason, Homer (together with Pindar, Euripides and Plutarch) is for Racine the essential inspiration for some of his later great plays, notably *Andromache* and *Iphigenia*. Inspiration in the sense of source: Homer's conclusions are Racine's starting-points.

In the *Iliad*, Homer had shown the desperate Andromache clutching her son and bidding her husband Hector not to leave her to fight the Greeks. 'Andromache,' he tells her,

'dear one, why so desperate? Why so much grief for me?
No man will hurl me down to Death, against my fate.
And fate? No man alive has ever escaped it,
neither brave man nor coward, I tell you –
it's born with us the day that we are born.'[10]

A Jansenist argument if there ever was one, which Racine explores in great depth in *Andromache*. The play follows the story of Hector's widow, allotted among the spoils of war to

Achilles' son Neoptolemus (also known as Pyrrhus). Fate has wrought a chain of unrequited loves: that of the Greek envoy Orestes for the Greek Princess Hermione, of Hermione for Pyrrhus, of Pyrrhus for Andromache and of Andromache for her dead husband Hector. Orestes declares his position clearly: 'I give myself blindly to the fate [*destin*] that drags me along.'[11] But Racine realized that this statement was too simple: something more than the power of fate is at play. The first edition of *Andromache* was published in 1667. A year later, he revised the line for the 1668 edition. In the new version, Orestes says: 'I give myself blindly to the rapture [*transport*] that drags me along.'[12] Fate, yes, but in the form of rapture, an obsessive fate that grants each man and woman a peculiar emotional strength, an impulse greater than our realization that it will lead us to misfortune or catastrophe.

This 'emotional strength' is not to be confused with human instinct. An example of the dichotomy is made clear in the episode of Ulysses and the Cyclops in Book IX of the *Odyssey*. While the Cyclops is driven by cannibal appetite which he satisfies through brute force, Ulysses survives through his *metis*, a Greek word that means 'clear thinking', 'clever reasoning', 'cunning'. In the first case, the action and he who performs it are one; in the second, the actor is master of his acts.[13] Not that a hero must always override his instincts: on the contrary, they are proof of his humanity, but he must be conscious of them. After Ulysses is forced to watch in horror his companions being devoured by the monster Scylla, 'screaming out, flinging their arms towards me',[14] he and the survivors go ashore for the night and 'adeptly' prepare their supper. They eat, drink and only then do they recall their 'dear companions' and weep, and 'a welcome sleep came on them in their tears'.[15] Aldous Huxley, commenting on this passage, remarks that Homer's description of these men eating and drinking after seeing the slaughter of their friends, rings astonishingly true. 'Every good book,' says Huxley, 'gives us bits of the truth, would not be a good book if it did not. But the whole truth, no. Of the great writers of the past, incredibly few have given us that. Homer – the Homer of the *Odyssey* – is one of those few.'[16]

It is this individual God-granted emotional strength, managed through *metis*, that allows for human fate to be fulfilled in a myriad different ways. According to Racine, Andromache is forced to marry the victorious Pyrrhus, but she succeeds in both following her apparent fate (to incarnate Troy's victimhood after Hector's death) and in overturning Troy's defeat in the same action (since Pyrrhus effectively abdicates in her favour and that of Hector's son, by saying: 'I give you... my crown and my faith:/Andromache, reign over Epirus and me').[17] Giving herself to Pyrrhus, she will become his queen, while her son, a Trojan, will inherit the Greek throne. It is not love that prompts Andromache (who will pay for this *metis* with her life) but something else which she can neither identify nor ignore. To revise Pascal's phrase, God has both blinded and enlightened her, forced her to obey her fate and, at the same time, to assume consciously her rapture as well.

Racine's annotations, scribbled on the margins of his

copies of the *Odyssey* and the *Iliad*, give us a fair idea of his reading of Homer. Racine was especially interested in the methods by which Homer achieved verisimilitude. He notes, for instance, that Telemachus' kind reception of Athena in a stranger's guise (in Book I of the *Odyssey*) might have been inspired by a similar welcome granted to the wandering Homer on his own travels; he points out that the *Iliad*'s story takes forty-seven precisely timed days: five of fighting, nine of plague, eleven for Poseidon's sojourn in Ethiopia, eleven for Hector's funeral, and eleven for that of Patroclus. Racine's notes cover the subjects of food, dress, geographical descriptions, appropriate metaphors, the efficacy of certain gestures, the pleasure derived from weeping. In Book V, Ulysses has jumped overboard to escape the wave Poseidon has sent to destroy him. He has spent two days adrift at sea, and on the third day he sees land with 'the joy that children feel/when they see their father's life dawn again,/one who's lain on a sickbed racked with torment'.[18] But just as he is about to reach the rocky shore, Poseidon sends another battering wave that would have flayed him alive against the stones had Athena not intervened. Grasping the rocks, the skin of his hands ripped off in strips, striking the reef 'Like pebbles stuck in the suckers of some octopus/dragged from its lair',[19] Odysseus prays to the River God whose mouth he has reached:

'Hear me, lord, whoever you are,
I've come to you, the answer to all my prayers –
rescue me from the sea, the Sea-lord's curse!

Even immortal gods will show a man respect,
whatever wanderer seeks their help – like me –
I throw myself on your mercy, on your current now –
I have suffered greatly. Pity me, lord,
your suppliant cries for help!'[20]

Racine remarks that Seneca, during his painful exile in Corsica, summed up this passage in four words: '*Res est sacra miser*' ('Wretchedness is a sacred thing'). And Racine adds: 'This sentiment is made even more beautiful by the fact that it is engraved in the heart by Nature herself.'[21] It is also the sentiment at the heart of the poems of Homer.

Not all the combatants in the century-long *querelle* were driven by literary, philosophical or aesthetic motives. Some were political. Anne Dacier, daughter of a noted humanist and one of the best-known Greek scholars of her time, whose work on the *Iliad* was to influence Pope's translation a few years later, sided with the *anciens* and published in 1714 an *ancien* handbook, *On the Causes of the Corruption of Taste*.[22] Together with other scholars such as Pierre-Daniel Huet and Jacques-Bénigne Bossuet, she oversaw a series of Greek and Latin texts trimmed and purged for the use of the Dauphin, the eldest son of the king of France, and '*ad usum Delphini*' became an expression to denote an expurgated book. Although Dacier's editions of Homer were famous, the Homer *ad usum Delphini* timorously excised not only certain scenes that might have been considered ribald (Ulysses naked in front of Nausicaa in Book VI of the *Odyssey*) but several disrespectful references to kings as well (Achilles' insulting speech to Agamemnon in Book I of the *Iliad*). The *ancienne* Dacier thought that the Dauphin might be affected by a different kind of vulgarity than the one that offended the *moderne* Perrault.

Some motives were religious. For François de Salignac de la Mothe-Fénelon, Homer could serve as a source of inspiration to the young, but only if his stories were told in the appropriate pedagogical tone and with a devout Christian purpose. Gifted with a brilliant mind and an easy style of storytelling, Fénelon seemed to be destined to an exalted career as the tutor of the Dauphin. He was elected to the French Academy, appointed Archbishop of Cambrai in 1693, and enjoyed fame as the author of several literary books of instruction. But in 1696 he fell out of favour with Madame de Maintenon, King Louis XIV's second wife, for having befriended Madame de Guyon, a devout promoter of Quietism among the young. Quietism, a Christian doctrine linked to certain trends of Spanish mysticism, encouraged abandonment to the will of God and favoured silence over prayer.[23] Madame de Maintenon, and Fénelon's own teacher, Bossuet, feared that such passive habits would lead to moral indifference. To justify his position, Fénelon published in 1697 an *Explanation of the Maxims of the Saints*[24] in which he attempted to defend, point by point, the disputed doctrine, but his arguments did nothing to convince his opponents. Less than two years later, Bossuet managed to have the book condemned both by the pope and by the king. To add to the dishonour, at about the same time, Fénelon was discharged of his duties as royal tutor.

Before his fall from grace, Fénelon, in order to provide his royal pupil with a manual of mythology and civic morals, devised in 1699 a pedagogical fable in which he continued the story of Telemachus,[25] interrupted in Book IV of the *Odyssey*. In Homer's poem, Telemachus and Nestor's son, Pisistratus, arrive at the palace of Menelaus and Helen, where they hear the story which the Old Man of the Sea had told the king, that Ulysses has been captured by Calypso on a faraway island. In the *Odyssey*, Telemachus does not appear again until Book XV; Fénelon decided to recount the missing adventures of Ulysses' son. Accompanied by Athena disguised as the faithful Mentor, Telemachus is shipwrecked on Calypso's island, falls in love with a nymph, is rescued from the attachment by Mentor and finally reaches the port of Salente. Here Mentor establishes an ideal city-state, in which the good of the people and the independence of the Church take precedence over the pleasures and powers of the king. In the meantime, Telemachus is sent off on various missions (including a descent into the kingdom of Hades) until, at last, they both sail back to Ithaca where Telemachus and Ulysses are rejoined once again. In the climate of suspicion and fear of Versailles, the anonymously published *Adventures of Telemachus* was seen less as a pastiche of Homer than as a treasonable criticism of Louis XIV's regime. From his own cathedral pulpit, Fénelon was forced to read out the pope's ordinance against his *Explanation*, and lived the rest of his life exiled from the court. Fénelon died in 1715, only eight months before his fractious king.[26]

Eventually, the dispute between these various readings of Homer acquired an absurd reputation. In 1721, Charles de Secondat, baron of Montesquieu, author of the influential *De l'esprit des lois* ('On the Spirit of the Law') made fun of the French society of his time in an anonymously published epistolary novel that purported to be the gossipy correspondence between Usbek, a Persian traveller, and his friends back home, on subjects that ranged from the traditional and oppressive Oriental order to the silly *laissez-faire* of France. Remarking that he is shocked by seeing how Parisians waste their talent on puerile things, Usbek gives his friend Rhédi (who is in Venice) a telling example. 'When I arrived in Paris. I found them becoming heated in a quarrel about the flimsiest matter imaginable: the reputation of an ancient Greek poet, whose homeland for the past two thousand years remains unknown, as well as the time of his death. Both parties admit that he was an excellent poet; the only question was how much or how little merit was to be attributed to him. Each one wished to contribute something of his own; but, among these distributors of reputation, some carried more weight than others. That's what the quarrel was about!'[27]

In the end, the *querelle* was left appropriately unresolved. In 1757, the scholarly baron Frédéric-Melchior Grimm reached this conclusion: 'We can truthfully say, without wishing to depress the *modernes*, that nothing has made the sublime singer [Homer] so admirable as the work of his successors, from Virgil to Monsieur de Voltaire.'[28]

CHAPTER 12

Homer as Poetry

Have I not made blind Homer sing to me?

Christopher Marlowe, *Doctor Faustus*, 1604

A century earlier, at about the same time that the *querelle* had begun, Rembrandt van Rijn painted a portrait of a bearded man in a large-brimmed hat, rich sleeves and a gold chain, his right hand on the skull of an ancient bust. Though Rembrandt himself didn't give the painting a title, it came to be known as 'Aristotle contemplating a bust of Homer'. Around 1632, Rembrandt had moved from Leyden, his home town, to Amsterdam, where he had set himself up as a portrait painter. His reputation grew and with it his fortune, increased by his marriage to well-to-do Saskia van Uylenborch, who became the model for many of his paintings. But after 1642 his business declined and when, ten years later, the commission for the portrait came, he was only four years away from declaring bankruptcy. Rembrandt accepted with alacrity.

The work had been commissioned by a rich Sicilian merchant, Antonio Ruffo, who, when he received it, imagined from the pile of books in the background that the subject was an intellectual of some sort, and entered the painting in his inventory as 'a half-length of a philosopher made in Amsterdam by the painter Rembrandt (it appears to be Aristotle or [the doctor of the Church] Albertus Magnus).'[1] A third character appears in the composition: a helmeted head on a medallion hanging from a gold chain and recently identified as that of Alexander the Great, Aristotle's most famous pupil.[2] Alexander is the link between the philosopher and the poet: it was Aristotle who, according to Plutarch, prepared the edition of the *Iliad* that Alexander kept 'with his dagger under his pillow, declaring that he esteemed it a perfect portable treasure of all military virtue and knowledge'.[3] Simon Schama makes a good case for the bearded man being the Greek painter Apelles rather than Aristotle, but what matters is that the contemplated bust is indeed Homer. Rembrandt portrayed Homer on other occasions: in a drawing that shows him reciting his poems and in a preparatory sketch for a canvas (poorly preserved) that shows the bard with his hands on his cane and his eyes in shadow. These portraits, albeit imaginary, depict a flesh-and-blood person, made vividly present in the act of speaking or composing, his eyes convincingly blind while 'above them', writes Schama, 'within the shining skull of the poet, visions are nonetheless forming'.

The bust, however, is a convention, not Rembrandt's conception of a poet or even of the poet Homer, but the reproduction of a popular icon, a mass-produced trinket, equivalent to the Christ on a Lourdes crucifix, 'a portrait-type,' notes Schama, 'commonly, but entirely speculatively, identified as the bard'. An inventory of Rembrandt's possessions lists precisely such a bust. And yet, because it is not a particular interpretation of Homer, the bust serves in the painting as the symbol for an all-embracing idea of poetry, perhaps of all the literary arts. Aristotle or Apelles, or whoever the bearded man might be (and he is very much a particular man), is contemplating in Homer's bust an immemorial flow of emotions and thoughts, born out of the heartening belief that the experience of the world can be distilled and preserved in words and images that will reflect that experience in the eyes of a reader. The man in Rembrandt's portrait is contemplating, not a bust of Homer, but the creative act itself. In the same way that the art of poetry might have been, for the early bards, symbolically incarnated in a mythical being called Homer, now, more than two thousand years later, the icon of Homer had been turned upon itself and came to mean the art of poetry.

But what was meant by 'the art of poetry'? For Philip Sidney in the sixteenth century it was the art of imitation, 'a speaking picture, with this end: to teach and delight'.[4] For Francis Bacon, a century later, it was the art of sublimation. 'Poesy,' he wrote, 'was ever thought to have some participation of divineness, because it doth raise and erect the mind, by submitting the shows of things to the desires of the mind; whereas reason doth buckle and bow the mind unto the nature of things.'[5] For the eighteenth century it came to mean the art of inventiveness or invention, 'to be original with the *minimum* of alteration' as T. S. Eliot put it, though he also warned: 'It is dangerous to generalize about the poetry of the eighteenth century as about that of any other age; for it was, like any other age, an age of transition.'[6] And it is perhaps in translation that transition is best expressed and clearest seen, since, in a newly translated text, whatever is meant by 'originality' can be shown by comparison to previous efforts.

When Alexander Pope began his translation of the *Iliad*, his concern was neither literal faithfulness nor archaeological veracity, but a brave attempt to 'invent again' what the greatest of poets had invented for the first time; to achieve something close to perfection through an established literary correctness within which a poet's imagination could build its singular designs. For Pope, it was no Muse that inspired Homer but the poet's own creative genius. 'Homer,' he wrote in the Preface, 'is universally allowed to have had the greatest invention of any writer whatever... It is the invention that in different degrees distinguishes all great geniuses: the utmost stretch of human study, learning, and industry, which masters everything besides, can never attain to this.'[7]

Pope was largely self-educated. The son of a Roman Catholic London draper, he spent a difficult childhood afflicted with a tubercular disease of the spine, a recluse in his parents' home in Windsor Forest, which led him in later life to be both suspicious of and greedy for attention. At the age of sixteen, he wrote a series of pastorals in imitation of Theocritus and Virgil, embarking on a lifelong relationship with the ancient authors from whom he would draw both rhetoric and subject matter. In 1715, at the age of twenty-seven, he published the first volume of his translation of Homer's *Iliad*. Pope had imagined his enterprise as a long journey whose end seemed almost unattainable. Pope had no Greek – no doubt a stumbling-block for anyone attempting a translation of Homer – but he worked from the translations of others, namely those of Chapman, John Ogilby and Thomas Hobbes, as well as from John Dryden's unfinished *Iliad*, and from Latin versions which he could only more or less decipher since his Latin was far from perfect. He wrote diligently, constructing the book in the strict form of heroic couplets, elevating the tone when he felt that Homer was being too pedestrian. Every day, he would translate thirty or forty verses before getting out of bed, and then he would continue to revise them until the evening, when he would read through the finished pages 'for the versification only'. Before starting, he wrote out the sense of each of Homer's lines in prose, and only after grasping the full meaning would he proceed to shape it into verse. But however honed these mechanics, the process itself was never mechanical. The poet Richard Outram once explained that many poets work in this way:[8] constructing a poem from prose jottings of ideas and observations, their own but also those of other writers, and that from this word-skeleton the poem begins to take on its individual shape.

Homer made Pope financially independent. No author had ever made as much from a translation. The *Iliad*, published in six volumes, brought him £5,320 4s, the *Odyssey*

£3,500, a total profit of almost £9,000 – a fortune in those days. 'Thanks to Homer,' Pope said, he could 'live and thrive, indebted to no prince or peer alive.' Although his *Iliad* was met with high praise from the reading public, the academics were less enthusiastic. Edward Gibbon, who enjoyed the translation, said that it had 'every merit except that of likeness to the original',[9] and the despotic Master of Trinity College, Cambridge, Richard Bentley, judged it 'a pretty poem, Mr Pope, but you must not call it Homer'. Dr Johnson, however, not the least gifted of readers, called it 'the noblest version of poetry the world has ever seen'.[10] Henry Fielding, in his amusing *A Journey from this World to the Next*, imagined seeing Homer in Elysium, with the scholarly Madame Dacier sitting in his lap. '[Homer] asked much after Mr Pope, and said he was very desirous of seeing him; for that he had read his *Iliad* in his translation with almost as much delight, as he believed he had given others in the original.'[11]

But some critics disliked what they perceived as Pope's artificiality rather than his artifice, and made fun of his scruples in rendering Homer's vulgarities vulgar. William Hazlitt argued that Pope's 'chief excellence lay more in diminishing, than in aggrandizing objects... in describing a row of pins and needles, rather than the embattled spears of Greeks and Trojans'.[12] Leslie Stephen, in his biography of Pope, saw the problem clearly: 'Any style becomes bad when it dies; when it is used merely as tradition, and not as the best mode of producing the desired impression... In such a case, no doubt, the diction becomes a burden, and a man is apt to fancy himself a poet because he is the slave of the external form instead of using it as the most familiar instrument.'[13] But that was after Pope had triumphed; it was his successors who failed to match his achievements.

Pope took every precaution to deflect criticism. 'Our author's work,' he wrote of Homer in his Preface, 'is a wild paradise, where if we cannot see all the beauties so distinctly as in an ordered garden, it is only because the number of them is infinitely greater.' He then pushed as far as he could the botanical metaphor: 'It is like a copious nursery, which contains the seeds and first productions of every kind, out of which those who followed him have but selected some particular plants, each according to his fancy, to cultivate and beautify. If some things are too luxuriant, it is owing to the richness of the soil; and if others are not arrived to perfection or maturity, it is only because they are overrun and oppressed by those of a stronger nature.'[14] In other words, Homer's perfection cannot be fully transplanted by anyone.

'The concept of a *definitive text*,' wrote Jorge Luis Borges in 1932, 'belongs to either religion or weariness.'[15] A definitive translation, therefore, is only one that we have read more times than another. We grow accustomed to Edward FitzGerald or John Chapman, T. E. Lawrence or J. H. Voss, and because we are especially familiar with one of them, believe it to be truer and better than the rest. Pope's version is for most of his readers (those who enjoy his daring, inspired music) definitive. Almost any example will do to prove his excellence, such as this description from Book

XXIII, after Achilles has killed Hector and built a funeral pile for Patroclus. But the winds won't rise to feed the flames, and the goddess Iris must deliver Achilles' prayer to the winds Boreas and Zephyr.

> Swift as the word she vanish'd from their view;
> Swift as the word the winds tumultuous flew;
> Forth burst the stormy band with thundering roar,
> And heaps on heaps the clouds are tossed before.
> To the wide main then stooping from the skies,
> The heaving deeps in watery mountains rise:
> Troy feels the blast along her shaking walls,
> Till on the pile the gather'd tempest falls.[16]

Robert Fagles, whose translations are used throughout this book, has been widely praised for his accuracy and modern ring. In his version of the *Iliad* of 1990, he paints the same scene in six lines:

> Message delivered, off she sped as the winds rose
> with a superhuman roar, stampeding clouds before them.
> Suddenly reaching the open sea in gale force,
> whipping whitecaps under a shrilling killer-squall
> they raised the good rich soil of Troy and struck the pyre
> and a huge inhuman blaze went howling up the skies.[17]

Our modern ear recognizes Fagles' idiom, from the 'Message delivered' to the 'killer-squall', and the 'inhuman' for the huge blaze is very good; it all rings true. But Pope is not aiming for verisimilitude; rather a natural artificiality punctuated by cadenced rhymes, composing verses with a repetitive beat not unlike today's rap, attempting an art 'itself unseen, but in the effects, remains', as he had called for in his *Essay on Criticism*:

> First follow Nature, and your Judgment frame
> By her just Standard, which is still the same:
> ...
> Art from that Fund each just Supply provides,
> Works without Show, and without Pomp presides.[18]

Pope wrote at the closing (and also at the beginning) of a particular moment in English literature, with certain codes and conventions which he handled better than almost anyone, perhaps because he had invented many of them. 'By perpetual practice,' wrote Dr Johnson, 'language had in his mind a systematical arrangement; having always the same use for words, he had words so selected and combined as to be ready at his call.'[19] Pope's style was never 'external' to him, never mechanical: it only seemed so in the eyes of certain of his readers who either demanded scientific exactness from the poet, or had already become attuned to William Wordsworth's cadences, and who therefore felt that Pope's lines were strained and weak and nothing but decorative. William Cowper, a dreary minor poet, said that Pope 'Made poetry a mere mechanic art/And ev'ry warbler has his tune by heart.'[20] But, as George Steiner wisely maintained, 'Pope's detractors have been those who have not read him.'[21]

Matthew Arnold certainly had read Pope, and yet in spite of judging him a 'prodigious talent', found him wanting as a translator. 'Homer,' Arnold wrote in 1861, 'invariably composes "with his eye on the object", whether the object be a moral or a metrial one: Pope composes with his eye on his style, into which he translates his subject, whatever it is.'[22] Arnold was a keen reader, an astute critic, a gifted educator and sometimes a good poet. The son of a Rugby headmaster, he became first fellow of Oriel College, Oxford, and then inspector of schools, an appointment that allowed him, for thirty-five long years, to observe the conditions of education in England and led to his plea for better educational standards, following the Prussian model (*Schools and Universities on the Continent*, 1868) and to his arguments for a livelier artistic engagement (*Culture and Anarchy*, 1869). Arnold was, above all, a cosmopolitan, impatient with the provincialism and short-sightedness of English intellectual life. But it was, perhaps, in his discussion of the problems related to Homeric translation that he best demonstrated his critical skills.

Arnold's points of departure are the two main schools of thought regarding translation in general. The first (put forward by the classicist Francis William Newman, only better to condemn it) argued in 1861 that 'the reader should, if possible, forget that it is a translation at all, and be lulled into the illusion that he is reading an original work – something original (if the translation be in English) from an English hand.'[23] The second, strongly defended by Newman, argued that a translator should 'retain every peculiarity of the original, so far as he is able, with the greater care the more foreign it may happen to be', so that it might 'never be forgotten that he is imitating, and imitating in a different material'. The translator's first duty was 'a historical one, to be faithful'. Both sides, Arnold pointed out, would agree as to faithfulness, 'but the question at issue between them is, in what faithfulness consists'. Arnold reasonably noted that, even if Newman were to achieve his purpose and 'retain every peculiarity of his original', who would assure him that what he had done adhered to Homer's manner and habit of thought? 'The only competent tribunal in this matter, the Greeks,' Arnold pointed out, 'are dead.'[24]

Arnold advised any would-be translator to leave aside a number of questions – whether Homer ever existed, whether he was one or many, whether the Christian doctrine of the Atonement was foreshadowed in Homeric mythology – since, even if it were possible to answer them, they could be of no benefit to the translation. Nor should the translator assume that modern sentiment is applicable to ancient stories: whatever it was that the ancients believed, we must assume that it was something different from what we believe today. The translator of Homer should be four things: rapid in his telling, plain and direct in his expression, also plain and direct in his thought, and finally, eminently noble. These qualities, Arnold recognized, were probably 'too general to be of much service to anybody', except to a future poet who would try his hand at Homer and who 'will have (or he cannot succeed) that true sense for his subject, and that disinterested love of it, which are, both of them, so rare in literature, and so precious'.[25]

Newman dismissed Arnold's criticisms without really addressing them, using pedantic grammatical quibbles and abstruse semantic principles. He imagined that Arnold was being ironic when he was being reflective, and disrespectful when he was nothing but accurate. That most exacting of critics, A. E. Housman, writing in 1892, had this to say of Arnold's arguments: 'But when it comes to literary criticism, heap up in one scale all the literary criticism that the whole nation of professed scholars ever wrote, and drop into the other the thin green volume of Matthew Arnold's *Lectures on Translating Homer*, which has long been out of print because the British public does not care to read it, and the first scale, as Milton says, will straight fly up and kick the beam.'[26]

CHAPTER 13

Realms of Gold

> Talking it over, we agreed that Blake was no good because
> he learnt Italian at over 60 to study Dante, and we knew
> Dante was no good because he was so fond of Virgil, and
> Virgil was no good because Tennyson ran him, and as for
> Tennyson – well, Tennyson goes without saying.
>
> Samuel Butler, *The Notebooks*, 1912 (post.)

For the Romantic poets, it was not in literary straitjackets that poetry was to be found, but in wild inspiration, out in the fresh air and in the experience of country life. Form should mirror feeling. John Keats believed that time spent in natural surroundings would 'strengthen more my reach in Poetry, than would stopping at home among books, even though I should reach Homer'.[1] Keats, or at least so he said, had come to Homer through Chapman's 1598 translation of the *Iliad* in opulent fourteen-syllable lines. Keats' account of the discovery is justly famous.

Much have I travell'd in the realms of gold,
  And many goodly states & kingdoms seen:

Round many western islands have I been
Which bards in fealty to Apollo hold.
Oft of one wide expanse had I been told
    That deep-brow'd Homer ruled as his demesne;
    Yet did I never breathe its pure serene
Till I heard Chapman speak out loud and bold:
Then felt I like some watcher of the skies
    When a new planet swims into his ken;
Or like stout Cortez when with eagle eyes
    He star'd at the Pacific – and all his men
Look'd at each other with a wild surmise –
    Silent, upon a peak in Darien.[2]

Chapman, in his 'Preface to the Reader', argued that the English tongue was best suited for translating Homer, 'Prince of Poets', for 'Poesy is the flower of the Sun, and disdains to open to the eye of a candle'. This, for the Romantics, felt closer to the notion of the primordial ground-breaking Homer, the 'with-all-skill-enriched Poet'[3] whom no rigid poetic form could truly contain. Attacking Pope against Chapman was, they felt, a good way of defending Homer.

William Blake attacked all three, but especially Homer. Blake's relationship to Homer isn't easy to understand: Homer was both a poet to be lauded and a name to be reviled; both one of the Visionary Poets (Blake ranked him with Virgil, Milton and Dante)[4] and one of the 'superceded' classics; one of the 'Inspired Men'[5] society condemned as dangerous outsiders and also a figurehead for the 'classical' past, used by society for defending intellectual crimes such as trading and hoarding, translating and copying, while at the same time despising true creation. 'The Classics!' Blake raged. 'It is the Classics, & not Goths nor Monks, that Desolate Europe with Wars.'[6]

According to Blake, what set Homer 'in so high a rank of Art' was his craft in dealing with symbols. Homer, he wrote in about 1820, 'addressed to the Imagination, which is Spiritual Sensation, & but mediately to the Understanding or Reason'.[7] And yet, in Blake's view, Homer's poems had been degraded by readers who found in them contemporary morals. 'If Homer's merit,' Blake answered, 'was only in these Historical combinations & Moral sentiments he would be no better than *Clarissa*', Richardson's huge sentimental novel. And Blake added, beyond appeal: 'The grandest Poetry is Immoral, the Grandest characters Wicked!'[8] Homer's 'Poetry of the Heathen', however, was 'Stolen and Perverted from the Bible, not by Chance but by design, by the Kings of Persia & their Generals, the Greek Heroes, & lastly by the Romans.'[9] It is as if, for Blake, 'Homer' stood for various different notions unrelated and unrelatable to one another. Perhaps a clue to the ambiguous identity Blake lent Homer can be seen in one of the illustrations that he made for Dante's *Commedia*. The seventh image in the series is a depiction of the 'Father of Poetry', as Dante saw him, crowned in laurel, bearing a sword and attended by the six poets from antiquity. Except that instead of giving Homer his name, Blake wrote 'Satan' and then partly erased the caption.[10] Satan was, for Blake, the true hero of *Paradise Lost*.[11]

What Blake thought of Pope is clearer. He coupled him with Dryden, whose poetry he branded 'Monotonous Sing Song, Sing Song from beginning to end'.[12] His near contemporary, Lord Byron, disagreed. He had read Pope thoroughly and found him a greater revolutionary than any of Byron's fellow writers and, as a poet, 'a touchstone of taste'.[13] 'With regard to poetry in general,' he wrote to his publisher, John Murray, on 17 September 1817, 'I am convinced that [we] are all in the wrong, one as much as another; that we are upon a wrong revolutionary poetical system, or systems, not worth a damn in itself... I am the more confirmed in this by having lately gone over some of our classics, particularly *Pope*, whom I tried in this way... and I was really astonished (I ought not to have been so) and mortified at the ineffable distance in point of sense, harmony, effect, and even *Imagination*, passion, and *Invention*, between the little Queen Anne's man, and us of the Lower Empire.'[14]

Byron admired Pope's *Iliad*. He had read Homer in the original, and Pope's less than accurate rendering of Homer's Greek did not diminish for him the force of Pope's poetic language. In 1834, John Stuart Mill complained that the classical curriculum in England ignored history and philosophy in favour of philology and poetry, preferring to teach Homer rather than Plato.[15] Although this was not entirely true (the classic philosophy scholars of Oxford and Cambridge are proof to the contrary), Byron's Greece is indeed that of the

Iliad and the *Odyssey* rather than that of Socrates and his disciples.

For Shelley too, Greece was Homer. Homer's poems, he wrote in *A Defence of Poetry* in 1821, 'were the elements of that social system which is the column upon which all succeeding civilization has reposed. Homer embodied the ideal perfection of his age in human character; nor can we doubt that those who read his verses were awakened to an ambition of becoming like to Achilles, Hector, and Ulysses: the truth and beauty of friendship, patriotism, and persevering devotion to an object, were unveiled to the depths in these immortal creations.'[16] Except that, more than Shelley himself, it was his contemporaries who attributed to Shelley and to his fellow poets the ancient features of classical heroes: Shelley as Patroclus, Byron as Achilles, and something of this must have been felt by Byron when he chose to sail for Greece on 13 July 1823 'to seek in action the redemption he had not found in thought'.[17]

Of course, for both Shelley and Byron, Homer's Greece was more than just a catalogue of noble examples. Greece represented for Byron an idealized utopian past as well as the betrayed present in which the governments of Europe had allowed an usurper (the Ottoman Empire) to plunder the sacred inheritance.

Oh, thou eternal Homer! I have now
   To paint a siege, wherein more men were slain,
With deadlier engines and a speedier blow,

Than in thy Greek gazette of that campaign;
And yet, like all men else, I must allow,
 To vie with thee would be about as vain
As for a brook to cope with Ocean's flood;
But still we Moderns equal you in blood;

If not in poetry, at least in fact;
 And fact is truth, the great desideratum!
Of which, howe'er the Muse describes each act,
 There should be ne'ertheless a slight substratum.[18]

If Homer had created the model both of craft and theme, then, Byron believed, it was the modern poet's task to translate both elements into a contemporary idiom. The subjects of war and travel in the *Iliad* and the *Odyssey* were recast into *Childe Harold's Pilgrimage* (1812) and *Don Juan* (1819–24), in which both heroes have something of Ulysses in their make-up and become the privileged witnesses of less than heroic Troys. In *Don Juan*, for example, memory of Homer's story serves as a debasing mirror for the Siege of Ismail of 1790, when the Russian forces took over the Ottoman stronghold – a muddled feat which in turn reflects, for Byron, the political turmoil of Europe after Napoleon.

But now, instead of slaying Priam's son,
 We only can but talk of escalade,
Bombs, drums, guns, bastions, batteries, bayonets, bullets,
Hard words, which stick in the soft Muses' gullets.[19]

What was honourable combat in Homer's *Iliad* becomes, in the morally impoverished early decades of the nineteenth century, little more than official murder. With a side stab at Wordsworth in his 'Thanksgiving Ode', Byron comments:

> 'Carnage' (so Wordsworth tells you) 'is God's daughter':
> If *he* speak truth, she is Christ's sister, and
> Just now behaved as in the Holy Land.[20]

Literary craft was another matter. By and large, Byron's enjoyment of Homer did not prompt him to imitate the master. Only occasionally did Byron pick up a Homeric epithet or simile and make it his own, perhaps because he felt that the popular devices of one age lose both power and familiarity when applied in another.

Homer, like Milman Parry's *guzlars*, used formulae and conventions of various kinds to construct his work which (again, like the *guzlars*) he manipulated in order to convey, enlarge, contradict or subvert the meaning. It is impossible for us, at a distance of many centuries, to know how Homer's audience received these devices, whether they looked for faithful adherence to tradition or whether they expected an original twist to the formulae.

The Homeric conventions are of various kinds. Some are formulaic phrases, even entire lines of verse, to begin a story or introduce a teller, like the 'They lived happily ever after' or the 'Once upon a time' of folktales, as, for example: 'So Proteus said, and his story crushed my heart',[21] or 'When young Dawn with her rose-red fingers shone once more',[22] repeated throughout the works. Others are formal epithets (Parry called them 'ornamental epithets') that accompany a person or place as a title: 'Menelaus the red-haired king' or 'the strong-built city of Athens', equivalent to calling Richard Nixon 'Tricky Dick' or referring to Chicago as 'the windy city'. Certain translators (Robert Fitzgerald, for instance[23]) choose not to reproduce these conventions, possibly because they believe that, while Homer's listeners might have found the epithets almost inaudible but necessary, a modern audience would judge their repetition trite or tedious. Borges suggested that for the poet, to say 'divine Patroclus' was simply the conventional correct form of address, just as we say 'to go on foot' and not 'by foot'.[24] But these conventions no longer seem like conventions to us: the 'rose-red fingers' of Dawn may strike a new reader as delightfully quirky instead of formally expected.

Conventions also dictate the description of certain actions such as the killing of a soldier. When, in the *Iliad*, Laogonus is killed by Meriones, or Erymas by Idomeneus,[25] the chronicle of these deaths doesn't follow an individual course but a set pattern that begins with mentioning the point of impact ('under the jaw and ear', 'straight through the mouth') and ends with a traditional periphrasis for death ('hateful darkness gripped him', 'death's dark cloud closed down around his corpse'). They are not intended to be realistic descriptions. Rather, they are the equivalent of other established literary sequences in certain genre fiction, such as describing the crime early in a detective novel, and the suspects all gathered in one room at the end.

Perhaps the best known of these conventions, and the one that has had, for the readers of Homer, the strongest effect, is the extended or epic simile. Unlike an ordinary metaphor that catches qualities in one object which it ascribes to another, thereby creating a new literary space in which what is said and what is implied intermingle and increase, the epic simile places side by side two different actions that don't blend but remain visually separate, one colouring or qualifying the other. Of these, there are over two hundred in the *Iliad* alone. In Book XVI, after the Trojans, led by Hector, have succeeded in driving the Greeks back to their ships, Patroclus, dressed in Achilles' armour, counterattacks and pushes the Trojans back to their walls. The scene is one of gruesome savagery.

> As ravenous wolves come swooping down on lambs or kids
> to snatch them away from right amidst their flock – all lost
> when a careless shepherd leaves them straggling down the
>   hills
> and quickly spotting a chance the wolf pack picks them off,
> no heart for the fight – so the Achaeans mauled the Trojans.[26]

For Homer and his audience, wolves preying on sheep and the unreliable shepherd-god not paying due attention to his flock were no doubt common experiences, and the image must have soon become conventional through repeated usage. By the time the simile reached the eighteenth century, though wolves continued their ancestral butchery outside the city walls, the image had become more domesticated, and Byron's audience certainly had less direct experience than Homer's of the savagery of wolves. However, it is one of the few formulae that Byron chose to borrow from Homer. The first line of 'The Destruction of Sennacherib' echoes the savage image without dwelling on it:

The Assyrian came down like the wolf on the fold…[27]

The line is powerful, and manages to lend to a stale device a degree of vividness it perhaps never possessed: first we see the Assyrians descending, then our eyes are directed towards the wolf attacking sheep, and we are left to draw our own conclusions.

Sometimes a poet will reverse the process, and lead us upstream from the second element of the comparison to the first, without beginning with 'as'. This is a famous sonnet by the Argentinian poet Enrique Banchs; the beast in question is not a wolf but a tiger; the simile is the same:

Turning his iridescent side in sinuous step
The tiger passes sleek and smooth as verse
And fierceness polishes the hard and terse
Topaze of his vigorous cold eye.
He stretches the deceitful muscles out,
Malevolent and languid, of his flanks,
And lies down slowly on the dusky banks

Of scattered autumn leaves. Now all about
The jungle slumbers in the silent heat.
Between the silken paws the snub-nosed head,
The still eye fixed impassively ahead
While nervously the tail, with steady beat,
Thrashes a guarded threat against the straight
cluster of nearby branches. That's my hate.[28]

Violence and hatred like a wild beast, a wild beast like violence and hatred: not every reader is convinced by the comparison. In one of his comic poems, the American Ogden Nash poked fun at 'the kind of thing that's being done all the time by poets, from Homer to Tennyson':

What does it mean when we are told
That that Assyrian came down like a wolf on the fold?
In the first place, George Gordon Byron had enough
  experience
To know that it probably wasn't just one Assyrian, it was a
  lot of Assyrians.[29]

Nash's joke raises a serious point. No image is solely metaphorical; it elicits from the reader a literal interpretation at the same time as it conjures up a poetic coupling, none of which is ever exhaustive. As in Dante's multiple levels of reading, the Homeric image is simultaneously a conventional formula, a realistic description, a metaphor and an analogy.

Madame de Staël, Byron's brilliant contemporary, argued

that it was in fact those very images that rendered Homer great, not his ideas, which she found shallow. Against the classic models of the pagan world she set the new world of Christian northern Europe, Germany in particular – ancient form against Romantic feeling. 'Homer and the Greek poets,' she wrote in 1800, 'were remarkable for the splendour and variety of their images, but not for any deep thoughts of their mind... Metaphysics, the art of bringing ideas into widespread use, has much quickened the step of human spirit; but, in the act of making the road shorter, it may at times have stripped it of its more brilliant aspects. Every object presents itself in turn to Homer's gaze; he does not always choose wisely, but he always depicts it in an interesting fashion'.[30] In fact, like Pope, she praised Homer's invention. For Madame de Staël, Homer was a craftsman, not a thinker, a purveyor of splendid pictures, not of ideas.

CHAPTER 14

Homer as Idea

As learned commentators view
In Homer more than Homer knew.

Jonathan Swift, *On Poetry*, 1733

In 1744, the year of Pope's death, Giambattista Vico, former professor of rhetoric at the University of Naples and appointed historiographer of King Charles de Bourbon, published the third revised edition of his revolutionary *La scienza nuova* or *The New Science*. Misunderstood or ignored by his contemporaries, Vico proposed a cyclical theory of history that began with Homer and his poetic knowledge, and eventually returned to it, in an ever-ascending spiral. Philosophers in Vico's age offered two conflicting theories of knowledge: the first was based on evidence and argument, 'the philosophy of life and existence', while the second was centred on introspection and thought, 'the philosophy of the irrational'.[1] Vico offered a third possibility: the imagination, an independent power of the mind that he called *fantasia*. Poetic images, such as those created by Homer to tell 'true' stories but condemned as lies by Plato, were not 'concepts in poetic cloaks'. These *universali fantastici* or 'universal images born from the imagination' were to be considered on their own terms. Western philosophy had always seen these images as literary or rhetorical and, because they were not conceptual, they were regarded as 'not philosophical'. In contrast, Vico took Homer's side against Plato's rationalism and argued for a knowledge he called *sapienza poetica* or poetic wisdom, whose driving force was memory, the goddess Homer knew as Mnemosyne. 'Memory,' wrote Vico, 'has three different aspects: memory when it remembers things, imagination when it alters or imitates them, and invention when it gives them a new turn or puts them into proper arrangement and relationship. For these reasons, the theological poets called Memory the mother of the Muses.'[2] Later, James Joyce was to sum up Vico's notion as 'Imagination is the working over of what is remembered.'[3]

In Book II of the *Iliad*, when Homer is about to list the gathering of the Greek armies on the plain outside Troy, he stops his narrative and invokes the Muses. Partly, this is the literary device that became codified in the Middle Ages as *excusatio propter infirmitatem* ('an apology for one's own short-comings'); partly, it is a way of lending verisimilitude to the telling by shifting responsibility: 'It is not I who says this, but something greater than I, and therefore it must be true.'

Sing to me now, you Muses who hold the halls of Olympus!
You are goddesses, you are everywhere, you know all things –
all we hear is the distant ring of glory, we know nothing –

who were the captains of Achaea? Who were the kings?
The mass of troops I could never tally, never name,
not even if I had ten tongues and ten mouths,
a tireless voice and the heart inside me bronze,
never unless you Muses of Olympus, daughters of Zeus
whose shield is rolling thunder, sing, sing in memory
all who gathered under Troy.[4]

The Muses can 'sing in memory', that is to say, they can speak the truth embedded in memory. It is not the poet who knows, but the daughters of Mnemosyne, notably the Muse Urania, whom Homer calls the Muse of divination, and of the knowledge of good and evil (only later will she become the Muse of astronomy). From this concept, Vico developed the notion that poetic wisdom does not belong to one poet but to a people, and that 'there is no authorship to Homer's works in the ordinary sense of the word, but that the mind of the Greek people is their author'.[5] For Vico, Homer was not a person but 'an idea'.[6]

Some fifty years later, Friedrich August Wolf, who most probably had not read Vico, developed a similar theory about Homer and his poems. A pious legend has it that this son of a modest schoolteacher was the first student of philology of any German university and that, in order to discourage him from pursuing what appeared to be a fruitless career, the university authorities explained that, once he had graduated, there would only be a couple of poorly paid openings for a philology professor. Wolf answered that this didn't worry him, since he only required one. Indeed, at the age of twenty-four, he became professor of philology at the University of Halle, where he began to develop his Homeric theory. The resulting book, written in a complicated, almost impregnable Latin, was eventually published in 1795 as *Prolegomena ad Homerum*.[7]

At the time, German readers relied on two potent guides to ancient Greek culture. One was Johann Joachim Winckelmann, the celebrated classical scholar who had risen from cobbler's son to one of the most erudite men of his age, and who had summed up the Greek ideal as 'a noble naïvety and a calm greatness'.[8] The other was Johann Heinrich Voss whose magnificent translations of the *Odyssey* in 1781 and the *Iliad* in 1793 proved that modern German could serve as a powerful medium for epic poetry by employing a pattern of verses of varying lengths (dactylic hexameters) that allowed great freedom of expression and the full use of a rich vocabulary.

Wolf's arguments opposed both the reverential consecration of Winckelmann's Homer and the untouchable nobility of his verse in Voss's rendition, and called for a serious investigation of how books such as the *Iliad* and the *Odyssey* had come into being. With his *Prolegomena*, Wolf gave birth to the new science of classical studies or *Altertumswissenschaft*.

At about the same time, in France, in the aftermath of the *querelle*, the brilliant polymath Denis Diderot found in Homer an example of that which, in his opinion, should be left behind if enlightened progress was to be made. It was not that Homer didn't move him or that he thought the *Iliad* lacked the realism Diderot sought in art. He admitted, for example, that Homer was capable of powerfully conveying the horrors of war: 'I enjoyed the sight of crows in Homer gathered around a corpse, tearing the eyes out of its head and flapping their wings with delight.'[9] But Homer could be understood as a counter-argument to the Enlightenment's view of a world driven by rationality alone, a view put forward, for instance, in Diderot's *D'Alembert's Dream* of 1769. The book, intelligent and humorous, consists of a series of philosophical dialogues in which Diderot proposes a revised materialist account of human history and animal life, suggesting that emotions, ideas and thoughts could be explained through biological evidence, without recourse to theology or spirituality, and dismissing all uncritical reverence for the past. Diderot's *Encyclopédie*, in seventeen large volumes of text plus eleven of illustrations, edited together with Jean d'Alembert and published between 1751 and 1772, attempted to define 'science, art and craft' through rational methods only, and included under innocuous headings dangerous subjects such as religion and systems of government. Under the general entry for 'Greek Philosophy',[10] for instance, Diderot amused himself in dismissing Homer as 'a theologian, philosopher and poet' and quoted the unattributed view (which he admits, 'demonstrates a want of both philosophy and taste') that Homer was an author 'unlikely to be read much in the future'. Vico had suggested that Homer was the product of the heroic cycle in society's development. For

Diderot, Homer belonged to a primitive, superstitious age.

Even though they led to the same conclusion as Vico's, Wolf's arguments were strictly historical and philological. According to Wolf, the books we attribute to Homer are the fruit of a long development in which many poets and performers played a part, and he argued that the original source cannot ever be retraced, only surmised from much later echoes. For Wolf, the *Iliad* and the *Odyssey* were like archaeological sites, to be dug up and scrutinized in order to establish the different levels of their construction. Consequently, Homer was not the composer of his books but their end product, a colophon added by generations of bards to lend authority and coherence to the text. For Wolf too, Homer was 'an idea', but an idea that came to close, not to set in motion, the creative process.

Wolf's criticism sounded a warning note not only among literary critics but also among theologians. If the unity of the 'Bible of the Greeks' could be called into question, why not the Bible itself? If Scripture's purpose was not to tell stories but to tell the truth, following Cicero's prescription for the writing of history, 'that it shall not dare say anything false',[11] then even the Bible wasn't exempt from scientific scrutiny. Johann Wolfgang von Goethe thought that this was going too far, and that there was a line to be drawn between the criticism of Homer's writings and the criticism of God's word. 'They are now pulling to pieces the Five Books of Moses,' he complained, late in life, to his friend Johann Peter Eckermann, 'and if destructive criticism is noxious in anything, it is so in religious matters, because in these everything depends on faith, to which we can't return once we've lost it.'[12]

Goethe was very familiar with Wolf and his work. In the summer of 1805, he stopped in Halle and decided to attend one of Wolf's lectures. Wolf's daughter agreed to allow the illustrious visitor into her father's classroom. Goethe then told her that he wouldn't sit among the students but would hide behind a curtain to listen. This curious gesture might have an explanation. Goethe had met Wolf ten years earlier, immediately after reading the newly published *Prolegomena*. He liked the man as much as he disliked the book. To Friedrich Schiller, he wrote that Wolf's *Prolegomena* was 'interesting enough, though it sits with me badly. The idea might be good and the effort respectable, if only the gentleman, in order to dress its weak flanks, had not stripped the richest gardens of the Realm of Aesthetics and turned them into boring fortifications.'[13] At the same time (he didn't say this to Schiller), Wolf's dismantlement of Homer granted Goethe the right to aspire to the rank of epic poet himself. If, as Wolf argued, Homer did not exist as author, and if the *Iliad* and the *Odyssey* were a ragbag of different compositions, then surely a later poet, with some understanding and talent, might dig in them to find material with which to build new masterpieces. Goethe's unfinished poem 'Achilles', begun in 1799, stems from an exploratory reading of Homer in search of ideas for an epic. 'These days I was away in order to study the *Iliad*, to see whether between it and the *Odyssey* there might not lie an epic story. I only find tragic material, but is that really true or is it rather I who can't find the epic? The end of Achilles' life and its background allow for an epic handling... but the question arises, is it right to handle tragic material as if it were at best epic?'[14] Goethe found the project so daring that, writing to Wilhelm von Humboldt about his work, he refrains from mentioning particulars for fear of appearing 'too bold'.[15] The same reason may have prompted him not to make himself visible at Wolf's lecture.

If Homer, as Wolf maintained, was an idea, a collective noun, a concept, then for Goethe and his contemporaries it was one that changed with every age and with the needs and talents of every age, becoming an emblem of the time. In spite of Wolf's criticism, Homer's ancient Greece was a tempting replacement for their shattered world in the aftermath of the French Revolution, a world in which Germany held together precariously, torn by internal quarrels and enfeebled by religious differences. Johann Gottfried Herder in his histories of European philosophy, Christoph Martin Wieland in his historical novels and imaginary dialogues, Wilhelm Heinse in his utopist fiction, Friedrich Schlegel in his essays on classical antiquity, Karl Philipp Moritz in his guide to ancient mythology, and, above all, Friedrich Hölderlin in every one of his fragmented books – all, however different their visions, found in Homer and his universe a model for their ideal Germany where men were noble and brave, and poetry and philosophy their principal activities.[16]

For Goethe, Homer as a shifting mirror was the primordial example of the poet who first embodies the truth of his people and then allows himself to embody the truth of future men and women in faraway and inscrutable ages. Artists like Homer, whether they existed in flesh and blood or only as spirit, stood outside time because they were divine beings, intercessors between gods and men. To the poet's craft (Homer's and his own) Goethe lent the word *Schöpfertum*, 'creative activity',[17] an act of imaginative generation that sublimates the people's innermost needs and becomes defined through that which their nation wants. As a concept in search of a conceiver, Homer might have uttered the words which Goethe lends Christ in another context: 'Oh my people, how I yearn for you!'[18] – a god seeking believers. In Goethe's reading, the divine Homer brought for each new generation the possibility of a cultural redemption to which Goethe himself aspired for Germany. Perhaps exaggerating a little this relationship between the two poets, the literary historian Ernst Robert Curtius declared that 'The founding hero *(heros ktistes)* of European literature is Homer. Its last universal author is Goethe.'[19]

CHAPTER 15

The Eternal Feminine

All the argument is a cuckold and a whore.

William Shakespeare, *Troilus and Cressida*, 1609

Goethe started quite early making Homer his own: among the first books he read as a child were, together with the *Arabian Nights*, Fénelon's *Télémaque* and the *Iliad* and *Odyssey*.[1] By the age of twenty-one, in 1770, he was shamed by Herder, who had befriended the young student in Strasbourg, into perfecting his Greek by reading Homer with the help of a parallel Latin translation. The acquaintance with the original no doubt provided Goethe with the impetus of lending Homer's books to his hero in *The Sorrows of the Young Werther*, the sensationally popular novel that Goethe wrote three years later and in less than ninety days. Shortly after arriving in the country village where he will meet for the first time the love of his life (alas, promised to another man), Werther writes to the receiver of his confidences that he longs for no new books, he needs no guidance, he wants no encouragement: all he requires is 'a lullaby to cradle me and that I find plenty in my Homer'.[2] Homer provides for Werther (and for the young Goethe, if we may confuse in this instance author and fictional character) not instruction or information, not even a text to meditate upon, but a gratifying spectrum of vicarious emotions, 'from sorrow to joy, and from delicious melancholy to violent passion'.

The distinction between books that instruct and books that lull is one that Schiller was to address more than twenty years later, in an essay published in *Die Horen*, the magazine he had founded with Goethe's support. *On Naïve and Sentimental Poetry*³ separates writers into two categories: those who are at one with Nature, depicting it in the truest fashion, and those who, aware of their separation from Nature, long to return to it imaginatively. For Schiller, both Homer and Goethe belonged to the first category, while he himself chose the second. Carl Gustav Jung remarked in 1921 that Schiller's distinction was profounder than it appeared at first glance.⁴ What Schiller implied, said Jung, was not a distinction between fundamental classes of poets but between 'certain characteristics or qualities of the individual product. Hence it is at once obvious that an introverted poet can, on occasion, be just as naïve as he is sentimental.' Schiller, Jung argued, was not concerned with the question of 'types' but of 'typical mechanisms'.

Homer 'as naïve poet', Schiller had written, 'allows Nature to have unlimited hold over him'.⁵ For Jung, this meant that Homer unconsciously identified with Nature, creating by analogy an association between the subject poet and his thematic object, lending it his creative power and representing it in a certain way because that is the way it shapes itself within him. 'He is himself Nature: Nature creates in him the product.' For Schiller, according to Jung, Homer is his own poems.

Goethe's perception of Homer both embraced and expanded Schiller's. He too identified Homer with the Homeric creations but, for Goethe, the relationship was not a closed circle. Every reading of the *Iliad* and the *Odyssey* rescued from the mesh something of Homer's gift, freeing the ancient poet, over and over again, from Nature's 'unlimited hold'. This ongoing exchange regularly bore new fruit, as Goethe's own writings attested. Homer's poems provided the naïve (and sentimental) Goethe with copy for his plays, whether for entire conflated plots – Ulysses and the Phaeacians, or Ulysses and Circe, or for his *Nausicaa*, for example – or, more importantly, for the central material of his *Faust, Part Two*.

In April 1827, when Goethe was seventy-eight years old, he decided to include in the fourth volume of the authorized edition of his works (known as *Ausgabe letzter Hand* or *ALH*) a poetic fragment he called 'Helena: a classical-romantic phantasmagoria', subtitled 'An Intermezzo for *Faust*'. Writing to a French editor interested in including the fragment in a translated edition of *Faust*, Goethe stressed that it was essential to understand that both texts bore no resemblance to one another, and that the story of Faust and Helen of Troy was utterly different from that of Faust and Gretchen which, in another context, he described as a 'relationship that came to grief in the chaos of misunderstood learning, middle-class narrow-mindedness, moral disorder and superstitious delusions.'[6] A synopsis, written by Goethe a year earlier, explains how *Faust, Part Two* differs from *Faust, Part One*. 'The old legend,' wrote Goethe, 'tells us (and the scene is duly included in the puppet play) that Faust in his lordly arrogance requires Mephistopheles to procure for him the beautiful Helen of Greece, and that Mephistopheles after some demur consents to do so. In our own version, we felt in duty bound not to omit so significant a motif.'[7]

Goethe lends a tone of satire to the scene. Commanded by the German Emperor, Mephistopheles conjures up Paris and Helen at the imperial court. The courtiers are divided: the men criticize Paris while the women swoon over his hand-some features, and when the men admire Helen, the women make fun of her big feet and pale complexion. Faust, over-come by Helen's beauty, tries to cast Paris aside but, as he does, the apparitions vanish and the feast ends in a riot. Faust faints. When he wakes, he demands that Mephistopheles procure Helen for him and the two set off on a long, fantasti-cal journey to the Kingdom of the Dead. Persephone, moved by an eloquent plea, allows Helen to return to the Land of the Living on condition that she remain in an imaginary palace resembling that of Menelaus in Sparta: there Faust must try to seduce her. Faust succeeds and a child is born from their union, but the child is killed in an accident and his death draws Faust and Helen apart. The final acts see Faust back in the Emperor's realm where, as a reward for helping him defeat a rival, Faust is given a tract of imperial land covered by the sea. Faust ends his life blinded by Care for having despoiled and murdered an elderly couple who occupied part of his land. Mephistopheles, however, does not succeed in obtaining his soul, which is taken to heaven by mystical spirits led by the soul of Gretchen.

Helen begins with Homer and, it could be said, ends with Goethe. It is in the *Iliad* that she first appears as the beautiful woman 'for whom so many Argives/lost their lives in Troy, far from native land',[8] a land that now seems to her unreal: 'There was a world,' she wonders, 'or was it all a dream?'[9] But like the other women in Homer, Helen is not just a pawn in the war of men. Everything about her is complex, even her beauty, which is never described except through the eyes of her beholders. There is a moment of great pathos when the old men of Troy, aloft on a tower while the Greek armies gather outside the walls for what will be yet another bloody battle, realize that everything and everyone might be lost to the enemy and know that they might be spared if Paris's bride is returned to her rightful husband. And then they see Helen moving along the ramparts and say to one another:

'Who on earth could blame them? Ah, no wonder
the men of Troy and Argives under arms have suffered
years of agony all for her, for such a woman.
Beauty, terrible beauty!'[10]

Even though the protagonists of both the *Iliad* and the *Odyssey* are men, at the core of each poem are extraordinary women. In the *Odyssey*, Ulysses' troubled journey would be meaningless without Penelope at the end: not waiting idly but supporting his efforts to reach Ithaca with her unravelling of her tapestry, his advances in space counterpoised by her retreating strands in time. In the *Iliad*, Achilles defines the battle as 'fighting other soldiers to win their wives as prizes', since the long war hinges on kidnapped Helen, and progresses through the dispute over Chryseis (promised to Agamemnon) and Briseis (to Achilles). The action is driven by the fighting men, the justification they give for it lies with the women: the relationship between the two weaves the story into the future. Helen is magically aware of her emblematic role. She says to Paris:

> Zeus planted a killing doom within us both,
> so even for generations still unborn
> we will live in song.[11]

In the last years of the sixteenth century, Christopher Marlowe, inspired by the early German versions of the Faust story, was the first to dramatize in English, in his *Tragical History of Dr Faustus*, the legendary encounter between the wizard doctor whose 'study fits a mercenary drudge,/Who aims at nothing but external trash'[12] and the woman who is the world's paragon of beauty, describing her with the famous lines:

> Was this the face that launch'd a thousand ships,
> And burnt the topless towers of Ilium?
> Sweet Helen, make me immortal with a kiss.[13]

The 'thousand ships' belong to the catalogue of the Greek fleet in Book II of the *Iliad*, the 'topless towers' to the elders' watch in Book III and to the *Aeneid*, II:56, the kiss that makes its receiver 'immortal' comes from Helen's power as 'deathless goddess', also in Book III.[14] She is, as Marlowe interprets Homer's creation, the measure of comparison with all beauty, female or male, whether with the lovely Zenocrate in his *Tamburlaine* or with the handsome Gaveston in *Edward II*.

Two and a half centuries later, Edgar Allan Poe would equate Helen's immortal beauty with the immortality of the ancient world itself, whose knowledge reaches us 'from regions which are Holy Land', thereby closing a circle in which Homer's Helen can provide the exhausted intellectual (Faust or Poe) with all that which the world of books (including presumably those of Homer) cannot give him.

> Helen, thy beauty is to me
> Like those Nicaean barks of yore
> That gently, o'er a perfumed sea,
> The weary, wayworn wanderer bore
> To his own native shore.[15]

Helen, however, not only grants immortality; she is also an eternal *casus belli*, a tag repeated several times in the *Iliad*.

(though King Priam magnanimously tells her that he does not blame her but the gods: 'They are the ones who brought this war upon me.')[16] When Goethe has her appear in *Faust, Part Two*, she painfully recalls the suffering that has taken place because of her, and asks if she is cursed with the dreadful gift of always having men fight for her:

> Is it a memory? Has delusion seized my mind?
> Was I all that? And am I? And shall I still be
> The nightmare image, Helena the cities' bane?[17]

If Gretchen in *Faust, Part One* is the seduced innocent who ends up murdering her baby, then Helen in *Faust, Part Two* is her counterpart, the innocent seducer whose son dies because of his own recklessness. And yet, of all the main characters, only Helen appears condemned to an eternity in which she will always be, as she herself declares, 'so much admired and so much censured'. Helen is all ambiguity: upon seeing her, Faust cannot decide if this creature, 'conjured out of time',[18] is a dream or a memory. All he knows is that nothing but her love will fulfil him, and in fact Faust's only time of contentment is during his time in Helen's arms. Perhaps, for Goethe, it is this fulfilled love that justifies the decision of saving the 'great sinner Faust' in the end. And yet the doctor's salvation is not achieved through Helen's hand. *Faust, Part One* ends with a 'voice from above' declaring Gretchen redeemed and it is Gretchen's spirit who, in *Faust, Part Two*, leads the doctor's soul to heaven, to the 'Eternal

Feminine' of the last verses. Helen, the other incarnation of that same 'Eternal Feminine', must instead return to Homer's realm: she can appear, but not remain visible in Goethe's modern world which, in spite of its enthusiasm for the ancients, refuses (in Werther's words) 'to be guided or encouraged or sent into raptures.'[19]

Shortly before his death in 1832, Goethe finished the last section of his autobiography, *Dichtung und Wahrheit*. In it, he hails his century as one fortunate enough to have witnessed the rebirth of Homer. 'Happy is that literary age,' he wrote, 'when great works of art of the past rise to the surface again and become part of our daily dealings, for it is then that they produce a new effect. For us, Homer's sun rose again, and according to the requirements of our age… No longer did we see in those poems a violent and inflated heroic world, but rather the mirrored truth of an essential present, and we tried to make him as much ours as possible.'[20]

CHAPTER 16

Homer as Symbol

> What song the Syrens sang, or what name Achilles
> assumed when he hid himself among the women, though
> puzzling questions, are not beyond all conjecture.
>
> Sir Thomas Browne, *Urn Burial*, 1690 (posth.)

Friedrich Nietzsche had little time for Goethe's views on Homer, which he found 'incompatible with that element out of which Dionysian art grows – the orgiastic. Indeed I do not doubt that as a matter of principle, Goethe excluded anything of the sort from the possibilities of the Greek soul. Consequently Goethe did not understand the Greeks.'[1] Like Goethe, Nietzsche had read Homer very young. The gifted son of a pastor, he studied in both Bonn and Leipzig and was elected to the chair of classical philosophy at the University of Basel at the age of twenty-five. During his professorship, three years later, he wrote his first great book, *The Birth of Tragedy*, published in 1872, in which he began to outline his theory about the driving forces of Greek culture. But already in his inaugural lecture at Basel, in 1869, he had pronounced the question on Homer that unwittingly echoed Vico's and foreshadowed Jung's: 'Has a person been made out of an idea or an idea out of a person?'²

For Nietzsche, no one could read Homer's books as Homer wrote them: we read not the stories he told but interpreted versions of those stories. 'Why did the whole Greek world exult over combat scenes of the *Iliad*?' he asks in a posthumously published fragment. 'I fear that we do not understand these sufficiently in a "Greek" manner; indeed, that we should shudder if we were ever to understand them "in Greek".'³ What allows for these individual readings is that, at the core of ancient Greek culture, is a living tension between, on the one hand, a tendency towards order and individual fulfilment (which Nietzsche called 'Apollonian') and, on the other, violence and destructive rapture ('Dionysian'). In this context, Homer was for Nietzsche a creative Apollonian force that wrote his poems 'in order to persuade us to continue to live'.⁴ Homer's gods justify human life by sharing it with us mortals; for his heroes, the greatest pain is therefore to leave this life, especially when one is young. Nietzsche saw Homer as the 'total victory of the Apollonian illusion', an illusion that entails believing ourselves worthy of being glorified, and therefore imagining beautiful gods who are our own reflection. In this, he joins Schiller's characterization of Homer as a natural poet. 'By means of this mirage of beauty,' concludes Nietzsche, 'Hellenic "will" battled with the talent, correlative to the artistic talent, for suffering and the wisdom of suffering, and as a monument to its triumph stands Homer, the naïve artist.'⁵

Seventeen years after writing this, in 1889, in Turin, the syphilis from which Nietzsche had suffered for years manifested itself in serious mental disturbances. To the bewilderment of his hosts, Nietzsche locked himself in his room, pounded the piano night and day, pranced about naked, singing loudly, and performed autoerotic Dionysian rites. When a local doctor for the insane came to examine him, Nietzsche cried out: *'Pas malade! Pas malade!'* At last his friends convinced him to leave Turin and return to Basel. In 1900 he died in Weimar, dressed in a white robe and recognizing no one.[6]

Nietzsche's poetical reading of Homer had placed him on the opposite side of Wolf's unsentimental investigations, though both believed that Homer was an abstract noun, a classic concept rather than a historical person. Homer's poems were a different matter. Nietzsche (and perhaps Wolf as well) understood that one of the qualities of a classic is that it elicits from the reader a double sense of witnessed truth: that of poetic artifice and that of experienced reality, or, in Nietzschean terms, that of Apollonian illusion and that of Dionysian struggle.

Sigmund Freud, writing in 1915, some six months after the outbreak of the First World War, suggested that something like this split perception of the world manifested itself in our relationship with death.[7] He did not refer to Nietzsche: his biographer, Peter Gay, remarked that 'Freud treated Nietzsche's writings as texts to be resisted far more than to be studied.'[8] Freud did, however, follow Nietzsche in noting that the value we place on life after death was a development of post-Homeric times and, like Nietzsche, quoted in support of his theory the answer Achilles gave to Ulysses in the Underworld. For Ulysses (that is, the living, for whom death is still unimaginable), death is a form of heroic fulfilment. He says to Achilles that he should not grieve at having died because:

Time was, when you were alive, we Argives
honoured you as a god, and now down here, I see,
you lord it over the dead in all your power.[9]

As mentioned, Achilles furiously denies this: he does not believe in the necessary advent of death and in whatever value we may grant it. His only concern is life, which he no longer has, and against which he will trade any reward of fame or glory. And this is the same Achilles who, in the *Iliad*, telling the young son of Priam that he will not spare his life, is suddenly aware that one day he too will die:

… even for me, I tell you,
death and the strong force of fate are waiting.
There will come a dawn or sunset or high noon
when a man will take my life in battle too.[10]

Achilles knows that he is mortal and, at the same time, refuses to accept the final fact. Freud argued that, like Achilles, our unconscious 'does not believe in its own death; it behaves as if it were immortal. What we call our "unconscious" – the deepest strata of our minds, made up of instinctual impulses – knows nothing that is negative, and no negation; in it, contradictories coincide. For that reason it does not know its own death, for to that we can give only a negative content. Thus there is nothing instinctual in us which responds to a belief in death.' And Freud adds: 'This may even be the secret of heroism.'[11]

Homer and the ancient world (especially that of the Greek tragedians) provided Freud with a useful vocabulary of what he called 'symbols' and lent him key words for the abstract concepts he dealt with in his psychoanalytical investigations. These sometimes took on the concrete shape of art objects which he enjoyed collecting throughout his life. In his study, first in Vienna, then in London, he kept dozens of Egyptian, Greek and Roman figurines and pottery, 'strewn over every available surface: they stood in serried ranks on bookshelves, thronged table tops and cabinets, and invaded Freud's orderly desk, where he had them under his fond eye as he wrote his letters and composed his papers'.[12] It was as if the presence of signs from the past helped him find the words for naming that which the unconscious would not even deny. To one of his patients, he explained that his fondness for the ancient world served as a useful mirror for his practice. 'The psychoanalyst, like the archaeologist in his excavations, must uncover layer after layer of the patient's psyche, before coming to the deepest, most valuable treasures.'[13] But, as Peter Gay remarked, 'this weighty metaphor does not exhaust the significance of this addiction for Freud'.[14] Freud found in Homer and his world a constantly changing trove of symbolic readings which, as his own work proved, reflected the tension between contradictory revelations. As if echoing the dialogue between Andromache and Hector in Book VI of the *Iliad*, Freud wrote: 'We recall the old saying, *Si vis pacem, para bellum*. If you want to preserve peace, arm for war.' And he concluded: 'It would be in keeping with these times to alter it: *Si vis vitam, para mortem*. If you want to endure life, prepare yourself for death.'[15]

Freud drew cautious parallels between archaeological discoveries and psychological truths, suggesting symbolic links between, for instance, the memory of disappeared civilizations and the group psychology of certain social upheavals. 'If all that is left of the past are the incomplete and blurred memories which we call tradition, this offers an artist a peculiar attraction, for in that case he is free to fill in the gaps in memory according to the desires of his imagination.'[16] In the same way, Freud's psychoanalysis (one of his more intelligent disciples argued) confronts us 'with the abyss within ourselves' and forces on us 'the incredibly difficult task of taming and controlling its chaos'.[17]

Carl Gustav Jung tempered what he considered a reductive method in Freud's reading. For Jung, 'Those conscious contents which give us a clue to the unconscious background are incorrectly called *symbols* by Freud. They are not true symbols, however, since according to his theory they have merely the role of signs or symptoms of the subliminal processes. The true symbol differs from this and should be understood as an expression of an intuitive idea that cannot yet be formulated in any other or better way.'[18] For Jung, only certain images, fully denoting an idea in all its sprawling and even contradictory complexity (Plato's metaphors or Christ's parables) were 'genuine and true symbols'. Homer, who knew this, did not end the *Iliad* with the narrow image of death. Just before the closing verses, he joined the grief of the defeated to the grief of the victors, and conjured up the memorable image of both combined in one, that, as Jung thought, surely 'cannot yet be formulated in any other or better way'. Agreeing to let old Priam have the remains of Hector, Achilles instructs the serving-women first to 'bathe and anoint the body' so that the father will not see the corpse of his son in a shameful state. And then Achilles lifts Hector up in his own arms and lays him down on a bier and, as he does this, he calls to his beloved Patroclus, whose murder he sought to avenge by the killing of Hector, and addresses the ghost of his friend:

'Feel no anger at me, Patroclus, if you learn –
even there in the House of Death – I let his father
have Prince Hector back. He gave me worthy ransom
and you shall have your share from me, as always,
your fitting, lordly share.'[19]

In 1908, the English poet Rupert Brooke attempted to disclose both the symbolic or 'poetic' and the historical or 'realistic' readings of Homer in a double sonnet which he imagined as a possible forked ending for the *Iliad*. Though hardly a professional soldier (he died of blood poisoning in 1915 on his way to fight in the Dardanelles) Brooke is today mainly remembered as a war poet on the strength of the first lines of 'The Soldier', written in the year of his death: 'If I should die, think only this of me: / That there's some corner of a foreign field/That is for ever England.'

Brooke's Homeric poem, 'Menelaus and Helen', reads:

I

Hot through Troy's ruin Menelaus broke
  To Priam's palace, sword in hand, to sate
  On that adulterous whore a ten years' hate
And a king's honour. Through red death, and smoke,
And cries, and then by quieter ways he strode,
  Till the still innermost chamber fronted him.
  He swung his sword, and crashed into the dim
Luxurious bower, flaming like a god.

High sat white Helen, lonely and serene.
  He had not remembered that she was so fair,
And that her neck curved down in such a way;
And he felt tired. He flung the sword away,
  And kissed her feet, and knelt before her there,
The perfect Knight before the perfect Queen.

II

So far the poet. How should he behold
   That journey home, the long connubial years?
   He does not tell you how white Helen bears
Child on legitimate child, becomes a scold,
Haggard with virtue. Menelaus bold
   Waxed garrulous, and sacked a hundred Troys
   'Twixt noon and supper. And her golden voice
Got shrill as he grew deafer. And both were old.

Often he wonders why on earth he went
   Troyward, or why poor Paris ever came.
Oft she weeps, gummy-eyed and impotent;
   Her dry shanks twitch at Paris' mumbled name.
So Menelaus nagged; and Helen cried;
And Paris slept on by Scamander side.[20]

CHAPTER 17

Homer as History

... but where I sought for Ilion's walls,
The quiet sheep feeds, and the tortoise crawls.

Lord Byron, *Don Juan*, 1819–24

Heinrich Schliemann, an amateur archaeologist who died a decade before Nietzsche, shared this double vision of the *Iliad*, both as invention and as history. Schliemann was less interested in the truth of the person Homer (though Schliemann thought he had indeed existed) than in that of his poems. Schliemann believed that, if properly deciphered, Homer's books, poetical inventions as they were, could provide an accurate guide to the physical site of Troy.

According to Schliemann (who also confessed that he was prone to lying and exaggeration), his passion for Homer began in his early childhood, when his father would recite for him at bedtime the adventures of the Homeric heroes. The boy was so enthralled by the stories that, one Christmas when he was ten, he presented his father with the gift of 'a badly written Latin essay upon the principal events of the Trojan war and the adventures of Ulysses and Agamemnon'.[1]

Because of the family's position, the boy was unable to attend college; he was instead apprenticed, at the age of fourteen, to a village grocer and quickly forgot most of what he had learned at home.

One of the picturesque characters in Schliemann's village happened to be an apprentice miller, a young man who had once studied the classics but had since become a pitiful drunk. Rumour had it that he had been expelled from school for bad behaviour and that, to punish him, his father, a Protestant clergyman, had made him learn the miller's trade. In despair, the young man had taken to drink but had not, however, forgotten his Homer. One evening, the drunken miller staggered into Schliemann's shop and, in front of the astonished boy, recited one hundred lines of ancient Greek in resounding rhythmic cadence. Schliemann did not understand a single word but the music of the verses made such an impression on him that he burst into tears and asked the man to repeat them again and again, bribing him with tumblers of brandy. 'From that moment on,' he later confessed, 'I never ceased to pray God that by His grace I might yet have the happiness to learn Greek.'[2]

A chest ailment made it impossible for Schliemann to continue working at the grocer's and, in search of new employment, he travelled to Hamburg, where he found a position as a cabin boy on a ship bound for Venezuela. A storm stranded the ship on the Dutch coast and Schliemann, believing destiny had decreed that he live in Holland, settled down in Amsterdam as a filing clerk. He decided to study languages and learned in quick succession English, French, Dutch, Spanish, Italian, Portuguese and Russian, but not until 1856, at the age of thirty-four, did he begin to study his beloved Greek. Some time later, a number of successful business transactions left him with a huge fortune. In his accounts of these adventures, Schliemann doesn't tell us what those transactions were, but his vast correspondence reveals that he was involved in various unscrupulous dealings: the commerce of saltpetre for gunpowder during the Crimean War, the purchase of gold from the Californian prospectors during the gold-rush, the buying and selling of cotton during the American Civil War.[3] A rich man at last, Schliemann was now able to fulfil his dream of visiting ancient Greece and exploring the places described by Homer. In this he was astonishingly successful. In 1873, using the *Iliad* as his travel guide, Schliemann unearthed, beneath the town of Hisarlik in north-western modern Turkey, the fabled city of Troy – not one but nine strata of Trojan cities.

Contrary to Schliemann's own marvellous account, he did not immediately stumble on the site. From the seventeenth century on, readers had imagined that it was possible to find 'Priam's six-gated city', as Shakespeare called it in *Troilus and Cressida*. John Sanderson, Queen Elizabeth I's ambassador, wrote that twice he had set off in search of Troy, first in 1584 and then in 1591, unsuccessfully. Throughout the eighteenth and nineteenth centuries, the search continued intermittently. Robert Wood published a book in 1769, *Essay on the Original Genius of Homer*, that, though not proposing an exact location for the city, described the changes in the topography that would probably have taken place since Homer's time (changes which we now know to be correct).[4] Some fifty years later, the armchair archaeologist Charles Maclaren correctly suggested that Troy's location was in Hisarlik, but the first serious diggings of the site were begun by Frank Calvert, a scholarly Englishman who had lived in Turkey all his life. Schliemann, whose sights were at first fixed on another location, finally agreed with Calvert's choice and joined him in the excavations.

Calvert and Schliemann soon had a falling out. Calvert publicly expressed his opinion that there was missing in the site an essential link between two strata, between that of the prehistoric occupation of the city and that of the so-called Archaic style of approximately 700 BC. In other words, there was no evidence of roughly 1200 BC, the time of the Trojan War itself. Schliemann was furious and accused Calvert of being 'A foul fiend... a libeller and a liar'. A few weeks later, Schliemann was vindicated. On 31 May 1873 he uncovered, in the stratum he had argued was Homer's Troy, a treasure of copper cauldrons full of golden and silver cups and vases, copper lance-heads and an astonishing collection of gold jewellery: rings, bracelets, earrings, diadems and one ornate headband. To record the find, Schliemann had his wife photographed in what he called 'the Jewels of Helen'.[5] Though the jewels now appear to have been dated correctly to the time of Homer's Troy, the 'treasure' itself was probably found by Schliemann over various weeks, scattered about in a number of places and then gathered in order to make believe that they were all part of one lot. Most of Schliemann's finds were stored in Berlin, from where they mysteriously disappeared after World War Two. Until recently, all that remained of the gold of Troy were later finds: a pair of earrings, a necklace, a few rings and some pins, on display at the Archaeological Museum of Istanbul. Then, in 1993, the vanished treasure was discovered in the Pushkin Museum in Moscow, where it had been deposited by the Russian Army. Though a German-Russian treaty has since been signed, allowing for the return of Schliemann's finds to Berlin, in 2004 the Association of Russian Museum Directors blocked the procedures in retaliation for the looting of Russian museums by the soldiers of the Third Reich.

Professional archaeologists and academic classicists were enraged by Schliemann's audacity and attempted to dismiss his findings. Matthew Arnold called him 'devious'. The orientalist Joseph Arthur, Count de Gobineau said he was 'a charlatan'. Ernst Curtius, excavator of Olympia, branded him 'a swindler'. In these attacks there were at least four issues at play: first, what the academics considered the insolent intrusion of an amateur into their professional field; second, the highly disturbing notion that poetry might not be pure invention, but might instead provide accurate depictions of the material world it portrayed; third, the inevitable conclusion that the *Iliad* and the *Odyssey* might have their origin in days far beyond the heroic age of Greece, in the pre-classical and nebulous times outside the reach of the university curriculum. Finally, they questioned the veracity of Schliemann's assumptions, arguing that the ruins he had uncovered were not those of Homer's Troy (which now we know occupy the stratum identified as Troy VIIa).

To Schliemann's daring imagination, these academic quibbles must have sounded like a reproach made to someone who has discovered the rabbit-hole leading into Wonderland, that this was not the *actual* entrance through which Alice herself descended. But Schliemann persisted. He described the ruins he had uncovered as 'Troy, the city besieged by Agamemnon', and the precious objects he had unearthed as 'the treasure of King Priam', because, he wrote, they were 'called so by the tradition of which Homer is the echo; but as soon as it is proved that Homer and the tradition were wrong, and that Troy's last king was called "Smith", I shall at once call him so.'⁶ Whatever the criticism of the professionals, in the popular eye Schliemann became a hero, the discoverer of a world believed until then to be purely imaginary.

CHAPTER 18

Madame Homer

If [the critic Desmond MacCarthy] sincerely wishes to
discover a great poetess, why does he let himself be
fobbed off with a possible authoress of the *Odyssey*?…
I have often been told that Sappho was a woman, and
that Plato and Aristotle placed her with Homer and
Archilochus among the greatest of poets.

Virginia Woolf, 'The Intellectual Status of Women', 1920

Some twenty-five years after Schliemann's discoveries, in
1897, Samuel Butler published in London a little book called
*The Authoress of the Odyssey: Who and What She Was, When and
Where She Wrote.*[1] The son of a clergyman and grandson of a
bishop, Butler had by then tried his hand, mostly with fair
success, at a dozen different activities, from sheep farmer in
New Zealand (which gave him the setting for his utopian
fantasy *Erewhon*) to painter, theologian, poet, scientist, musi-
cian, classicist and novelist (his best work, *The Way of All
Flesh*, was published posthumously, in 1903). Butler believed
that a careful reading of the *Odyssey* could prove that the
author was, not a blind male bard, but a young unmarried

woman, and a native of Sicily. He placed her life roughly between 1050 and 1000 BC and argued that she had before her, while she worked, Homer's *Iliad* from which, from time to time, 'she quoted freely'. Butler dismissed Wolf's theories of a multilayered authorship, which he ridiculed as 'the nightmares of Homeric extravagance which German professors have evolved out of their own inner consciousness', but he conceded that two distinct poems, 'with widely different aims', had been cobbled together to make the *Odyssey* as we know it. With happy nonchalance, Butler said that he had based his theory on a comment made in passing by the scholar Richard Bentley (who had so flippantly dismissed Pope's translation) that the *Iliad* was written for men and the *Odyssey* for women. Butler denied this notion of an exclusive audience, arguing that the *Odyssey* 'was written for any one who would listen to it', but maintained, however, that 'If an anonymous book strikes so able a critic as having been written for women, a *prima facie* case is established for thinking that it was probably written by a woman.'

The idea had come to Butler in 1886. He had been writing the libretto (and much of the music) for a secular oratorio based on the travels of Ulysses, and decided to re-read the *Odyssey* in the original, something he hadn't done for many years. 'Fascinated, however, as I at once was by its amazing interest and beauty, I had an ever-present sense of a something wrong, of a something that was eluding me, and of a riddle which I could not read. The more I reflected upon the words, so luminous and so transparent, the more I felt a darkness behind them that I must pierce before I could see the heart of the writer – and this was what I wanted; for art is only interesting in so far as it reveals an artist.'[3]

Once certain of his intuition, Butler found in the *Odyssey* the facts to sustain it. For example, he discovered in the poem mistakes that, he said, 'a young woman might easily make, but which no man could hardly fall into'. Among these, he listed: believing that a ship had a rudder at both ends (in Book IX); that well-seasoned timber can be cut from a growing tree (Book V); that a flying hawk could tear its prey while in the air (Book XV). He then proceeded to map out carefully the palace of Ulysses to prove that only a woman would know what took place in all quarters of the building and, when certain descriptions presented problems, he argued again that only a woman would have no qualms about 'shifting the gates a little' for the purpose of her story. Finally, 'When Ulysses and Penelope are in bed... and are telling their stories to one another, Penelope tells hers first. I believe a male writer would have made Ulysses' story come first and Penelope's second.'[4]

Butler then considered a problem which scholars have been confronting since the early days of Homeric commentary: that Ulysses' description of Ithaca doesn't correspond exactly to any known Greek island:

Sunny Ithaca is my home. Atop her stands our seamark,
Mount Neriton's leafy ridges shimmering in the wind.
Around her a ring of islands circle side-by-side,

Dulichion, Same, wooded Zacynthus too, but mine
lies low and away, the farthest out to sea,
rearing into the western dusk
while the others face the east and breaking day.[5]

The topographical references Homer gives us for Ithaca are detailed and vivid, but they don't match the ones of the Ithaca we know today. It has often been suggested that Homer, composing his poem somewhere in Asia Minor, had just invented the description of Ulysses' home which he had never seen, or was misinformed about it. A recent theory suggests that Ithaca was in fact an island that has now become part of the mainland: the westernmost tip of Cephalonia, known as Paliki.[6] Butler imagined instead that there was, in Homer's time, another island called Ithaca, which he located in the area around Trapani in Sicily. Butler chose 'the lofty and rugged island of Marettimo'[7] as the most likely candidate.

Classicists and historians received the book in scornful silence or with finger-wagging disapproval. As late as 1956, the American historian Moses I. Finley accused Butler of taking for granted 'that not only was the author(ess) of the *Odyssey* a Victorian novelist, but that the values and emotions of the characters in the poem were identical with those of his own time'.[8] The criticism is fair. And yet, quirky and unconvincing as Butler's theory might be, it established a precedent for a particular relationship to the classics that would become almost commonplace among writers of the twentieth century. Instead of viewing the work as a hallowed summit readers can never quite reach and in whose shadow they strive, as Goethe had suggested,[9] Butler proposed a level ground on which both share a common space that can be entered, inhabited, renamed and reshaped in an endlessly renewed process. The process itself was, of course, not original, and yet its shameless appropriation had a pleasing cheek about it. But then Butler never lacked self-confidence. He once remarked to his friend William Ballard that when Perseus had come to free Andromeda, the dragon had never felt in better health and spirits, and was looking remarkably well. Ballard said he wished that this fact appeared in the poets. Butler looked at him and observed: 'Ballard, I also am "the poets"'.[10]

Writing in the same ironic vein, in 1932 T. E. Lawrence imagined Homer, the author of the *Odyssey*, not as a young Sicilian lady but as an old British gentleman. '[A] bookworm, no longer young, living from home, a mainlander, city-bred and domestic. Married but not exclusively, a dog-lover, often hungry and thirsty, dark-haired. Fond of poetry, a great if uncritical reader of the *Iliad*, with limited sensuous range but an exact eyesight which gave him all his pictures. A lover of old bric-à-brac, though as muddled an antiquary as Walter Scott... He loved the rural scene as only a citizen can. No farmer, he had learned the points of a good olive tree. He is all adrift when it comes to fighting, and had not seen deaths in battle. He had sailed upon and watched the sea with a palpitant concern, seafaring being not his trade. As a minor sportsman he had seen wild boars at bay and heard tall yarns of lions... Very bookish, this house-bred man. His work smells of the literary coterie, of a writing tradition. His note-books were stocked with purple passages and he embedded these in his tale wherever they would more or less fit. He, like William Morris, was driven by his age to legend, where he found men living untrammelled under the God-possessed skies. Only, with more verbal felicity than Morris', he had less poetry.'[11]

Like Butler and Lawrence, the writers who followed began to establish a companionable relationship with Homer. In our time, Margaret Atwood, perhaps with an eye on Butler, took up Homer's account of Ulysses' return and re-imagined it from the point of view of Penelope and her maids.[12] In Book XXII of the *Odyssey*, after Ulysses shoots Antinous, one of the two leading suitors, and reveals himself to the rest of the astonished men, he begins killing them one by one with the assistance of Telemachus, the swineherd Eumaeus and the cowherd Philoetius. The goatherd Melanthius tries to arm the surviving suitors but is quickly found out, tortured and put to death. Ulysses, having run out of arrows, puts on his armour and finishes off the suitors with his sword and spear, while the twelve maids who have slept with them are strung up by their necks with a ship's cable. After the mas-sacre, Ulysses purges his palace, halls and court, with cleans-ing fumes. Atwood found the story unsatisfactory. There are, said Atwood, 'two questions that must pose themselves after any close reading of the *Odyssey*: what led to the hanging of the maids, and what was Penelope really up to? The story as told in the *Odyssey* doesn't hold water: there are too many inconsistencies.'[13]

Butler thought that these 'inconsistencies' were simply due to the fact that Homer was a woman. 'All readers,' Butler wrote, 'will help poets, playwrights and novelists, by making believe a good deal, but we like to know whether we are in the hands of one who will flog us uphill, or who will make as little demand upon us as possible.' And in the scene of the killing of the suitors and the hanging of the maids, Butler argued that the former mode prevailed, since in his opinion, the authoress of the *Odyssey* identified herself here with Penelope (though Butler believed that she depicted herself in the poem as Nausicaa). 'She does not care how much she may afflict the reader in his efforts to believe her – the only thing she cares for is her revenge. She must have every one of the suitors killed stone dead, and all the guilty women hanged, and Melanthius first horribly tortured and then cut in pieces. Provided these objects are attained, it is not necessary that the reader should be able to believe, or even follow, all the ins and outs of the processes that lead up to them.'[14]

Atwood doesn't find the mechanics of the scene implausible, only the story itself. For Atwood's Penelope, the killing of the maids is the result of a terrible error. In her version, when Ulysses asks the nurse Eurycleia to choose twelve of the fifty household maids to be sacrificed, the old woman, not knowing Penelope's plot, chooses the twelve faithful ones who pretended, following Penelope's instructions, to be rude to their queen. And then Penelope imagines a more sinister explanation. 'What if Eurycleia was aware of my agreement with the maids – of their spying on the Suitors for me, of my orders to them to behave rebelliously? What if she singled them out and had them killed out of resentment at being excluded and the desire to retain her inside position with Odysseus?'[15]

Whichever the cause, the twelve maids killed 'as doves or thrushes beating their spread wings/against some snare rigged up in thickets'[16] (as Homer movingly describes them) haunt the reader's imagination, and Atwood's version links their story to contemporary accounts of mass rapes, and the attendant ostracism from their own people, of women in Bosnia, Rwanda and Darfur, and many other of today's battlefields. If, as Butler suggested, the author of the *Odyssey* was a woman, she would have no doubt been aware that rape is (like anger, revenge and plunder) a weapon of war. According to Atwood, the fury of the murdered maids haunts Ulysses like a curse throughout eternity, infecting him with the constant wish 'to be anywhere and anyone else'. As we have seen, Dante and Tennyson echo that curse.

Readers will never be quite certain whether Butler put forward his authorship proposal in earnest or not. If it wasn't, then he had more of a talent to be witty than to recognize the wit of others. After he told William Thackeray's eldest daughter, Lady Ritchie, of his *Odyssey* theory, she responded by announcing that she had one of her own: that the sonnets of Shakespeare had been written by Anne Hathaway. Butler didn't get the joke. He repeated the story, shaking his head and muttering, 'Poor lady, that was a silly thing to say.'[17]

In the years following the publication of Butler's book, though in academic circles the old questions kept being batted about (was Homer a singular or plural author, or was he an author at all?), in fiction and poetry Homer began to be treated as a living author rather than as a resident of Olympus, and the legacy of Greece and Rome as common contemporary property to be pilfered at will. If Butler too was 'the poets', then the identification worked both ways, and Homer became (in Butler's eyes, at least) an ancient Butler. Rudyard Kipling, for whom our understanding of the present is helped by mirroring what we know of the past, believed that it was useful to make these far-fetched associations: to learn from the merits and faults of the Roman Empire to criticize the Empire of Queen Victoria, to read in the stories of the Middle Ages how to live better lives in our own times, to find in Horace and in Shakespeare models for the present writer's craft. His portrait of Homer illustrates the point very clearly:

> When 'Omer smote 'is bloomin' lyre
>   He'd 'eard men sing by land an' sea;
> An' what he thought 'e might require,
>   'E went an' took – the same as me!
>
> The market-girls an' fishermen,

The shepherds an' the sailors, too,
They 'eard old songs turn up again,
  But kep' it quiet – same as you!

They knew 'e stole; 'e knew they knowed.
  They didn't tell, nor make a fuss,
But winked at 'Omer down the road,
  An' 'e winked back – the same as us![18]

CHAPTER 19

Ulysses' Travels

Mr Gladstone read Homer for fun, which I thought
served him right.

Winston Churchill, *My Early Life*, 1930

Since Homer was now a man of a thousand faces – a young
Sicilian woman, a literary gentleman, an uneducated busker
– he could then just as easily be an Irishman in exile. His
heroes could fight the daily battles of an ordinary Dublin citizen. They could travel the labyrinthine city from adventure
to adventure like a soldier returning home or like a son in
search of his father. They could be our contemporaries, since
Homer had foreseen everything and, as the German poet
Durs Grünbein remarked, 'the present is wind in the eyes of
Homer'.[1] They could feel surrounded by an ever-tempting
sea that lent its colour, wine-dark or snot-green, to its poets.
They could attempt to be, if not good (James Joyce used the
German word '*gut*') then at least '*gutmütig*' – decent.[2]

Like Butler, Joyce assumed that he too was 'the poets', and
at first the young Joyce was of two minds about allowing
Homer into their company. To the writer Padraic Colum, the

twenty-year-old Irishman declared that he had no interest in Homer, whose epics, he felt, were 'outside the tradition of European culture'.[3] In his eyes, the only European epic was Dante's *Commedia*. Possibly this extreme view was the result of his Irish Catholic upbringing, since the Counter-Reformation ideology, with its profound distrust of Greek, lived on strongly in most Catholic countries. Joyce had studied Latin at school: later, when living in Trieste, he picked up a few words of modern Greek but deeply regretted his ignorance of Homer's tongue. To his friend Frank Budgen, a civil servant posted in Zurich, he said: 'But just think, isn't that a world I am peculiarly fit to enter?'[4]

Joyce wanted to do more than enter it: he wished to rebuild it from scratch, on Irish ground and with Irish materials. William Butler Yeats, in an essay written in 1905, which Joyce had with him in Trieste, had suggested that the time was ripe for a new writer to revisit the ancient world of the *Odyssey*. 'I think that we will learn again,' he said with visionary wisdom, 'how to describe at great length an old man wandering among enchanted islands, his return home at last, his slowly gathering vengeance, a flitting shape of a goddess, and a flight of arrows, and yet to make all these so different things… become… the signature or symbol of a mood of the divine imagination.'[5] In Yeats' rallying call, and in Vico, Joyce found confirmation of his intuition. Philological synchronicities bolstered his confidence. The *Odyssey* begins with Ulysses on Calypso's island, Ogygia. Joyce discovered that Ogygia was the name that Plutarch had long ago given to

Ireland.[6] Although Joyce had told Vladimir Nabokov in 1937 that basing his *Ulysses* on Homer's poem was 'a whim' and that his collaboration with Stuart Gilbert in preparing a Homeric correspondence to *Ulysses* was 'a terrible mistake'[7] (Joyce deleted the Homeric titles of his chapters before *Ulysses* was published in book form), Homer's presence is very obviously noticeable throughout the novel. Nabokov suggested that a mysterious character who keeps appearing in *Ulysses*, described only as 'the man in the brown macintosh' and never clearly identified, might be Joyce himself lurking in his own pages.[8] It might just as well be Homer, come to supervise the renovation of his works.

Following Joyce's dismissal of his inspiration, Nabokov argued that the relationship between the *Odyssey* and *Ulysses* was nothing but fodder for critics. And yet it would be absurd not to recognize the deliberate parallels and *hommages*, quotations and borrowings from Homer in the novel, some with direct reference to his poems, others via Dante and Virgil. In the process of association, however, they all become Joycean, as in the beautiful use of Homeric epithets in Joyce's description of the Citizen Cyclops:

> The figure seated on a large boulder at the foot of a round tower was that of a broadshouldered deepchested stronglimbed frankeyed redhaired freelyfreckled shaggybearded widemouthed largenosed longheaded deepvoiced barekneed brawnyhanded hairylegged ruddyfaced sinewyarmed hero.[9]

Joyce manages to be funny and respectful of Homer at the same time, not falling into the kind of parodic imitation that amused A. E. Housman:

O suitably attired in leather boots
Head of a traveller, wherefore seeking whom
Whence by what way how purposed art thou come
To this well-nightingaled vicinity?[10]

Joyce told Budgen that he was writing a book based on the *Odyssey* and that it would deal with eighteen hours in the life of an 'all-round character'.[11] He contended that no such person had ever been described. Christ, Hamlet, Faust, all lacked the complete experience of life. He dismissed Christ as a bachelor who had never lived with a woman, Hamlet as being only a son, and neither husband nor father, and Faust as someone neither young nor old, without home or family, cumbered with Mephistopheles 'always hanging round him at his side or heels'. There was one, however, whom, he thought, might fill the bill. Ulysses was 'son to Laertes... father to Telemachus, husband to Penelope, lover of Calypso, companion in arms to the Greek warriors around Troy, and King of Ithaca. He was subjected to many trials, but wisdom and courage came through them all.'[12] Furthermore, Joyce reminded Budgen that while Ulysses was a brave soldier on the battlefield, determined to see the battle to the end, he had also been a war dodger who had tried to escape from military service by pretending to be mad and ploughing his field with an ass and an ox yoked together. (He was trapped by the recruiting sergeant who laid the baby Telemachus in front of the plough – a counterpoint to the story in which Achilles' mother hides him among the women to prevent him from joining the army, and he is recognized by Ulysses when the transvestite hero chooses, from a number of gifts, a shield and spear instead of jewellery.)[13]

Ulysses is indeed one of the most complex characters in Homer's poems. In the *Iliad*, he is a cautious, reasonable warrior. He is also an able diplomat capable of taking Agamemnon's offer of reconciliation to Achilles, and a master of rhetoric who knows how to play dumb in order to better surprise his audience. Priam's old counsellor, Antenor, describes Ulysses speaking in public, standing at first stiff and still with his eyes on the ground and then bursting into speech.

> You'd think him a sullen fellow or just plain fool.
> But when *he* let loose that great voice from his chest
> and the words came piling on like a driving winter blizzard –
> then no man alive could rival Odysseus![14]

Quoting Antenor's description, the Mexican critic Alfonso Reyes argued that Ulysses' intellectual dexterity rendered him dangerous in the eyes of authority, like a certain South American diplomat who told Reyes that whenever he returned to his country, he imagined the dictator-in-office thinking to himself: 'I must distrust this man, he knows his grammar.'[15]

In the *Odyssey*, Ulysses has become a crafty hero surviving by his wits, somewhat similar to the trickster figure in folktales. But he is never maliciously deceitful: his mocking of the Cyclops in Book IX, for instance, when he says that his name is Nobody, is fully justified by the monstrous behaviour of the creature. Nor is he ever willingly unfaithful: his true love is Penelope, and if he becomes the lover of Circe and Calypso it is explicitly in spite of himself, because as a mortal he cannot resist the advances of a goddess. However, when Princess Nausicaa shows that she is attracted to him, he politely turns her down.

But once the stories of Ulysses travelled to Rome, the nature of the hero changed. There had been Greek antecedants of this other Ulysses as far back as 415 when Euripides depicted him in *The Trojan Women* as a violent, bullying military man. He became an unscrupulous, vainglorious character, associated in the Roman mind with the clever Levantine Greeks against whom the Romans had a deep-rooted prejudice.[16] Virgil depicted him as a heartless plunderer, a sort of Greek Moriarty, 'that master-craftsman of crime'.[17] It is in the guise of this third personality that Ulysses enters the literature of Europe. Dante condemns Ulysses, together with his comrade Diomedes, to the eighth Circle of Hell in which the Counsellors of Fraud, spiritual thieves who advise others to thieve, writhe enveloped in everlasting flames: the rapacious ardour that consumed them from inside now consumes them from the outside, and if in life they used their tongues to make others burn with greed, now the tongues (of fire) burn them. And it is here that Dante intuitively has Ulysses fulfil Tiresias's prophecy, which Dante, ignorant of Homer, can never have known. In the Underworld, the soothsayer Tiresias announces not what will be but what may be: the possibilities of the foreseeable future are always more than one and the outcome depends on the hero's choice. Tiresias tells Ulysses that if he fulfils certain conditions he will reach Ithaca and kill his wife's suitors, but that staying at home may not be his lot. Ulysses, Tiresias says, will feel the urge to 'go forth once more'[18] and undertake one last, fatal journey. The description that Dante gives Ulysses of his final adventure is among the most beautiful verses Dante ever wrote and no English translation does it proper justice.[19]

More than six centuries later, Alfred, Lord Tennyson imagined a vigorous, moving version that is not at all unfaithful to Dante's achievement and which ends:

Old age hath yet his honour and his toil;
Death closes all: but something ere the end,
Some work of noble note, may yet be done,
Not unbecoming men that strove with Gods.
The lights begin to twinkle from the rocks:
The long day wanes: the slow moon climbs: the deep
Moans round with many voices. Come, my friends,
'Tis not too late to seek a newer world.
Push off, and sitting well in order smite
The sounding furrows; for my purpose holds
To sail beyond the sunset, and the baths

Of all the western stars, until I die.
It may be that the gulfs will wash us down:
It may be we shall touch the Happy Isles,
And see the great Achilles, whom we knew.
Though much is taken, much abides; and though
We are not now that strength which in old days
Moved earth and heaven; that which we are, we are;
One equal temper of heroic hearts,
Made weak by time and fate, but strong in will
To strive, to seek, to find, and not to yield.[20]

Tennyson, steeped in the classics at Cambridge, takes Dante's condemned king back to his Homeric source. Ulysses, who 'cannot rest from travel', must relinquish his role as the rogue too-clever-for-his-own-good and again assume the identity of a hero. 'I am become a name', he says, summing up his long journey from the soldier-survivor who called himself 'Nobody', to the returned king anxious to sail once more. 'Among the many things that Ulysses has been,' wrote the Peruvian novelist Mario Vargas Llosa, 'there is one constant in Western literature: the fascination with human beings that do away with limits, who, instead of bowing to the servitude of what is possible, endeavour, against all logic, to seek the impossible.[21]

In a long poetic version of the *Odyssey* by the Greek novelist Nikos Kazantzakis, Ulysses becomes a bleaker version of his Tennysonian counterpart. He is a wanderer in search of self-knowledge, a chameleon figure who is (the line is Tennyson's) 'a part of all that I have met'. He is a king, a soldier, a lover, the unhappy founder of a utopian community in Africa, but he is never successful in his enterprises. And yet, for this Ulysses, failure is less important than experience. Like that other man of many parts, Frankenstein's monster, who ends his days in the icy waste of the Arctic, Kazantzakis's Ulysses is washed up on the icy waste of Antarctica, and his last words echo Dante's in the *Commedia*:

> Then flesh dissolved, glances congealed, the heart's pulse
>   stopped,
> and the great mind leapt to the peak of its holy freedom,
> fluttered with empty wings, then upright through the air
> soared high and freed itself from its last cage, its freedom.
> All things like frail mist scattered till but one brave cry
> for a brief moment hung in the calm benighted waters:
> 'Forward, my lads, sail on, for Death's breeze blows in a
>   fair wind!'[22]

A South American contemporary of Tennyson, the Argentinian José Hernández composed in 1872 an epic poem whose hero, Martín Fierro, is a Ulyssean gaucho, an army dodger like Ulysses had tried to be. Fierro is accompanied in his adventures by Sergeant Cruz who, like Ulysses' friend Diomedes when faced with the brave Glaucus in the *Iliad*,[23] refuses to fight Fierro and becomes his intimate friend. Fierro's morals are less those of the

Homeric king than that of the scoundrel in Virgil or the sinner in Dante. Fierro's world is ruled by cunning and violence, as proclaimed in the lessons taught by a cynical old gaucho, El Viejo Vizcacha ('Old Badger', a sort of South American Nestor). For example:

Become a friend of the judge
Don't give him reason to complain,
And when he decides to be mad
You should meekly bow your head,
Because it's always good to have
A post against which to scratch your back.[24]

Joyce's version of the king of Ithaca, the Dublin Jew Leopold Bloom, occupies a middle ground, neither that of the Tennyson hero nor that of the Dante adventurer. Being a Jew, he is endemically an exile, both inside and outside the Irish fold, a condition Joyce himself, as an Irish artist, experienced. But Bloom's Jewishness brings him close to another Ulysses, the Wandering Jew of medieval legend. Between 1902 and 1903, Victor Bérard, one of the most original of French classicists, published two massive volumes of scholarship, *The Phoenicians and the Odyssey*,[25] suggesting that Homer's poem had Semitic roots and that all its geographical names were actual places that could be revealed by finding an equivalent Hebrew word. For instance, Homer calls Circe's island both Nesos Kirkes and Aiaia. Aiaia means nothing in Greek but in Hebrew it means 'Island of the She-Hawk', which in Greek translates as Nesos Kirkes.[26] For Bérard, Homer was Greek, but since the Phoenicians were the best sailors of the ancient world, he made his seafaring Ulysses a Phoenician, that is to say, Semitic. Without distinguishing between the various Semitic people, Joyce helped himself to Bérard's theory to justify his conception of Ulysses-Bloom as a milder version of the Wandering Jew (as Buck Mulligan calls him in the novel),[27] whose name in the Middle Ages is Cartaphilus or Ahasuerus. Joyce had read Eugène Sue's potboiler version, *Le juif errant*, before leaving Ireland in 1904 and was familiar with the story. According to the legend, as Christ paused by his door carrying the Cross to Calvary, Ahasuerus (or Cartaphilus) cried out to him, 'Walk faster!' To which Christ replied: 'I will go, but you will walk until I come again!'[28] The curse echoes that of Poseidon who condemns Ulysses to wander 'time and again off course'.[29]

Joyce's *Ulysses* is not an interpretation of Homer, neither is it a retelling, even less a pastiche. Dr Johnson, writing in 1765, argued that 'The Pythagorean scale of numbers was at once discovered to be perfect; but the poems of *Homer* we yet know not to transcend the common limits of human intelligence, but by remarking, that nation after nation, and century after century, has been able to do little more than transpose his incidents, new-name his characters, and paraphrase his sentiments. The reverence due to writings that have long subsisted arises therefore not from any credulous confidence in the superior wisdom of past ages, or gloomy persuasion of the degeneracy of mankind, but is the consequence of acknowledged and indubitable positions, that what has been longest known has been most considered, and what is most considered is best understood.'[30] Joyce did other than acknowledge Homer's position: he re-imagined the story of the primordial journey undertaken by every man in every age. His coupling was less between Ulysses and Bloom than between Homer and Joyce himself, less between the creations than between the creators. Other writers made Homer theirs through translation, transposition, projection. Joyce did it by starting again.

CHAPTER 20

Homer Through the Looking-Glass

No ancient poem is on the subject of soap-bubbles.

Lewis Carroll, *Symbolic Logic*, 1895

Every age re-imagines the classics in its own proper idiom. In 1954, the Italian novelist Alberto Moravia noted that, in the post-war world, Homer was conceived as 'pure popular spectacle' which, in contemporary terms, meant film. In his novel *Il Disprezzo* (*Contempt*) the narrator translates various episodes of the *Odyssey* into the cinematographic versions he has seen: Ulysses spying on Nausicaa in the water becomes the peepshow 'Beauties in the Bath', the Cyclops is *King Kong*, Circe is Antinéa in Wilhelm Pabst's 1932 film, *The Mistress of Atlantis*.

In the years preceding the Second World War, 'pure popular spectacle' was the theatre and Homer's poems served as explicit, even dangerous cautionary fables for the plots. Jean Giraudoux – the official spokesman for French culture in the French Ministry of Foreign Affairs, a darling of the Fascist periodical *Je suis partout* and a lover of German language and literature – made frequent use of Homer's stories in his dramas. During the war his political position was ambiguous, but after the war he was regarded as a patriot, and his work was included, for instance, in an anthology of Resistance literature, *La Patrie se fait tous les jours* of 1947.[1] His two-act play *La Guerre de Troie n'aura pas lieu* ('The Trojan War Will Not Take Place', sometimes translated as *Tiger at the Gates*) is one of the best-known French dramas of the twentieth century. It was written in 1935, the year Hitler promulgated the anti-Jewish laws in Nuremberg and the Fascist 'Croix de Feu' organization was founded in France. It was not the author's favourite. Giraudoux had conceived it as a prelude to the *Iliad*, set in a remote age 'when the characters have not yet entered the realm of legend',[2] and for a specific audience (that of Louis Jouvet's Théâtre de l'Athénée in Paris) who supposedly knew its classics.

'The Trojan War will not take place,' says Andromache to Cassandra as the curtain rises. Hector has convinced Paris that Helen should be returned to her husband. But King Priam and the old poet Demokos argue that this 'incarnation of beauty' must be kept in Troy. The Greek embassy arrives, led by Ulysses and Oiax, and Hector attempts to negotiate Helen's return. But an insulting remark by Oiax serves as an excuse for Demokos to incite the populace to attack the Greeks. Furious, Hector kills the old poet who, before dying, accuses Oiax of the deed. Oiax is then murdered by the populace. Cassandra's last words are: 'The Trojan poet is dead...

Now the Greek poet can begin.'[3] Demokos leaves the stage to Homer. Giraudoux stops where the *Iliad* starts.

'I wanted to write a tragedy,' said Giraudoux. 'Most of the characters, we know, are destined to be killed, not in my play but in the course of history, and therefore a sort of shadow hovers over them.'[4] The menacing shadow is incarnated in the constant presence on stage of Cassandra, aware of the inevitable catastrophe. Giraudoux's characters are not Homer's. Priam and Hecuba are not the united couple of the *Iliad* but hold opposing views on the imminent crisis. Hecuba is a sharp-tongued, level-headed crone, dead set against the war; Priam, a proud and senile warmonger, dazzled by Helen, his son Paris's prize catch. Helen is a complex figure in whom certain critics[5] saw an image of the absurdity of fate, and whose indefinable beauty arouses the lust of the Council of Elders, a crowd of arrogant, greedy old men that includes Demokos. Paris is a young prig, Ajax (renamed Oiax) a bullying fool. Giraudoux had conceived Ulysses as a diplomat with evil intentions, a smooth talker, someone much more dangerous than the pompous Demokos: early audiences, surprisingly, saw him as a philosopher-warrior, a man of measured words and good will. Hector is among the most humane of the play's characters, torn between hatred of the war and a taste for violence, darkly aware that his own fate is part of a greater design which he is incapable of conceiving.

In spite of its seamless construction, *La Guerre de Troie n'aura pas lieu* remains unconvincing, and even efforts such as Harold Pinter's remarkable 1982 adaptation for the National

Theatre in London during the Falklands War lacked dramatic power. Giraudoux had proposed to write a tragedy, 'the affirmation of a horrible link between humankind and a destiny greater than human destiny itself'.[6] In this he failed, perhaps because, as the novelist Marguerite Yourcenar remarked, 'His characters, rather than myths, are caricatures of myths.'[7] Doris Lessing once noted that 'Myth does not mean something untrue, but a concentration of truth.'[8] It may be that in Giraudoux the myths appear too diffuse, too diluted.

In 1990, the Caribbean poet Derek Walcott attempted the opposite procedure. His re-imagined *Odyssey* in a Caribbean setting is a concentration of endless readings of Homer's *Ulysses*. In his Nobel Prize acceptance speech, Walcott denied that his *Omeros* was an epic in the strict sense of the word, but rather a collection of epic fragments arranged in three-line stanzas that echo Dante's *terza rima* in the *Commedia*.[9] Its idiom is a mixture of contemporary English and Creole and, though its characters bear the names of Homer's heroes, they are also the names that slave-owners commonly gave to the black population of the islands: Philoctete, Helen, Achille, Hector. The *Odyssey* begins *in medias res*, when Ulysses is already halfway through his travels; likewise, *Omeros* begins halfway through the *Odyssey*, with the first line of Book XI ('Now down we came to the ship')[10] which becomes, in Walcott's idiom: 'This is how, one sunrise, we cut down them canoes.'[11] (Already Ezra Pound had chosen the same device: the first of his *Cantos* starts: 'And then we went down to the ship...')[12]

In *Omeros*, the visit to the Underworld becomes a dream voyage to Africa, the land of the protagonist's roots, where a vision of the past shows him his ancestors being captured by the slavers. The visitor is not Ulysses but Achille, victim of sun-stroke, whose rage at witnessing the ancient abduction is like that of his namesake after the death of Patroclus, confused with a hatred towards Patroclus' murderer. Towards the slavers, he feels 'the same/mania that, in the arrows of drizzle, he felt for Hector',[13] and towards the slaves, a terrible grief:

> … Warm ashes made his skull white
> over eyes sore as embers, over a skin charred as coal,
> the core of his toothless mouth, groaning to the firelight,
>
> was like a felled cedar's whose sorrow surrounds its bole.
> One hand clawed the pile of ashes, the other fist thudded on
> the drum of his chest, the ribs were like a caved-in canoe
>
> that rots for years under the changing leaves of an almond,
> while the boys who played war in it become grown men who
> work, marry, and die, until their own sons in turn
>
> rock the rotted hulk, or race in it, pretending to row,
> as Achille had done in the manchineel grove as a boy.[14]

If Walcott's Achille is a blend of several Homeric heroes, his bard is a blend of several poets: Homer certainly, but also Joyce, incarnated in a blind West Indian veteran who spends his days singing to himself in the shade of a pharmacy near the beach, his khaki dog on a leash:

> the blind man sat on his crate after the pirogues
> set out, muttering the dark language of the blind,
> gnarled hands on his stick, his ears as sharp as the dog's.
>
> Sometimes he would sing and the scraps blew on the wind
> when her beads rubbed their rosary. Old St Omere.
> He claimed he'd sailed round the world. 'Monsieur Seven
>   Seas'
>
> they christened him, from a cod-liver-oil label
> with its wriggling swordfish. But his words were not clear.
> They were Greek to her. Or old African babble.[15]

To the Homeric characters in *Omeros*, Greek is as foreign as the tongues of Africa, and Africa, for Walcott, is an Ithaca to which Ulysses will never return. Read after Joyce's novel, Homer's *Odyssey* is not only a poem of homecoming but also one of everlasting exile.

Of course, the shadow of the homecoming, of the expected and longed-for return, is constantly present in *Omeros* as it is in *Ulysses* and in the *Odyssey*. In fact, the *Odyssey* can be read as the endless story of a return that can only be achieved through its repeated telling, and which exists in prerequisite form even before the adventures begin. Fifteen years before *Omeros* was published, Italo Calvino perceptively noted that the *Odyssey* is a collection of numerous *Odysseys* fitted one into another like Chinese boxes.[16] It begins with Telemachus' search for a story that does not yet exist, the story that will, at the end of the poem, become the *Odyssey*. First, in Menelaus' account to Telemachus, the Old Man of the Sea begins the telling at the very point where Ulysses himself begins it, on Calypso's island. When he stops, Homer resumes the story and follows his hero until he reaches the court of the Phaeacians. Here the blind bard Demodocus sings to his audience (of which Ulysses, as we have seen, is part) a couple of Ulysses' adventures: Ulysses weeps and, picking up the narrative, tells how he reached the Underworld and how the ghost of Tiresias revealed to him what would happen next. As Calvino points out, the story of Ulysses' return is the real story of the *Odyssey*, a story which, throughout his adventures, Ulysses must not forget.

The Alexandrian poet Constantine Cavafy, who died in 1933, also understood that Ulysses' return is the prerequisite of the *Odyssey*. Cavafy wrote as an inheritor of the Hellenistic tradition, someone who read Homer as if able to discard its innumerable layers of post-Homeric exegeses and reach the source. In Cavafy's writing, Ulysses and Achilles are neither modern nor fabled or distant figures. When, for example, he says, 'Our efforts are like those of the Trojans', he is able to convince the reader that his experience is indeed first-hand and that the Trojan suffering is alive in his presence. The metaphor is clear, and yet it does not read as metaphor.

Yet we're sure to fail. Up there,
high on the walls, the dirge has already begun.
They're mourning the memory, the aura of our days.
Priam and Hecuba mourn for us bitterly.[17]

Ithaca, Cavafy reminds us, is not only the point of arrival but also, we often forget, that of departure: it has created the distance between the exile and the return. The length and intensity of the journey back increase the value of the remote final goal.

Laestrygonians, Cyclops,
wild Poseidon – you won't encounter them
unless you bring them along inside your soul,
unless your soul sets them up in front of you.

...

Ithaka gave you the marvellous journey.
Without her you wouldn't have set out.
She has nothing left to give you now.

And if you find her poor, Ithaca won't have fooled you.
Wise as you will have become, so full of experience,
you'll have understood by then what these Ithakas mean.[18]

Ithaca, the city Ulysses cherishes in his memory, has allowed the *Odyssey* to run its course. Opposed to it is the anonymous port in Cavafy's poem 'The City', a starting-point that was unthinkingly left behind, an Ithaca abandoned because it seemed unsatisfactory, unrewarding, and which therefore offers Ulysses no adventures, no experience, nothing but the difficulties without the journey.

> You won't find a new country, won't find another shore.
> This city will always pursue you.
> You'll walk the same streets, grow old
> in the same neighbourhoods, turn grey in these same houses.
> You'll always end up in this city. Don't hope for things
>   elsewhere:
> there's no ship for you, there's no road.
> Now that you've wasted your life here, in this small corner,
> you've destroyed it everywhere in the world.[19]

Like Ithaca in the *Odyssey*, Troy in the *Iliad* is both a city and an emblem for the story of a war whose beginning and end are not chronicled in the poem: less than seven weeks, a mere fifty-two days, are accounted for in the seemingly everlasting conflict, providing in its fragmented nature a useful mirror for our own anguished centuries.

The 1981 novel *Famous Last Words*, by the Canadian writer Timothy Findley, takes place in this eternal battlefield.[20] It tells the story of a group of men and women lost in a nightmare place that evokes Cavafy's nameless city, through which they all obediently move without understanding the purpose or destination of their movements. The setting is the Second World War; the narrator, Hugh Selwyn Mauberley, the poet-hero invented by Ezra Pound for his collection of semi-autobiographical poems published in 1920.[21] 'I didn't know quite how to tell this story,' Findley confessed, 'until I realized that if I were Homer, I'd have recognized this wasn't just the story of men and women – but of men and women and the gods to whom they are obedient – and told best through the evocation of icons. So what I must do is transpose this story, which is history, into another key – which is mythology.'[22]

Findley's chosen mythological model is the *Iliad*. For Findley, every one of our wars (whether between the British and the Germans, democracy and fascism, or between the upper and the lower classes) is also a war between Greeks and Trojans, a symbolic struggle which in the eye of its literate chronicler, Homer-Mauberley, dissolves into particular stories of singular men and women struggling under the whims and passions of a pantheon of mad gods. In this complex *roman à clef*, Mauberley is Homer, commissioned to turn historical characters from gossip-column subjects into mythological icons. Mrs Simpson is a half-willing Helen, yoked to a dithering Paris (the weakling Edward VII) and fated to be rescued by various brutal or righteous Agamemnons and Menelauses. Hera and Zeus are Churchill and Hitler, Athena is Ezra Pound, the murderous Achilles is the Nazi Harry Reinhardt who, instead of a telltale heel, sports alligator shoes and who (a new twist in the story) will kill his creator by plunging a pickaxe into Mauberley's eye, rendering him as blind as tradition depicts Homer.

Findley's Homer is neither conventionally good nor just. He is an admirer of absolute power, someone willing to collaborate in the setting up of a puppet government in which the Duke and the Duchess of Windsor are to play king and queen; willing to take part in a cabal that, under the code name 'Penelope', waits for the right moment to unleash their evil plan on the world; willing to forsake his writing for a cheap plot of parodic characters. Mauberley is the iconic transgressor, political, sexual and artistic. He has allied himself with the Fascists, he is sexually ambiguous, his literary ambition 'to describe the beautiful' is stubbornly opposed to the current 'roar of bombast and rhetoric'. Mauberley is a hungry, haunted, burrowing creature at odds with the world and with himself. 'What power-hungry people do,' Findley once said, 'can be embraced very generally by my use of the term "fascist," because I think that's what fascism is: all power-hungry people can touch the rest of the people where they are hungry to be powerful too, but no, they can never be powerful without the powerful iconic people doing things for them, and in their name.'[23] In other words, the power-hungry heroes of Troy can never be powerful without the gods tugging at their strings.

On the walls of one of the rooms of the Grand Elysium Hotel (the name that, in modern mythology, Greta Garbo's celebrated film gives to besieged Troy)[24] Mauberley writes out the story of his life: 'All I have written here is true,' his confession states, 'except the lies.' Mauberley's story (like Homer's) will be read and judged by others who will come after him, and then will be left to crumble into dust like the walls of the hotel itself. 'This is the way the world ends,' Eliot had written in 'The Hollow Men', 'Not with a bang but a whimper'[25] – a line that Pound repeated in his 'Canto 74'[26] and then added: 'To build the city of Dioce whose terraces are the colour of stars.' Dioce was a Medan king who, after being made ruler by the people because of his fair judgements, built a visionary city that was meant to be an earthly paradise. Pound, an admirer of Mussolini, imagined that the Italian dictator would create, like Dioce, an ideal state after the cataclysm of the war. The future world imagined by Findley's Mauberley is like this Diocean Troy, first destroyed by the Greeks and later resurrected in the Rome of Aeneas, of Augustus, of the Renaissance and finally (according to Fascist ideology) in the Rome of Mussolini whose triumph Pound-Mauberley wished for and whose threat is still present. In Mauberley's words on the final page of Findley's novel:

> Imagine something mysterious rises to the surface on a summer afternoon – shows itself and is gone before it can be identified... By the end of the afternoon, the shape – whatever it was – can barely be remembered. No one can be made to state it was absolutely thus and so. Nothing can be conjured of its size. In the end the sighting is rejected, becoming something only dimly thought on: dreadful but unreal... Thus, whatever rose towards the light is left to sink unnamed: a shape that passes slowly through a dream.

Waking, all we remember is the awesome presence, while a shadow lying dormant in the twilight whispers from the other side of reason: I am here. I wait.[27]

CHAPTER 21

The Never-ending War

> *Rumsfeld:* I liked what you said earlier, sir. A war on
>   terror. That's good. That's vague.
> *Cheney:* It's good.
> *Rumsfeld:* That way we can do anything.
>
> David Hare, *Stuff Happens*, 2006

If, as Calvino suggests, there exists a story that is the *Odyssey's* implicit prelude, then the *Iliad* too may contain such a primordial narrative: the *tacit* story of war, not just the Trojan War. In September 2005, over the course of three evenings, almost 3,000 people filled the largest theatre space in the Rome Auditorium to listen to a dramatized reading of the *Iliad* which the Italian novelist Alessandro Baricco had published the previous year. Baricco, author of the bestselling novel *Silk*, lent to the various characters of Homer's poem a stage and a voice to tell the Siege of Troy. In a postscript to the published text,[1] Baricco insisted that these were not ordinary times in which to read the *Iliad* but times of war, everyday wars of large and small conflicts that bring in their wake the whole warrior array, from murder and torture to proclamations of good intent and acts of heroism. In these times, said Baricco, to read the *Iliad* in public is a trifle, but not any trifle. 'To say it clearly, I mean that the *Iliad* is a story of war, without care and without measure. It was composed in praise of a warring humanity, and it did it in such a memorable way that it should last throughout eternity and reach the last descendant of our last descendants, still singing the solemn beauty and the irredeemable emotion that war once was and always will be. In school, perhaps, the story is told differently. But at its heart lies this: the *Iliad* is a monument to war.'

Baricco gives several reasons for his definition. First, the compassion with which Homer has transmitted the arguments of the defeated. In a story written from the point of view of the victors, he reminds us that what remains, above all, is the humanity of the Trojans: Priam, Hector, Paris, even minor characters such as Pandarus (killed by Diomedes) and Sarpedon (killed by Patroclus). Many of the voices we hear are not from the soldiers but from the women: Andromache, Helen, Hecuba. Isn't it astonishing, asks Baricco, that in a male warrior society such as that of the Greeks, Homer decided to preserve so strongly the voice of women and their desire for peace? Baricco points out that the women are Scheherazades: they know that, as long as they continue to speak, war does not take place. Even the men must realize that Achilles delays his entry in the war by staying with the women, and that all the time they are arguing about how to fight, they don't fight. When Achilles and the other men finally enter into battle, they do so blindly, fanatically devoted to their duty. But before that happens comes the long and slow time of women. 'Words,' says Baricco 'are a weapon with which they manage to freeze the war.'

Reading through the *Iliad*, Baricco suggests that our infatuation with the beauty of war hasn't waned: if war is hell, however atrocious this might sound, it is a beautiful hell. War in our time, though cursed and abominated, is far from being considered an absolute evil. Our only escape from its malevolent attraction (and this is Baricco's moving proposal) is to create an alternative beauty that may compete with our longing for war, something built day after day by thousands of artisans. If we do this, says Baricco, we will succeed in keeping Achilles away from the homicidal fighting: not through fear or horror, but by tempting him with a different kind of beauty, more dazzling than the one that attracts him now and infinitely less violent. This, then, is the *Iliad*'s necessary prelude.

Baricco's hopeful argument has a long and venerable opposition, dating back almost to the time of Homer himself. For Heraclitus, war was not an undesirable attraction but the combatant energy that held the world together, and he reproached Homer for not lending war sufficient encouragement. 'Homer should be turned out of the canon and whipped. He was wrong in saying: "Would that strife might perish from among gods and men!" He did not see that he was praying for the destruction of the universe, for, if his prayer were heard, all things would pass away.'[2] Furthermore, Heraclitus argued, 'We must know that war is what is common to all beings, and that it is driven by justice;

therefore, everything is born from and made necessary through discord.'³ Dante considered this vigorous notion from a different point of view. Since the goal of law is the common good, Dante reasoned, and this cannot be obtained through injustice, any war undertaken 'for the common good' must be just. In Dante's eyes, Rome's conquest of the world was just, since it must have been effected 'not through violence but through law'.⁴ In our day, those who speak of 'necessary losses' and 'collateral damage' follow the same argument.

Baricco lays his finger on a terrible paradox. We know that the murderous violence of war is terrible, and yet something in us loves the spectacle. When Ulysses and Telemachus attack the treacherous suitors, Homer compares the vengeful king and his son to eagles attacking small birds that cringe under the clouds:

> ... the eagles plunge in fury, rip their lives out – hopeless,
> never a chance of flight or rescue – and people love the
> sport.⁵

People love the sport. Writing in 1939 on the notion of force in the *Iliad*, Simone Weil noted that the prevailing feeling throughout the poem is one of bitterness, 'the only justifiable bitterness, for it springs from the subjections of the human spirit to force, that is, in the last analysis, to matter. This subjection is the common lot, although each spirit will bear it differently, in proportion to its own virtue. No one in

the *Iliad* is spared by it, as no one on earth is. No one who suc-
cumbs to it is by virtue of this fact regarded with contempt.
Whoever, within his own soul and in human relations,
escapes the domination of force, is loved but loved sorrowfully, because of the threat of destruction that constantly
hangs over him.'[6] Only someone who has suffered through
war, injustice, misfortune, someone who has learned how far
'the domination of force' extends 'and knows how *not* to
respect it, is capable', according to Weil, 'of love and justice'.
Perhaps this is what Dante had in mind.

To expose soldiers to this paradox, in the first year of the
Second World War, the poet and critic Herbert Read compiled
an anthology, *The Knapsack*, small enough to be packed into a
kit. Three extracts from Chapman's Homer begin his selection: the invocation to Ares from his translation of Homer's
Battle of the Frogs and Mice, Agamemnon taking up arms in
Book XI of the *Iliad*, and the forging of Achilles' shield in
Book XVIII. Read said that he was guided in his choice by
both a wish to avoid the 'sustained tone of moral seriousness'
and a 'certain abstractness' in the idealism of other war
anthologies, as well as a desire to show 'the dialectic of life,
the contradictions on which we have to meditate if we are to
construct a workable philosophy'. 'In war,' Read argued and
in the daily struggle of everyday life, it is a workable philosophy that each man has to construct for himself if he is to preserve a serene mind.'[7] The wish for a 'serene mind' occurs in
the invocation to Ares in the *Battle*.

On the one hand, we cannot deny the benevolent ideals

that sometimes lead to war, the heroism and altruism with which it is sometimes fought, and the freedom from oppression that is sometimes its consequence. With the excuse of best intentions, Homer lovingly describes the sword piercing the flesh, the spurting blood, the broken teeth, the marrow oozing from the severed bones, and Ajax speaks of 'the joy of war'[8] and Paris strides into battle 'exultant, laughing aloud'.[9] On the other hand, the slaughter, the destruction, the suffering of every kind brought on by war, cannot be defended[10] and, doubtlessly, Homer loathed war. 'Atrocious', 'scourge of men', 'lying, two-faced', he calls it. And Zeus himself speaks of 'the horrid works of war'.[11] Pity and mourning, and a plea for compassion, are never far from the battlefield. It is not by chance that supplications (first, of the priest of Apollo, Chryses, for his daughter taken by Agamemnon, and last, of King Priam for the body of his son Hector) begin and end the *Iliad*.

The extraordinary power of the *Iliad* comes from the fact that it holds the tension between these two truths. Emile Zola, writing from the perspective of nineteenth-century realism, refused Homer any such subtlety. 'In his books, the heroes are nothing but gang bosses. There, women are raped, people are duped, they insult one another for months, they cut one another's throats, they drag around the corpses of their enemies. Read the novels of Fenimore Cooper about the Indians, and you'll see the similarities.'[12] Zola was mistaken: Homer is never merely descriptive and certainly never commonplace. It is easy, for a modern reader, to confuse the use of conventional epithets with conventional descriptions, but the fact that the epithets themselves are fixed by convention does not mean that they are synonymous: Homer knew sixty-odd ways to say 'so-and-so died' and they are all different.

War, Homer explicitly tells us, has its place in the universe, as represented in the shield that the smithy-god Hephaestus has crafted for Achilles.[13] It is divided into five circles. In the middle are the earth, the sky and the sea. Next come two cities, one at peace, showing everyday activities such as a wedding and a lawsuit, the other under siege, depicting men preparing an ambush while the elders, the women and the children cower behind the walls. The third circle shows the four seasons; the fourth, a ritual dance; and finally, the fifth and last is an image of Ocean, the river that in Homer's time was also the edge of the world. Framed by the cosmos, the world of humankind naturally includes the activity of war, counterpoised to the arts of peace. Achilles' shield (like the whole of the *Iliad*, and also the *Odyssey*) shows how fully Homer understood our ambiguous relationship to violence, our desire for it and our hatred of it, the beauty we ascribe to it and the horror it makes us feel, so that when faced with it, we are forced to look both ways. Two examples from the *Iliad* will illustrate the point.

Book VI begins with the Greek and Trojan forces battling on the plain of Troy, between the rivers Simois and Xanthus. One of the Trojans called Adrestus (there are three of that name) is caught alive by Menelaus after his horses have bolted and he is hurled to earth from his chariot. Menelaus rises over him, 'his spear's long shadow looming', and Adrestus hugs his captor's knees and begs him to spare him for a rich ransom. Adrestus' pleas move the king and, just as he is about to hand him back to an aide to be taken as prisoner to the ships, Agamemnon appears and chides him for his weakness. Menelaus, we must remember, is the injured party, Helen's husband; Agamemnon, though supreme commander of the Greek army, is only Menelaus' brother. And Agamemnon says:

> Why such concern for enemies? I suppose you got
> such tender loving care at home from the Trojans.
> Ah would to god not one of them could escape
> his sudden plunging death beneath our hands!
> No baby boy still in his mother's belly,
> not even he escape – all Ilium blotted out,
> no tears for their lives, no markers for their graves![14]

Goaded by his brother, Menelaus shoves Adrestus with his fist and Agamemnon stabs the fallen man 'in the flank and back'. Adrestus falls down dead, face up, and Agamemnon 'dug a heel in his heaving chest/and wrenched the ash spear out'.[15]

A second example. Almost at the end of the *Iliad*, the angry Achilles pursues Hector outside the walls of Troy. Both are soldiers, both have blood on their hands, both have loved ones who have been killed, both believe that their cause is just. One is Greek, the other Trojan, but at this point their allegiances hardly matter. Now they are two men intent on killing one another. They run past the city walls and past the double springs of the river Scamander. And at this point, Homer breaks off his description of the fighting and pauses to remind us:

And here, close to the springs, lie washing-pools
scooped out in the hollow rocks and broad and smooth
where the wives of Troy and all their lovely daughters
would wash their glistening robes in the old days,
the days of peace before the sons of Achaea came...
Past these they raced...[16]

The scene of war, says Homer, is never only that of war: it is never only that of men acting out in the present the events of the day. It is always the scene of the past as well, a display of what men secretly once were, revealed now in their ultimate moments. Confronted with the imminence of violent death, war also confronts them with the memory of days of peace, of the happiness that life can, and should, grant us. War is both things: the experience of an awful present and the ghost of a beloved past.

Also, reparation for the future. Priam's supplication to Achilles fulfils not just a traditional obligation or a sentimental act of mourning. It takes place so that a circle might be closed, and so that those who have suffered might be comforted. In the Underworld, when Ulysses meets the unfortunate Elpenor who was killed just before leaving Circe's island

and left unburied, the ghost addresses his old captain with these words:

> My lord, remember me, I beg you! Don't sail off
> and desert me, left behind unwept, unburied, don't,
> or my curse may draw god's fury on your head.
> No, burn me in full armour, all my harness,
> heap my mound by the churning grey surf –
> a man whose luck ran out –
> so even men to come will learn my story.[17]

This is, in essence, what allows war to acquire its redemptory sense: the knowledge that the dead can help us not to forget injustice. From Priam's plea to have the body of his son restored and Elpenor's to have his body cremated, to today's demands that war graves be opened in Latin America, Bosnia, Spain and dozens of other places, our healthy impulse is to restore to the dead their rightful role as memorials. In this way, as Homer knew, we can, simultaneously, both loudly abominate their loss and lovingly honour their sacrifice.

Shortly before his death in 1955, the American poet Wallace Stevens wrote this Homeric definition of war:

> War has no haunt except the heart,
> Which envy haunts, and hate, and fear,
> And malice, and ambition, near
> The haunt of love...[18]

CHAPTER 22

Everyman

> They say Ulysses, tired of astonishments,
> Wept for love at once again seeing his Ithaca
> Humble and green. Art is like that Ithaca
> Of green eternity, not of mere astonishments.
>
> Jorge Luis Borges, *Arte poética*, 1958

In 1949, in Buenos Aires, Jorge Luis Borges published a short story called 'The Immortal', later included in the volume *The Aleph*,[1] and inspired perhaps by his reading of Rudyard Kipling's *Kim* and H. G. Wells's *The Country of the Blind*. It begins with an epigraph taken from Francis Bacon: 'Solomon saith: *There is no new thing upon the earth*. So that as Plato had an imagination, *that all knowledge was but remembrance*, so Solomon giveth his sentence, *that all novelty is but oblivion*.'

In London, in the early days of June 1929, the Princess of Lucinge received from the antiquarian bookseller Joseph Cartaphilus of Smyrna the six volumes of the first edition of Pope's *Iliad*. The man, she said, had singularly vague features and spoke several languages badly. Later she heard that he had died at sea, on board the *Zeus*, and that he had been buried on the island of Ios. In the *Iliad's* last volume she found a manuscript written in a Latinized English.

The manuscript tells the story of a Roman tribune who, stationed in Thebes, witnesses one sleepless night the arrival of a rider coming from the east. The man, bloodied and exhausted, falls from his horse and asks the name of the city's river; the tribune tells him it is called the Egypt. The rider explains that the river for which he searches is another, a secret river at the edge of the world that purifies men of death, and on whose farthest shore rises the City of the Immortals. The man dies and the tribune is filled with the desire to find the city. At the head of two hundred men, he sets out in search of it. The lands they cross are wild and strange; the men mutiny; the tribune escapes after being shot with an arrow. Feverish, he wanders in the desert; when he wakes, he finds himself, hands tied, in a stone niche carved out on the slope of a mountain. At the foot of the mountain is a brackish stream; beyond it rises the City of the Immortals. There are other niches on the slope and in the valley, as well as shallow holes in the sand; from these he sees grey, naked men emerge into the sunlight. The tribune guesses that these are the Troglodytes, a tribe that lacks speech and eats serpents. Devoured by thirst, the tribune throws himself down the slope and drinks from the stream. Before losing consciousness, he inexplicably repeats a few Greek words:

And men who lived in Zelea under the foot of Ida,
a wealthy clan that drank the Aesepus' dark waters –[2]

After many days and nights he manages to cut his bonds and shamefully begs or steals his first ration of serpent's meat. The desire to enter the City of the Immortals continues to haunt him. One day, he decides to escape the Troglodytes at the time when most of them leave their holes to look towards the west, without even noticing the sunset. At midnight he reaches the city and sees with relief ('because man so abominates novelty and the desert') that one of the Troglodytes has followed him.

But the City of the Immortals, built on a sort of plateau, shows no points of entrance, no stairs or gates. The fierce sun forces him to take refuge in a cave. Here he finds a well and a flight of steps that leads into the lower darkness; the tribune descends and loses himself in a labyrinth of identical galleries and chambers. After many attempts, he emerges into the city itself and sees, looming ahead, a palace of many shapes and heights. He feels that this building is older than man, older than the earth itself, and that its age suited the labours of immortal craftsmen. He thinks: 'This palace was built by the gods.' Then he explores it, and corrects himself: 'The gods who built this are dead.' He notices its peculiarities and pronounces: 'The gods who built this were mad.' The tribune realizes that the city is not a labyrinth like the one he was lost in underground. 'A labyrinth is a house built to confuse men; its architecture, rich in symmetries, is subject to this purpose.' The architecture of the palace lacks any purpose whatsoever: corridors lead nowhere, windows are unreachable, doors lead to wells, staircases run upside down. Horrified, he escapes.

When he comes out of the cave, he finds the Troglodyte lying at the entrance, tracing incomprehensible signs in the sand. The tribune feels that the creature has been waiting for him; that night, on the way back to the Troglodyte village, he decides to teach him a few words. The Troglodyte reminds him of the dog Argos in the *Odyssey*; he decides to give him the dog's name. Day after day, the tribune attempts to teach Argos to speak. First months, then years pass, unsuccessfully. At last, one evening, it starts to rain. The entire tribe, in ecstasy, greets the falling water. The tribune calls to Argos who has begun to whimper. Suddenly, as if discovering something lost and forgotten long ago, the Troglodyte utters a few words: 'Argos, dog of Ulysses.' And then, still not looking at the tribune, quotes a line by Homer, 'a dog on piles of dung from mules and cattle'. The tribune asks him what he knows of the *Odyssey*. Because the Troglodyte's Greek is poor, he must repeat the question. 'Very little,' the Troglodyte answers. 'Less than the poorest bard. Eleven hundred years must have gone by since I invented it.'

That night the truth is revealed to him. The Troglodytes are the Immortals; the brackish stream, the river sought by the rider. As to the famous city, the Immortals had destroyed it nine centuries ago and from its ruins they had built the senseless city the tribune had seen 'as a parody or an inversion, and also as a temple to the irrational gods who govern the world and of whom we know nothing, except that they are not like men'. That was the last physical endeavour of the Immortals. Judging all enterprise fruitless, they decided to live in thought only, in pure speculation. After building the city, they forgot it and went to dwell in the caves.

Homer tells the tribune the story of his old age, and of the voyage he undertook, like that of Ulysses, to discover the land of men who ignore the sea and don't eat salt. He lived for a century in the City of the Immortals and, when they tore it down, he advised building the other one, as he had sung the Battle of the Mice and the Frogs after singing the Trojan War. 'It was like a god creating first the cosmos and afterwards chaos.'

The tribune realizes that drinking from the stream has made him immortal too, and sadly reflects that being immortal is something banal: with the exception of man, every creature enjoys immortality, because it ignores death. The divine, terrible, incomprehensible thing is to know that you are immortal. The slightest thought is the beginning or the end of an invisible design; an evil act may be performed so that in the future good may come of it. Given an infinite time, every action is just, but also indifferent: there are no moral or intellectual merits. Homer composed the *Odyssey*; after an endless number of years, the impossibility would be not to compose, even once, the *Odyssey*. For the Immortals, therefore, everything must take place again, nothing can happen only once, nothing is precarious. The tribune and Homer part company at the gates of Tangiers: they do not say farewell.

The tribune recalls some of his further adventures: taking part in the battle of Stamford in 1066, although he cannot remember on what side he fought; having been a scribe in

Bulaq who copied out the story of Sindbad; having played chess in a Samarkand prison and studied astrology in Bikaner and Bohemia. In 1714, in Aberdeen, he subscribed to Pope's translation of the *Iliad* which he read with great delight; in 1729 he discussed the poem with a professor of rhetoric called Giambattista. On 4 October 1921, the ship taking him to Bombay stopped on the Eritrean coast; on the outskirts of the port he tasted the water from a clear stream: as he rose, a thorn pierced the back of his hand. The pain made him realize that, once again, he was mortal. That night he slept until dawn.

The story offers two conclusions. The second concerns a commentary on the published manuscript (by a certain Dr Cordovero) attempting to prove that the text is apocryphal, and attributing it to the pen of the antiquarian Joseph Cartaphilus; a postscript, dated 1950, finds such allegations inadmissible. The first conclusion, by the tribune himself, addresses the uncanny tone of the narrative. The events he has described, he says, seem fantastic because they belong, in fact, to two different men. A Roman tribune would not refer, as he does in the beginning, to the Theban river as Egypt. Homer, however, would: in the *Odyssey*, he invariably says Egypt instead of Nile. The words the tribune utters after drinking the immortal waters belong to the *Iliad*, Book II, lines 935–6. The particular mention of the transcription of Sindbad's adventures and of the reading of Pope's *Iliad* are moving details, but not if said by a Roman tribune; spoken by Homer, however, how extraordinary to discover that he has copied out the story of another Ulysses and that he has read, in a barbarian tongue, his own *Iliad*! When the end approaches, the narrator says, no images remain in the mind, only words, and it isn't surprising that time should have mingled the words which represented one man with those uttered by another. The manuscript concludes with this confession: 'I have been Homer; soon, I shall be Nobody, like Ulysses; soon, I shall be every man, I shall be dead.'

Homer is a cipher. Since he has no proven identity and his books reveal no obvious clues to their composition, he can bear, like his *Iliad* and his *Odyssey*, an infinity of readings. Homer may be what we mean by the vast word 'antiquity' – a vicious circle that assumes the definition of what it seeks to define – or what we mean by the word 'poetry', or by 'humanity'. Homer may stand for that obscure early time of our common histories of which we have a few magnificent artefacts, but no true knowledge of how those artefacts were understood or felt. It is impossible to guess what sense Homer and his contemporaries might have had of the notion of a shared immortality, of every human being living out a segment of an endless human life in which, given enough time, each one will do and feel what everyone else has done or felt.

The chronology we have invented for ourselves prompts us to imagine that our sense of the world and of ourselves evolves, and that there is progress of feeling and imagination as there is development of technology and invention. We see ourselves as better than our ancestors, those savages of the

Bronze Age who, though they wrought fine cups and bangles and sang beautiful songs, massacred each other in horrible wars, possessed slaves and raped women, ate without forks and conceived gods who threw thunderbolts. It is difficult for us to imagine that, such a long time ago, we already had words to name our most bewildering experiences and our deepest and most obscure emotions. The phantom figure we call Homer exists somewhere in the dark distance, like the ruins of a building whose shape and purpose we ignore. And yet, here and there, in his books, lie perhaps the inklings of an answer.

Hector, attempting to explain to Andromache why he must fight, acknowledges however that,

… in my heart and soul I also know this well:
the day will come when sacred Troy must die,
Priam must die and all his people with him,
Priam who hurls the strong ash spear…[3]

To which Achilles has unwittingly responded earlier:

One and the same lot for the man who hangs back
and the man who battles hard. The same honour waits
for the coward and the brave. They both go down to Death,
the fighter who shirks, the one who works to exhaustion.[4]

The communality of death, the arbitrary dealings of fate, are notions general enough for us to indulge in the commonplace that they are shared by all humankind, and belong to all places and all times. For the reader of Homer, however, at a distance of two and a half millennia, certain details in the poems render them magically singular, distil them into something intimately familiar, make them ours: Athena, knowing that Ulysses has suffered endlessly for ten long years, heartlessly saying to his son that 'It's light work for a willing god to save a mortal/even half the world away';[5] Achilles the warrior cursing war after the death of Patroclus;[6] the monstrous Cyclops tenderly placing each suckling lamb under its dam;[7] the dog Argos dying of heartbreak on seeing his master return after such a long absence;[8] Ulysses and Penelope in bed, telling each other their stories, husband and wife unable to fall asleep till all is told;[9] Andromache glancing back, again and again, at Hector departing for battle;[10] Priam and Achilles eating together and admiring, one the young man's beauty, the other, the old man's nobility.[11] How astonishing that, in a language we no longer know precisely how to pronounce, a poet or various poets whose faces and characters we cannot conceive, who lived in a society of whose customs and beliefs we have but a very vague idea, described for us our own lives today, with every secret happiness and every hidden sin.

A Greek author who called himself, after the philosopher, 'Heraclitus', composed in the first century AD a series of commentaries on Homer under the title *Homeric Allegories*. The first of these reads: 'From the very earliest infancy young children are nursed in their learning by Homer, and swaddled in his verses. We water our souls with them as though they were nourishing milk. He stands beside each of us as we start out and gradually grow into men, he blossoms as we do, and until old age we never grow tired of him, for as soon as we set him aside we thirst for him again; it may be said that the same limit is set to both Homer and life.'[12]

NOTES

A Note on Translations and Editions

1 Samuel Butler, *The Authoress of the Odyssey: Who and What She Was, When and Where She Wrote* [1897], Second Edition With a New Preface by Henry Festing Jones, London, Jonathan Cape, 1922.

Introduction

1 Gustave Flaubert, 'Dictionnaire des idées reçues' in *Bouvard et Pécuchet*, introduction par Rayond Queneau, Paris, Editions du Point du Jour, 1947.

2 Cf. André Gide, *Oscar Wilde: In Memoriam*, Paris, Mercure de France, 1910.

3 Quoted in Henry Solly, *These Eighty Years, or The Story of an Unfinished Life*, vol. II, chapter 2, page 81, London, Simpkin Marshall & Co., 1893.

4 Virginia Woolf, 'On Not Knowing Greek' in *The Common Reader: First Series*, London, The Hogarth Press, 1925.

5 Emanuel Geibel, 'Kriegslied' in *Heroldsrufe: Zeitgedichte, Gesammelte Werke*, Band 4, Stuttgart, Cotta, 1893.

6 Simone de Beauvoir, *La femme rompue*, Paris, Gallimard, 1963.

7 *The Iliad of Homer*, translated by T. S. Brandreth, 2 vols, London, W. Pickering, 1846.

8 'Mucho más que libros', *Semana*, 4 June 2001, Bogotá.

9 *Iliad*, Book XXIV, lines 594–9.

10 *Iliad*, XXIV: 613–20.

Chapter 2

1 Mustafá El-Abbadi, *Life and Fate of the Ancient Library of Alexandria*, Paris, Unesco, 1990.

2 Herodotus, *The Histories*, edited by A. R. Burn, London, Penguin Books, 1954, Book II, section 117.

3 Athenaeus, *The Deipnosophists*, translated and edited by Charles B. Gulick, London, William Heinemann, 1950, Book VIII, section 347e.

4 F. Zeitlin, 'Visions and Revisions of Homer' in S. Goldhill (ed.), *Being Greek under Rome*, Cambridge and New York, Cambridge University Press, 2001.

5 Herodotus, *The Histories*, V: 58.

6 *Iliad*, VI: 198–9.

7 Cf. Bruce Heiden, 'The Placement of Book Divisions in the Iliad' in *Journal of Hellenic Studies*, 1998. Also Minna Skafte Jensen, 'Dividing Homer: When and How were the *Iliad* and the *Odyssey* Divided into Songs?' in *Symbolae Osloenses*, 1999, both quoted in J. Haubold, *Homer's People: Epic Poetry and Social Formation*, Cambridge and London, Cambridge University Press, 2000.

8 Jean Irigoin, 'Homère, l'écriture et le livre' in *Europe*, 79e année, No. 865, May 2001, Paris. A contrary argument is given by Bruce Heiden in the article mentioned above.

9 Thomas Heywood, *The Hierarchy of the Blessed Angells. Their*

names, orders and offices; the fall of Lucifer with his angells [1635], New York, Da Capo Press, 1973.

10 Miguel de Cervantes Saavedra, *El Ingenioso Hidalgo Don Quijote de la Mancha*, Buenos Aires, Edición y notas, Celina S. de Cortázar e Isaías Lerner, Universitaria de Buenos Aires, 1969, II: 74.

11 'Hymn to Delian Apollo' in *The Homeric Hymns*, translated by Jules Cashford with an Introduction and Notes by Nicholas Richardson, London and New York, Penguin Books, 2003, v. 175.

12 [Thomas Blackwell], *An Enquiry into the Life and Writings of Homer*, second edition, London, J. Oswald, 1736.

13 Herodotus, *Vie d'Homère*, mise en français d'Amyot par J.-J. van Dooren, Paris, Librairie Ancienne Edouard Champion, 1926.

14 John Milton, *Paradise Regained*, in *Complete Poems and Major Prose*, edited by Marritt Y. Hughes, Indianapolis and New York, The Odyssey Press, 1957, Book IV, line 259.

15 *Héraclite, Fragments: Citations et témoignages*, traduction et présentation par Jean-François Pradeau, 2e édition corrigée, Paris, Flammarion, 2004.

16 Herodotus, *Vie d'Homère*, op. cit.

17 *Héraclite, Fragments: Citations et témoignages*, op. cit.

18 *Odyssey*, Book VIII, lines 51–99.

19 *Odyssey*, VIII: 302–410.

20 *Odyssey*, VIII: 552–84.

21 *Odyssey* I: 178.

22 *Odyssey*, VIII: 87.

23 T. E. Lawrence, 'Translator's Note' in *The Odyssey of Homer*, translated into English prose by T. E. Shaw (Colonel T. E. Lawrence), New York, Oxford University Press, Galaxy Books, 1956.

24 Albert B. Lord, *The Singer of Tales*, Cambridge, Mass., Harvard University Press, 1960. A novel by the Albanian writer Ismail Kadaré, *The File on H* gives a fictional account of their adventure.

25 Plato, *Ion*, translated by Lane Cooper, in *The Collected Dialogues of Plato, Including the Letters*, edited by Edith Hamilton and Huntington Cairns, Princeton, NJ, Princeton University Press, 1963.

26 Plato, *Ion*, op. cit.

27 Claude Mossé, *La Grèce archaïque d'Homère à Eschyle*, Paris, Editions du Seuil, 1984.

28 Thomas De Quincey, 'Homer and the Homeridae' in *The Works of Thomas De Quincey*, vol. 13, edited by G. Lindop et al., London, Pickering and Chatto, 2001–3.

29 J. M. Foley, *Homer's Traditional Art*, University Park, Penn., Penn State University Press, 1999.

30 Gilbert Murray, *Five Stages of Greek Religion*, third edition with a new Introduction by the author, New York, Doubleday, 1951.

31 Strabo, *Geography*, translated by H. L. Jones, London, William Heinemann, 1960, Book I, section 73.

32 Aristotle, *Metaphysics*, translated by Hugh Tredennik and edited by G. C. Armstrong, London, William Heinemann, 1930.

33 Paul Veyne, *Les Grecs ont-ils cru à leurs mythes?*, Paris, Editions du Seuil, 1983.

34 John Burnet, *Early Greek Philosophy*, Edinburgh, Adam and Charles Black, 1892.

35 Cf. Jacqueline de Romilly, *La Grèce antique contre la violence*, Paris, Editions de Fallois, 2000.

36 Plutarch, 'Alcibiades' in *Lives*, vol. I, the Dryden translation, edited and revised by Arthur Hugh Clough, New York, Random House, 1992.

Chapter 3

1 Plato, *Republic*, translated by Paul Shorey, in *The Collected Dialogues of Plato*, op. cit., Book X.

2 Ibid.

3 Aldous Huxley, *Brave New World*, London, Chatto & Windus, 1933.

4 Plato, *The Lesser Hippias*, translated by Benjamin Jowett, in *The Collected Dialogues of Plato*, op. cit.

5 Miguel de Cervantes Saavedra, *Don Quijote de la Mancha*, op. cit.

6 Aristotle, *Poetics*, IV, translated by Samuel Henry Butcher, New York, Walter J. Black, 1943.

7 Cicéron, *L'Orateur: Du meilleur genre d'orateurs*, texte établi et traduit par Albert Yon, Paris, Les Belles Lettres, 2002, III.

8 John Milton, *Areopagitica: A Speech of Mr. John Milton*, first published 1644, New York and London, G. P. Putnam's Sons, 1928.

9 Strabo, *Geography*, Book 13, chapter 1, section 45.

10 Irad Malkin, *The Returns of Odysseus: Colonization and Ethnicity*, Berkeley, Calif., University of California Press, 1998.

11 *Iliad*, XI: 747–53.

Chapter 4

1 J. Irgoin, 'Les éditions des poètes à Aléxandrie' in *Sciences exactes et sciences appliqués à Alexandrie*, Actes du coloque international de St-Etienne, St-Etienne, Université de St-Etienne, 1996.

2 Gregory Nagy, 'Aristarchean Questions' in *Bryn Mawr Classical Review*, VII, 14, Bryn Mawr, PA, 1998.

3 Tomas Hägg, *The Novel in Antiquity*, Berkeley and Los Angeles, University of California Press, 1983.

4 Horace, *Epîtres*, II: 1, 'À Auguste' in *Oeuvres*, Paris, Garnier Frères, 1967.

5 Pliny attributes this remark to his friend Atilius. 'A Novius Maximus', *Lettres I–IX* [II: 14] edited by A. M. Guillemin, 3 vols, Paris, Les Belles Lettres, 1927–8.

6 Peter Levi, *Horace: A Life*, London, Duckworth, 1997.

7 Horace, Epîtres II: 1, 'À Auguste' in *Oeuvres*, op. cit.

8 Horace, Epîtres I: 2, 'À Lollius' in *Oeuvres*, op. cit.

9 Quintilian, *The Orator's Education*, edited and translated by Donald A. Russell, Cambridge, Mass. and London, Harvard University Press, 1970, Book 10, in vol. IV.

10 *Iliad*, II: 931–2.

11 Cf. Claudia Moatti, *La Raison de Rome: Naissance de l'esprit critique à la fin de la République*, Paris, Editions du Seuil, 1997.

12 Peter Levi, *Virgil: His Life and Times*, London, Duckworth, 1998.

13 Manuel Sanz Morales, *Mitógrafos griegos*, Madrid, Akal, 2002.

14 Tim Whitmarsh, *Ancient Greek Literature*, Cambridge, Polity, 2004.

15 Virgil, *Aeneid*, A New Verse Translation by C. Day Lewis, Oxford, Oxford University Press, 1952, Book VI, lines 847–53.

16 Hermann Broch, *Der Tod des Vergil* [1945], Zurich, Rhein Verlag, 1958.

17 Virgil, *Aeneid*, 1: 283–4.

18 *Iliad*, XX: 210–11.

19 Stesichorus of Sicily in the sixth century BC and Hellanicus of Lesbos in the fifth century BC, among others.

20 Cf. Niall Rudd, Introduction to *Horace: Satires and Epistles* and *Persius: Satires* London, Penguin Books, 1973.

21 Lucretius, *On the Nature of Things*, Introduction by Wendell

Clausen, translated by H. A. J. Munro, New York, Washington Square Press, 1965.

22 Lewis Carroll, 'What the Tortoise said to Achilles' in *Mind*, April 1895, in *The Complete Works of Lewis Carroll*, London, The Nonesuch Press, 1922.

23 *The Iliads of Homer, Prince of Poets, Never Before in Any Language Truly Translated, Done According to the Greek by George Chapman*, London, George Newnes and New York, Charles Scribner's Sons, 1904.

24 Quoted in *Homer in English*, edited with an Introduction and Notes by George Steiner, London, Penguin Books, 1996.

25 Alexander Pope, *The Iliad and the Odyssey of Homer*, edited by the Revd H. F. Cary, New York, George Routledge and Sons, 1872.

26 Quoted in *Homer in English*, op. cit.

27 *Iliad*, in two volumes, with an English translation by A. T. Murray, Cambridge, Mass. and London, Harvard University Press, 1924; reprinted 2001.

28 *The Iliad: the Story of Achilles*, translated by W. H. D. Rowse, London, Thomas Nelson and Sons, 1938.

29 H. D. F. Kitto, *The Greeks*, London, Penguin Books, 1951.

30 *The Iliad of Homer*, translated by Richard Lattimore, Chicago, Chicago University Press, 1951.

31 Robert Lowell, *Imitations*, London, Faber and Faber, 1962.

32 Juan de Mena, *La Ilíada de Homero*, Edición crítica de las *Sumas de la Yliada de Omero* y del orìginal latino reconstruìdo, acompañada de un glosarìo latino-romance, por T. González Rolán, María F. del Barrio Vega y A. López Fonseca, Madrid, Ediciones Clásicas, 1996.

33 Homer, *Ilias*, in der Übertragung von Johann Heinrich Voss, mit einem Nachwort von Ute Schmidt-Berger, Munich, Artemis & Winkler, 1957.

34 Homère, *Iliade*, traduction de Leconte de Lisle, Paris, Profrance, 1998.

35 Haroldo do Campos, *Homero, Ilíada*, Introduçao e organizaçao Trajano Vieira, São Paulo, Editora Arx, 2001.

36 Juan Valera y Alcalá Galiano, *Cartas dirigidas al Sr. D. Francisco de Paula Canalejas*, Madrid, Revista Ibérica, 1864.

37 *Odyssey*, XI: 555–8.

38 Nancy Sherman, *Stoic Warriors: The Ancient Philosophy Behind the Military Mind*, Oxford and New York, Oxford University Press, 2005.

39 Stendhal, *La Chartreuse de Parme*, Paris, Le Divan, 1927, Book II, chapter 18.

40 Giacomo Leopardi, *Zibaldone di pensieri*, vol. I, Milan, Mondadori, 1997, §289.

41 Virgil, *Aeneid*, VXII: 837–9.

Chapter 5

1 J. Steinmann, *Saint Jerôme*, Paris, Editions du Cerf, 1958.

2 Matthew 6: 21.

3 St Jerome, 'Letter to Eustochium on Guarding Virginity' in *The Collected Works of Erasmus*, vol. 61, *Patristic Scholarship: The Edition of St Jerome*, edited, translated and annotated by James F. Brady and John C. Olin, Toronto, Buffalo, London, University of Toronto Press, 1992.

4 St Jerome, 'Letter to Magnus, Roman Orator' in *The Collected Works of Erasmus*, vol. 61, op. cit.

5 Erasmus, 'Life of Jerome' in *The Collected Works of Erasmus*, vol. 61.

6 St Augustine, *Confessions*, translated with an Introduction by

R. S. Pine-Coffin, London, Penguin Books, 1961, Chapter 1, section 13.

7 Ibid., I: 14.

8 Horace, *Epîtres*, I: 2, 'À Lollius' in *Oeuvres*, Paris, Garnier Frères, 1967.

9 St Augustine, *The City of God*, translated by Henry Bettenson, London, Penguin Books, 1972, Book I, chapter 1, section 3.

10 St Augustine, *Confessions*, op. cit., I: 13 and 16.

11 Heinrich Heine, *Sämtliche Werke*, zweiter Band. Herausgegeben von Prof. Dr Ernst Elster, Leipzig und Wien, Mayers Klassiker-Ausgaben, 1890.

Chapter 6

1 James J. O'Donnell, *Cassiodorus*, Berkeley, University of California Press, 1979.

2 Edward Gibbon, *The Decline and Fall of the Roman Empire*, vol. III, New York, Random House, 1983, p. 53. The earlier information on the Royal College is also to be found in Gibbon.

3 Michel Psellus, *Fourteen Byzantine Rulers* (the *Chronographia*), translated, with an Introduction, by E. R. A. Sewter, London, Penguin Books, 1966, Book VI.

4 William V. Harris, *Ancient Literacy*, Cambridge, Mass., and London, Harvard University Press, 1989.

5 Quoted in Harris, *Ancient Literacy*.

6 J. M. Wallace-Hadrill, *The Barbarian West: AD 400–1000, The Early Middle Ages*, revised edition, New York, Harper & Brothers, 1962.

7 Armando Petrucci, 'La concezione cristiana del libro fra VI e VII secolo' in *Libri e lettori nel medioevo: Guida storica e critica*, a cura di Guglielmo Cavallo, Rome, Laterza, 1989.

8 *Venetus Marcianus: Facsimile of the Codex*, with a Preface by John Williams White and an Introduction by Thomas W. Allen, Boston, Mass., Archeological Institute of America, 1902.

9 *Odyssey*, XI: 138–43.

10 Cf. Alan James, *Introduction* to Quintus of Smyrna, *The Trojan Epic: Posthomerica*, Baltimore and London, Johns Hopkins University Press, 2004.

11 Ibid.

12 The information on Dictys and Dares is taken from *The Trojan War: The Chronicles of Dictys of Crete and Dares the Phrygian*, translated with Introduction and Notes by R. M. Frazer, Fr., Bloomington and London, Indiana University Press, 1966.

13 Ronald T. Ridley, *The Historical Observations of Jacob Perizonius*, Rome, Bardi Editore, 1988.

14 Benoît de Sainte-Maure, *Le Roman de Troie*, extraits du manuscrit Milan, Bibliothèque ambrosienne, D55, édités, présentés et traduits par Emmanuèle Baumgartner et Françoise Vieillard, Paris, Letters Gothiques, Librairie Générale Française, 1998.

15 John Lydgate, *The Troy Book* [1412–20], edited by Robert R. Edwards, Kalamazoo, Western Michigan University, 1998.

16 Geoffrey Chaucer, *Troilus and Criseyde* [c. 1385] in *Complete Works*, edited from numerous manuscripts by Walter W. Skeat, Oxford and London, Oxford University Press, 1912.

17 Robert Henryson, *The Testament of Cresseid* [c. 1500] edited by Hugh MacDiarmid, London and New York, Penguin Books, 1989.

18 William Caxton, *Recuyell of the Historyes of Troye* [1474] edited with a critical Introduction, index and glossary by H. O. Sommer, 2 vols, London, D. Nutt, 1894.

19 Ben Jonson, 'To the Memory of My Beloved, the Author, Mr. William Shakespeare' in *Complete Works*, edited by P. Simpson

and E. Simpson, Oxford and London, Oxford University Press, 1986.

20 William Shakespeare, *Troilus and Cressida* [1609] in *Complete Works*, edited by W. J. Craig, Oxford, London, New York and Toronto, Oxford University Press, 1969.

Chapter 7

1 Lakhdar Souami, 'Présentation' in Jahiz, *Le cadi et la mouche: Anthologie du Livre des Animaux*, Paris, Sindbad, 1988.

2 Mas'udi, *Muruj al-Dhahab*, quoted in Houari Touati, *L'armoire à sagesse: bibliothèques et collections en Islam*, Paris, Aubier, 2003.

3 The story is told by the tenth-century scholar Ibn al-Nadim in his *al-Fihrist*, quoted in Johannes Pedersen, *The Arabic Book*, translated by Geoffrey French, Princeton, NJ, Princeton University Press, 1984.

4 Odyssey, XII: 95.

5 G. Strohmaier, 'Homer in Baghdad' in *Byzantinoslavica*, vol. 41, Prague, Institute of Slavonic Studies, 1980, pp. 196–200.

6 Quoted in Dimitri Gutas, *Greek Thought, Arabic Culture: The Graeco-Arabic Translation Movement in Baghdad and early 'Abbasid Society (2nd–4th/8th–10th centuries)*, Routledge: London and New York, 1998.

7 The 'death-bed meditations' are associated with the *wasaya* or 'testament' genre in Islamic medieval literature. Cf. Juan Vernet, *Lo que Europa debe al Islam de España*, Barcelona, El Acantilado, 1999.

8 Cf. Jörg Kraemer, 'Arabische Homerverse' in *Zeitschrift der Deutschen Morgenländischen Gesellschaft*, Band 106, Heft 2, Wiesbaden, Kommissionverlag Franz Steiner, 1956.

9 Patricia Crone, *Medieval Islamic Political Thought*, Edinburgh,

Edinburgh University Press, 2004, chapter XIV.

10 Cf. Robert Irwin, *Night and Horses and the Desert: An Anthology of Classical Arabic Literature*, London, Allen Lane, 1999.

11 Anonymous, *The Subtle Ruse: The Book of Arabic Wisdom and Guile*, translated by René Khawam, London, 1976, quoted in Robert Irwin, *Night and Horses and the Desert*.

12 A. I. Sabra, 'The Appropiation and Subsequent Naturalisation of Greek Science in Medieval Islam: a Preliminary Statement' in *The History of Science*, vol. 25 (1987) quoted in Patricia Crone, *Medieval Islamic Political Thought*, op. cit.

13 Wilhelm Grimm, 'Die Sage von Polyphem' quoted in William Hansen, *Ariadne's Thread: A Guide to International Tales Found in Classical Literature*, Ithaca and London, Cornell University Press, 2002.

14 Donald K. Fry, 'Polyphemus in Iceland' in *The Fourteenth Century, Acta IV*, 1977, quoted by Hermann Pálsson, 'Egils Saga Einhenda ok Ásmundar Berserkjabana' in *Dictionary of the Middle Ages*, vol. 4, Joseph R. Strayer (ed.), New York, Charles Scribner's Sons, 1989.

15 F. Gabrieli, 'The Transmission of Learning and Literary Influences to Western Europe' in *The Cambridge History of Islam*, Cambridge, Cambridge University Press, 1970.

16 Juan de Mena, 'Proemio', *La Ilíada de Homero*, op. cit.

Chapter 8

1 Quoted in E. R. Curtius, *Europäische Literatur und Lateinisches Mittelalter*, XI, Bern, A. Francke AG, 1948.

2 Francesco Petrarca, *Familiarum rerum*, edited by V. Rossi, Florence, 1937.

3 Dante Alighieri, *Commedia, Inferno*, a cura di Emilio Pasquini e

Antonio Quaglio, Milan, Garzanti, 1987, IV: 80–99.

4 *Iliad*, I: 232.

5 Cf. Robin Lane Fox, *Pagans and Christians in the Mediterranean World from the Second Century AD to the Conversion of Constantine*, New York, Alfred A. Knopf, 1986.

6 Seneca, 'On the Shortness of Life' in *The Stoic Philosophy of Seneca*, translated with an Introduction by Moses Hadas, New York, Doubleday & Co., 1958.

7 Albertino Mussato, *Historia Augusta de gestis Henrici VII*, quoted in Cristophe Carraud, Petrarque, *La vie solitaire*, préface de Nicholas Mann, introduction, traduction et notes de Christophe Carraud, Grenoble, Jérôme Millon, 1999.

8 Francesco Petrarca, *Secretum meum* in *Prose*, edited by Guido Martellotti et al. Milan, R. Ricciardi, 1955.

9 Dante Alighieri, *Commedia, Paradiso*, II: 7–9.

10 Virgil, *Aeneid*, I: 8.

11 Dante Alighieri, *Commedia, Inferno* I: 7–9.

12 G. K. Chesterton, 'Tricks of Memory' in *The Glass Walking Stick and Other Essays* by G. K. Chesterton, London, Methuen, 1955.

13 Jean-Christophe Saladin, *La Bataille du grec à la Renaissance*, 2e tirage revu et corrigé, Paris, Les Belles Lettres, 2000.

14 Francesco Petrarca, *Familiarum rerum*, XVIII: 2.

15 Jacob Burckhardt, *The Civilization of the Renaissance in Italy*, translated by S. G. C. Middlemore, New York, Random House, 1954.

16 George Steiner, 'Introduction' to *Homer in English*, op. cit.

Chapter 9

1 *Odyssey*, X: 539–41 and 550–52.

2 *Odyssey*, X: 553–95.

3 *Odyssey*, XI.

4 *Odyssey*, XXIV: 13–14.

5 Pindar, fragment 129 in *Works*, edited by Sir J. E. Sandys, Cambridge, Mass., and New York, Harvard University Press and William Heinemann, 1972.

6 *Odyssey*, XI: 555–8.

7 *Odyssey*, XI: 43–8.

8 *Odyssey*, XI: 723–6.

9 Jean le Fèvre uses the expression *danse macabré* [*sic*] for the first time in 1376, in his poem *Le respit de la mort*. Cf. Paul Binski, *Medieval Death: Ritual and Representation*, Ithaca, NY, Cornell University Press, 1996.

10 Hellmut Rosenfeld, *Der mittelalteriche Totentanz*, Wien, Böhlau Verlag, 1954.

11 *Iliad*, VI: 171–5.

12 Virgil, *Aeneid*, A New Verse Translation by C. Day Lewis, op. cit., VI: 306–14.

13 Dante Alighieri, *Commedia, Inferno*, III: 112–14.

14 André Malraux, *La voie royale*, Paris, Bernard Grasset, 1930.

15 Cf. Eugenio N. Frongia, 'Canto III: The Gate of Hell' in *Lectura Dantis: Inferno*, edited by Allen Mandelbaum, Anthony Oldcorn and Charles Ross, Berkeley, University of California Press, 1998.

16 John Milton, *Paradise Lost* [1667], in *Paradise Lost and Other Poems* (newly annotated by Edward Le Comte), New York, New American Library, 1961, Book I, lines 302–4.

17 Paul Verlaine, 'Chanson d'Automne' in *Poèmes saturniens*, Paris, Alphonse Lemerre, 1866.

18 Gerard Manley Hopkins, 'Spring and Fall' in *Poems and Prose of Gerard Manley Hopkins*, selected with an Introduction and Notes by W. H. Gardner, London, Penguin Books, 1953.

19 Dante Alighieri, *Le Opere di Dante*. Testo critico della Società Dantesca Italiana, ed. M. Barbi et al., Milan, Società Dantesca Italiana, 1921/22.

20 Ecclesiastes, I: 4.

21 Percy Bysshe Shelley, 'Ode to Naples', *The Complete Poems*, with Notes by Mary Shelley, New York, Random House, 1994, I: 1.

22 For the first observation, cf. E. Auerbach, *Dante als Dichter der irdischen Welt*, Berlin, De Gruyter, 1969; for the second, C. S. Singleton (translator), Introduction to *The Divine Comedy*, London, Routledge and Kegan Paul, 1971–5.

23 Cf. Claude Fauriel, *Dante et les origines de la langue et de la littérature italiennes: Cours faits à la Faculté de lettres de Paris*, Paris, Jules Mohl, 1854.

Chapter 10

1 Dante Alighieri, *Commedia, Inferno*, IV: 143–4.

2 Dante Alighieri, *Commedia, Inferno*, IV: 76–8.

3 Dante Alighieri, *Commedia, Inferno*, IV: 37–9.

4 John Pope-Hennessy, *The Portrait in the Renaissance*, Princeton, NJ, Princeton University Press, 1979.

5 Raphael completed this particular room in 1511. Cf. Jean-Pierre Cuzin, *Raphaël, vie et oeuvre*, Paris, Bibliothèque des arts, 1983.

6 Susy Marcon and Marino Zorzi (eds), *Aldo Manuzio e l'ambiente veneziano 1494–1515*, Venice, Il Cardo, 1994.

7 Vespasiano da Bisticci, *Vite di uomini illustri*, edited by P. d'Ancona e E. Aeschlimann, Milan, Arnoldo Mondadori, 1951.

8 Leonardo Bruni, 'The Study of Literature' in *Humanist Educational Treatises*, edited and translated by Craig W. Kallendorf, Cambridge, Mass. and London, Harvard University Press, 2002, §20.

9 Battista Guarino, 'A Program of Teaching and Learning' in *Humanist Educational Treatises*, op. cit., §19.

10 Aeneas Silvius Piccolimini, 'The Education of Boys' in *Humanist Educational Treatises*, op. cit., §33.

11 Francisco Bethencourt, 'A fundação' in *História das Inquisições: Portugal, Espanha e Itália, séculos XV-XIX*, São Paulo, Companhia das Letras, 2000.

12 J. N. D. Kelly, *The Oxford Dictionary of Popes*, Oxford and New York, Oxford University Press, 1988.

13 Jean-Christophe Saladin provides a breakdown of these terms by author in *La Bataille du grec à la Renaissance*, op. cit.

14 Quoted in Jean-Christophe Saladin, *La Bataille du grec à la Renaissance*, op. cit.

15 Neil Kent, *The Soul of the North: A Social, Architectural and Cultural History of the Nordic Countries, 1700–1940*, London, Reaktion Books, 2000.

16 Oliver Goldsmith, *The Vicar of Wakefield* [1766], Introduction by Frederick W. Hilles, New York, E. P. Dutton & Co., 1951.

17 Quoted in Henry Kamen, *The Disinherited: The Exiles Who Created Spanish Culture*, Penguin/Allen Lane: London, 2007.

18 Pedro Mexía, *Silva de varia lección*, edición de Isaías Lerner, Madrid, Editorial Castalia, 2003.

19 Isaías Lerner, 'Prólogo' a Pedro Mexía, *Silva de varia lección*, op. cit.

20 Francisco de Quevedo, *Las zahúrdas de Platón*, quoted in Raimundo Lida, *Prosas de Quevedo*, Barcelona, Editorial Crítica, 1980.

21 Francisco de Quevedo, *Defensa de Epicuro*, quoted in Lida, op. cit.

22 Cf. Octavio Paz, *Sor Juana Inés de la Cruz, o Las trampas de la fe*, Mexico, Fondo de Cultura Económica, 1988.

23 Sor Juana Inés de la Cruz, 'El Sueño' in *Antología poética*, selección e introducción José Miguel Oviedo, Madrid, Alianza, 2004.

24 Francis Bacon, '*De Sapientia Veterum*' [1609] translated into English as 'The Wisdom of the Ancients' [1619] in *Bacon's Essays including his Moral and Historical Works*, London and New York, Frederick Warne and Co., 1892.

Chapter 11

1 Michel de Montaigne, 'Les Essais' in *Collection de moralistes français*, publié avec des commentaires par Amaury Duval, vol. IV, Paris, Chez Chassériau, 1822, II: 36.

2 Charles Perrault, *Parallèle des anciens et des modernes* [1688–97], Geneva, Slatkine, 1971.

3 *Iliad*, XI: 656.

4 Princess Nausicaa, daughter of King Alcinous, in *Odyssey*, VI: 70–73.

5 Charles-Augustin Sainte-Beuve, *Réflexions sur les lettres*, Paris, Plon, 1941.

6 Jean Racine, 'Remarques sur l'*Odysée*' in *Oeuvres complètes*, présentation, notes et commentaires par Raymond Picard, Paris, Gallimard, 1950, tome II: VI, 2.

7 Louis Racine, 'Mémoires contenant quelques particularités sur la vie et les ouvrages de Jean Racine' in *Oeuvres complètes*, tome I.

8 Charles-Augustin Sainte-Beuve, *Port-Royal*, Paris, Gallimard, 1954–5, vol. I: II [1867].

9 Blaise Pascal, *Pensées*, nouvelle édition revue avec soin, Paris, Imprimerie d'Auguste Delalain, 1820, II: XIV: 11.

10 *Iliad*, VI: 580–84.

11 Jean Racine, *Andromaque* in *Oeuvres complètes*, tome I, op. cit., I: 1.

12 Raymond Picard, introduction à Jean Racine, *Andromaque* in *Oeuvres complètes*, tome I, op. cit.

13 Jean-Pierre Vernant, 'Catégories de l'agent et de l'action en Grèce ancienne' in *Religions, histoires, raisons*, Paris, François Maspero, 1979.

14 *Odyssey*, XII: 278.

15 *Odyssey*, XII: 336.

16 Aldous Huxley, 'Tragedy and the Whole Truth' in *The Complete Essays*, vol. III, 1930–35, edited with commentary by Robert S. Baker and James Sexton, Chicago, Ivan R. Dee, 2001.

17 Jean Racine, *Andromaque* in *Oeuvres complètes*, tome I, op. cit., V: 3.

18 *Odyssey*, V: 436–8.

19 *Odyssey*, V: 476–7.

20 *Odyssey*, V: 490–97.

21 Jean Racine, 'Remarques sur l'*Odysée*' in *Oeuvres complètes*, op. cit.

22 Anne Dacier, *Des causes de la corruption du goût* [1714], Geneva, Sladkine, 1970.

23 Jean-Robert Armogathe, *Le Quiétisme*, Paris, Presses Universitaires de France, 1973.

24 François de Fénelon, *Explication des maximes des saints*, in *Oeuvres*, 2 vols, Paris, Gallimard, 1997.

25 François de Fénelon, *Les Aventures de Télémaque*, in *Oeuvres*, op. cit.

26 James Herbert Davis, Jr., *Fénelon*, Boston, Twayne, 1979.

27 Montesquieu, *Lettres persanes*, XXXVI, Établissement du texte, prèface, chronologie, bibliographie et notes par Laurent Versini, Paris, GF-Flammarion, 1995.

28 Baron Frédéric-Melchior Grimm, 'Lettre du 1er juin 1757' in *Correspondance littéraire*, II [1820], Paris, Mercure de France, 2001.

Chapter 12

1 All information on the painting is taken from Simon Schama's *Rembrandt's Eyes*, New York, Alfred A. Knopf, 1999.

2 Julius S. Held, 'Rembrandt's Aristotle' in *Rembrandt Studies*, Princeton, 1991, quoted by Simon Schama.

3 Plutarch, 'Alexander' in *Lives*, vol. II.

4 Sir Philip Sidney, *The Defence of Poesy* [1595] in *The Renaissance in England*, edited by H. E. Rowlands and H. Baker, Lexington, Mass., D. C. Heath, 1954.

5 Sir Francis Bacon, *The Advancement of Learning* [1605] edited by Michael Kiernan, Oxford and New York, Oxford University Press, 2000.

6 T. S. Eliot, 'Poetry in the Eighteenth Century' in *The Pelican Guide to English Literature*, vol. 4, edited by Boris Ford, London, Penguin Books, 1957.

7 Alexander Pope, *The Iliad and the Odyssey of Homer*, edited by the Revd H. F. Cary, New York, George Routledge and Sons, 1872.

8 Richard Outram, private correspondence.

9 Edward Gibbon, *Memoirs of My Life*, edited by Betty Radice, London, Penguin Books, 1998.

10 Samuel Johnson, 'Pope' in *Lives of the English Poets* [1779–81], vol. II, with an Introduction by Arthur Waugh, Oxford and London, Oxford University Press, 1912.

11 Henry Fielding, 'A Journey from This World to the Next' [1743] in *The Complete Works of Henry Fielding, Esq. with an Essay on the Life, Genius and Achievement of the Author*, by William Ernest Henley, London, William Heinemann, 1903.

12 William Hazlitt, *Lectures on English Poets* in *Selected Essays*, edited by Geoffrey Keynes, London, The Nonesuch Press, 1946.

13 Leslie Stephen, *Pope*, London, Macmillan and Co., 1909.

14 Pope, *The Iliad and the Odyssey of Homer*, op. cit.

15 Jorge Luis Borges, 'Las versiones homéricas' in *Discusión*, Buenos Aires, Manuel Gleizer, 1932.

16 Pope, *The Iliad and the Odyssey of Homer*, op. cit., Book XXIII.

17 Homer, *The Iliad*, translated by Robert Fagles, Introduction and Notes by Bernard Knox, London, Penguin Books, 1990, XXIII: 243–8.

18 Pope, *Essay on Criticism*, lines 68–9, 74–5, in *The Poems of Alexander Pope* (ed. John Butt), London, Methuen & Co, 1963.

19 Samuel Johnson, 'Pope' in *Lives of the English Poets*, op. cit.

20 William Cowper, *Table Talk*, London, John Sharpe, 1825, Book I, section 656.

21 *Homer in English*, edited with an Introduction and Notes by George Steiner, London, Penguin Books, 1996.

22 Matthew Arnold, *On Translating Homer*, London, Smith, Elder & Co., 1896.

23 Ibid.

24 Ibid.

25 Ibid.

26 A. E. Housman, 'Introductory Lecture' [1892] in *The Name and Nature of Poetry and Other Selected Prose*, edited by John Carter, Cambridge and London, Cambridge University Press, 1961.

Chapter 13

1 John Keats, 'Letter to Benjamin Bailey', 18 July 1818, in *The Complete Works of John Keats*, vol. IV, edited by H. Buxton Forman, Glasgow, Gowars & Gray, 1901.

2 John Keats, 'On First Looking into Chapman's Homer' in *The Poems of John Keats*, Arranged in Chronological Order with a

Preface by Sidney Colvin, vol. I, London, Chatto & Windus, 1924.

3 *The Iliads of Homer, Prince of Poets, Never Before in any Language Truly Translated, Done According to the Greek by George Chapman*, London, George Newnes, 1904.

4 William Blake, 'On Virgil' in *The Complete Writings of William Blake*, edited by Geoffrey Keynes, Oxford, Oxford University Press, 1957.

5 William Blake, 'Preface' to *Milton: A Poem in 2 Books to Justify the Ways of God to Man*, in *The Complete Poems*, edited by Alicia Ostriker, London and New York, Penguin Books, 1977.

6 William Blake, 'On Homer's Poetry' in *The Complete Writings of William Blake*, op. cit.

7 William Blake, 'Letter to the Rvd. Dr. Trusler, 23 August 1799', *The Poetry and Prose of William Blake*, edited by David V. Erdman, commentary by Harold Bloom, Garden City, New York, Doubleday & Co., 1965.

8 William Blake, 'On Boyd' in *The Complete Writings of William Blake*, op. cit.

9 William Blake, 'On Dante' in *The Complete Writings of William Blake*, op. cit.

10 *The Illuminated Blake*, edited by David V. Erdman, Garden City, New York, Doubleday & Co., 1974.

11 Cf. William Blake, 'The Marriage of Heaven and Hell: The Voice of the Devil' in William Blake, 'On Boyd' in *The Complete Writings of William Blake*, op. cit.

12 William Blake, 'Public Address', pp. 60 and 20, *The Poetry and Prose of William Blake*, op. cit.

13 Lord Byron, 'Letter to Octavius Gilchrist, 15 September 1821' in *Byron: A Self-Portrait: Letters and Diaries, 1789–1824*, edited by Peter Quennell, 2 vols, New York, Charles Scribner's Sons, 1950.

14 Lord Byron, 'Letter to John Murray, 17 September 1817', *Byron: A Self-Portrait*, op. cit.

15 John Stuart Mill, 'Notes on Some of the More Popular Dialogues of Plato' in *The Collected Works of John Stuart Mill*, edited by J. M. Robson, vol. XI, Toronto, Toronto University Press, 1978.

16 Percy Bysshe Shelley, 'A Defence of Poetry' in *Essays and Letters*, edited by Ernest Rhys, London, Walter Scott, 1887.

17 Herbert Read, *Byron*, London, Longmans, Green & Co., 1951.

18 Lord Byron, *Don Juan*, VII: 633–44 in *Byron: The Oxford Authors*, edited by Jerome J. McGann, Oxford and New York, Oxford University Press, 1986.

19 Lord Byron, *Don Juan*, VIII: 621–4 in *Byron: The Oxford Authors*, op. cit.

20 Lord Byron, *Don Juan*, VIII: 70–72.

21 *Odyssey*, IV: 605.

22 *Odyssey*, II: 1.

23 The *Odyssey* [1961] and the *Iliad* [1974] translated by Robert Fitzgerald, New York, Farrar, Straus & Giroux, 2004.

24 Jorge Luis Borges, 'Las versiones homéricas', in *Discusión*, op. cit.

25 *Iliad*, XVI: 703–7 and 407–13.

26 *Iliad*, XVI: 415–19.

27 Lord Byron, 'The Destruction of Sennacherib' in *The Poetical Works, The Only Complete and Copyright Text in I Volume*, edited with a Memoir by E. H. Coleridge, London, John Murray, 1905.

28 Enrique Banchs, 'El tigre' in *La urna* [1911], Buenos Aires, Proa, 2000.

29 Ogden Nash, 'Very Like a Whale' in *Selected Verse*, New York, Random House, 1946.

30 Madame de Staël, *De la littérature considerée dans ses rapports avec les institutions sociales* [1800] edited by P. van Tiegham, 2 vols, Geneva and Paris, Librairie Garnier, 1959.

Chapter 14

1 Donald Phillip Verene, *Vico's Science of Imagination*, Ithaca and London, Cornell University Press, 1981.

2 Giambattista Vico, *La scienza nuova*, §819, Turin, Torinese, 1952.

3 Richard Ellmann, *James Joyce*, new and revised edition, Oxford and New York, Oxford University Press, 1982.

4 *Iliad*, II: 573–82.

5 Donald Phillip Verene, *Vico's Science of Imagination*, op. cit.

6 Giambattista Vico, *La scienza nuova*, op. cit., §873.

7 Ulrich Joost, 'Friedrich August Wolf' in Walther Killy, *Literatur Lexicon*, Band XII, Munich, Bertelsmann, 1992.

8 Johann Joachim Winckelmann, *Gedanken über die Nachahmung der griechischen Werke in der Malerei und Bildhauerkunst* [1755], Stuttgart, Philipp Reclam, 1995.

9 Denis Diderot, 'Salon de 1767' in *Oeuvres complètes*, annotées par J. Assézat et M. Tourneux, Paris, Garnier frères, 1875–9.

10 Cf. 'Grecs (philosophie des)' in *L'Encyclopédie de Diderot et d'Alembert*, edition facsimile, Milan, Franco Maria Ricci, 1977–8.

11 Cicéron, *L'Orateur: Du meilleur genre d'orateurs*, II: 62.

12 Johann Peter Eckermann, *Gespräche mit Goethe in den letzten Jahren seines Lebens* [1837–48] Herausgegeben von Fritz Bergemann, 2 Bände, Frankfurt-am-Main, Suhrkamp Verlag, 1981.

13 J. W. von Goethe, 'Brief an Schiller', 17 Mai 1795, in *Werke*, Band 2, textkritisch durchgesehen von Erich Trunz, Munich, C. H. Beck, 1981.

14 J. W. von Goethe, 'Brief an Schiller', 27 December 1797, in *Werke*, Band 2, op. cit.

15 J. W. von Goethe, 'Brief an Humboldt', 26 Mai 1799, in *Werke*, Band 2, op. cit.

16 Among many others: Herder's *Auch eine Philosophie der Geschichte zur Bildung der Menschheit* (1774), *Alteste Urkunde des Menschengeschlechts* (1774), *Ideen zur Philosophie der Geschichte der Menschheit* (1784–91) etc., Wieland's *Geschichte des Agaton* (1766–7), *Die Abderiten* (1774), *Neue Götter-Gespräche* (1791) etc., Heinse's *Ardinghello* (1789), Schlegel's *Über die Diotima* (1795), *Uber das Studium der griechischen Poesie* (1797), *Die Griechen und Römer* (1798) etc., Karl Philipp Moritz's, *Die Götterlehre* (1791), Hölderlin's *Hyperion* (1797–9), *Empedocles* (1797–1800) etc.

17 Cf. E. R. Curtius, *Europäische Literatur und Lateinisches Mittelalter*, XVIII, Bern, A. Francke AG, 1948.

18 J. W. von Goethe, 'Der ewige Jude' in *Goethes Poetische Werke*, Band 2, Stuttgart, J. G. Cotta'sche Buchhandlung Nachfolger, 1950–54.

19 E. R. Curtius, *Europäische Literatur und Lateinisches Mittelalter*, I, op. cit.

Chapter 15

1 Nicholas Boyle, *Goethe, the Poet and the Age*, vol. I, 'The Poetry of Desire', Oxford and New York, Oxford University Press, 1992.

2 J. W. von Goethe, *Die Leiden des Jungen Werther*, I, in *Werke*, Band 6, textkritisch durchgesehen von Erich Trunz und kommentiert von Benno von Wiese, Munich, C. H. Beck, 1981.

3 Friedrich Schiller, 'Über naïve und sentimentalische Dichtung' in *Schillers Werke*, herausgegeben von Ludwig Bellermann, Achter Band, Leipzig and Vienna, Bibliographisches Institut, 1905.

4 Carl Gustav Jung, 'Schiller's Ideas on the Type Problem' in *Psychological Types*, a Revision by R. F. C. Hull of the Translation

by H. G. Baynes, vol. 6 of the *Collected Works*, Princeton, NJ, Princeton University Press, 1971.

5 Friedrich Schiller, 'Über naïve und sentimentalische Dichtung' in *Schillers Werke*, op. cit.

6 Quoted in David Luke's Introduction to J. W. von Goethe, *Faust, Part II*, translated by David Luke, Oxford and New York, Oxford University Press, 1994.

7 Ibid.

8 *Iliad*, II: 189–90.

9 *Iliad*, III: 219.

10 *Iliad*, III: 187–90.

11 *Iliad*, VI: 424–6.

12 Christopher Marlowe, *Doctor Faustus* (1588?, first published 1604), lines 62–3, in *The Plays of Christopher Marlowe*, Oxford and London, Oxford University Press, 1939.

13 Christopher Marlowe, *Doctor Faustus*, lines 1354–6.

14 *Iliad*, III: 191.

15 Edgar Allan Poe, 'To Helen' (1848) in *Poems*, vol. X of *The Complete Works of Edgar Allan Poe*, collected and edited by Edmund Clarence Stedman and George Edward Woodberry, New York, Charles Scribner's Sons, 1914.

16 *Iliad*, III: 200.

17 Goethe, *Faust, Part II*, translated by David Luke, op. cit., lines 8838–40.

18 Ibid., line 6197.

19 Goethe, *Die Leiden des Jungen Werther*, I, in *Werke*, Band 6, op. cit.

20 J. W. von Goethe, *Dichtung und Wahrheit* in *Werke*, Band 9, textkritisch durchgesehen von Liselotte Blumenthal und kommentiert von Erich Trunz, Munich, C. H. Beck, 1981.

Chapter 16

1 Friedrich Nietzsche, 'What I Owe to the Ancients', Part 2, in *Twilight of the Gods*, in *The Portable Nietzsche*, edited and translated by Walter Kaufmann, London, Penguin Books, 1954.

2 Friedrich Nietzsche, 'Homer und die klassische Philologie' in *Werke in drei Bänden*, herausgegeben von Karl Schlechta, Munich, Carl Hanser Verlag, 1973.

3 Friedrich Nietzsche, 'Homer Contest' in *The Portable Nietzsche*, op. cit.

4 Friedrich Nietzsche, *The Birth of Tragedy Out of the Spirit of Music*, translated by Shaun Whiteside, edited by Michael Tanner, new revised edition, London and New York, Penguin Books, 2003.

5 Ibid.

6 Lesley Chamberlain, *Nietzsche in Turin*, London, Quartet Books, 1996.

7 Sigmund Freud, 'Our Attitude Towards War' in *Civilization, Society and Religion: Group Psychology, Civilization and Its Discontents and Other Works*, translated from the German under the general editorship of James Strachey, London, Penguin Books, 1985.

8 Peter Gay, *Freud: A Life for Our Time*, New York and London, W. W. Norton & Co., 1988.

9 *Odyssey*, XI: 550–52.

10 *Iliad*, XXI: 123–6.

11 Freud, 'Our Attitude Towards War', op. cit.

12 Gay, *Freud: A Life for Our Time*, op. cit.

13 Quoted in Gay, *Freud: A Life for Our Time*, op. cit.

14 Ibid.

15 Freud, 'Our Attitude Towards War', op. cit.

16 Sigmund Freud, 'Moses and Monotheism' [1939] in *The Origins of Religion*, translated from the German under the general editorship of James Strachey, London, Penguin Books, 1985.

17 Bruno Bettelheim, *Freud and Man's Soul*, New York, Alfred A. Knopf, 1983.

18 Carl Gustav Jung, 'On the Relation of Analytical Psychology to Poetry' in *The Spirit in Man, Art and Literature*, translated by H. G. Baynes, Princeton, Princeton University Press, 1966.

19 *Iliad*, XXIV: 695–9.

20 Rupert Brooke, *The Collected Poems*, with an introduction by George Edward Woodberry, New York, Dodd, Mead & Co., 1923.

Chapter 17

1 Heinrich Schliemann, *Troy and Its Remains: A Narrative of Researches and Discoveries Made on the Site of Ilium and in the Trojan Plain*, edited by Philip Smith [translated by L. Dora Schmitz, 1875], New York, Arno Press, 1976.

2 Ibid.

3 Michael Wood, *In Search of the Trojan War*, London, BBC Books, 1985.

4 Ibid.

5 Ibid.

6 Quoted in Philip Smith's Introduction to Schliemann, *Troy and Its Remains*.

Chapter 18

1 Samuel Butler, *The Authoress of the Odyssey: Who and What She Was, When and Where She Wrote* [1897], Second Edition With a

New Preface by Henry Festing Jones, London, Jonathan Cape, 1922.

2 Ibid.

3 Ibid.

4 Ibid.

5 *Odyssey*, IX: 23–9.

6 Robert Bittlestone, *Odysseus Unbound: The Search for Homer's Ithaca*, Cambridge, Mass., and London, Cambridge University Press, 2006.

7 Butler, *The Authoress of the Odyssey*, op. cit.

8 Moses Finley, *The World of Odysseus* [1956], London and New York, Pelican Books, 1962.

9 J. W. von Goethe, *Dichtung und Wahrheit*, op. cit.

10 Samuel Butler, *The Notebooks*, Selections arranged and edited by Henry Festing Jones, London, Jonathan Cape, 1912.

11 T. E. Lawrence, 'Translator's Note' in *The Odyssey of Homer*, op. cit.

12 Margaret Atwood, *The Penelopiad: The Myth of Penelope and Odysseus*, Edinburgh and New York, Canongate, 2005.

13 Ibid.

14 Butler, *The Authoress of the Odyssey*, op. cit.

15 Atwood, *The Penelopiad*, op. cit.

16 *Odyssey*, XXII: 494–5.

17 Mary Josefa MacCarthy, *A Nineteenth-Century Childhood*, London, William Heinemann, 1924.

18 Rudyard Kipling, 'When 'Omer Smote 'Is Bloomin' Lyre' in *The Seven Seas*, London, Methuen & Co., 1896.

Chapter 19

1 Durs Grünbein, *Galilei vermißt Dantes Hölle und bleibt an den*

Maßen hängen, Frankfurt-am-Main, Suhrkamp Verlag, 1996.

2 Quoted in Richard Ellmann, *James Joyce*, new and revised edition, Oxford and New York, Oxford University Press, 1982.

3 Quoted in ibid.

4 Quoted in ibid.

5 W. B. Yeats, 'The Autumn of the Body' in *Ideas of Good and Evil*, quoted by Richard Ellmann, *The Consciousness of Joyce*, Toronto and New York, Oxford University Press, 1977.

6 Cf. Ellmann, *The Consciousness of Joyce*.

7 Ibid.

8 Vladimir Nabokov, 'Ulysses' in *Lectures on Literature*, edited by Fredson Bowers, Introduction by John Updike, New York and London, Harcourt Brace Jovanovich, 1980.

9 James Joyce, *Ulysses*, London, Sydney, Toronto, The Bodley Head, 1960, p. 382.

10 A. E. Housman, 'Fragment of a Greek Tragedy' [1883] in *Trinity Magazine*, Oxford, February 1921.

11 Quoted in Ellmann, *James Joyce*, op. cit.

12 Quoted in ibid.

13 Neither story is in Homer: Ulysses' is told by Hyginus, *Fabulae* 95, Achilles' in Apollodorus (attr.) *The Library*. Cf. Robert Graves, *The Greek Myths*, revised edition, London and New York, Penguin Books, 1960.

14 *Iliad* III: 265–8.

15 Alfonso Reyes, 'Odiseo' en *Algunos ensayos*, prólogo y selección Emmanuel Carballo, México, Universidad Nacional Autónoma de México, 2002.

16 Michael Grant, *History of Rome*, London, Weidenfeld Nicolson, 1978.

17 Virgil, *Aeneid*, II: 164.

18 *Odyssey*, XI: 138.

19 Dante Alighieri, *Commedia, Inferno*, XXVI: 90–142.

20 Alfred, Lord Tennyson, 'Ulysses' in *Selected Poems*, chosen and edited by Michael Millgate, Oxford and New York, Oxford University Press, 1963.

21 Mario Vargas Llosa, 'Odiseo en Mérida', *El País*: Madrid, 30 July 2006.

22 Nikos Kazantzakis, *The Odyssey: A Modern Sequel*, translated by Kimon Friar, New York, Simon & Schuster, 1985.

23 *Iliad*, VI: 277.

24 José Hernández, *Martín Fierro*, 'La vuelta de Martín Fierro', Prólogo por las profesoras María Teresa Gramuglio y Beatriz Sarlo; notas por el profesor Andrés Avellaneda, Buenos Aires, Centro Editor de América Latina, 1979, 15: 2319–24.

25 Victor Bérard, *Les Phéniciens et l'Odysée*, 2 vols, Paris, Armand Colin, 1902–3.

26 Richard Ellmann, *The Consciousness of Joyce*, op. cit.

27 James Joyce, *Ulysses*, op. cit., p. 279.

28 George K. Anderson, *The Legend of the Wandering Jew*, third printing, Hanover and London, Brown University Press, 1991. Anderson argues that to associate Bloom with the Wandering Jew is an oversimplification.

29 *Odyssey*, 1: 2.

30 Samuel Johnson, *A Preface to Shakespeare* [1765] in *The Major Works*, edited by Donald Greene, Oxford and New York, Oxford University Press, 2000.

Chapter 20

1 Jean Paulhan and Dominique Aury (eds), *La patrie se fait tous les jours*, Paris, Editions de Minuit, 1947.

2 Jean Giraudoux, 'Note sur le texte' in *Théâtre complet*, edited by Jacques Body, Paris, Gallimard, 1982.

3 Jean Giraudoux, *La guerre de Troie n'aura pas lieu* in *Théâtre complet*, op. cit.

4 Quoted by Colette Weil, 'Préface' in Jean Giraudoux, *La guerre de Troie n'aura pas lieu*, Paris, Grasset, 1991.

5 Cf. Marie-Jeanne Durry, *L'Univers de Giraudoux*, Paris, Mercure de France, 1961.

6 Jean Giraudoux, 'Bellac et la tragédie', quoted by Colette Weil, 'Préface' in Jean Giraudoux, *La guerre de Troie n'aura pas lieu*, op. cit.

7 Marguerite Yourcenar, *Les yeux ouverts: entretiens avec Mathieu Galey*, Paris, Editions du Centurion, 1980.

8 Doris Lessing, *African Laughter: Four Visits to Zimbabwe*, London, HarperCollins, 1992.

9 Derek Walcott, *The Antilles: Fragments of Epic Memory: The Nobel Lecture*, New York, Farrar, Straus & Giroux, 1993.

10 *Odyssey*, XI: 1.

11 Derek Walcott, *Omeros*, London, Faber and Faber, 1990, I: 1:1.

12 Ezra Pound, *The Cantos*, revised edition, London, Faber and Faber, 1975, I: 1.

13 Walcott, *Omeros*, op. cit., III: 27: 3.

14 Ibid., III: 27: 3.

15 Ibid., I: 3: 2.

16 Italo Calvino, *Perché leggere i classici*, Milan, Arnoldo Mondadori, 1991.

17 C. P. Cavafy, 'Trojans' in *Collected Poems*, bilingual edition, translated by Edmund Keeley and Philip Sherrard, edited by George Savidis, London, The Hogarth Press, 1975.

18 Cavafy, 'Ithaka' in ibid.

19 Cavafy, 'The City' in ibid.

20 Timothy Findley, *Famous Last Words*, Toronto and Vancouver, Clarke, Irwin & Co.,1981.

21 Ezra Pound, *Hugh Selwyn Mauberley*, London, Faber and Faber, 1920.

22 Timothy Findley, 'Famous Last Words' in *Inside Memory: Pages From a Writer's Workbook*, Toronto, HarperCollins, 1990.

23 David Ingham, 'Bashing the Fascists: The Moral Dimensions of Findley's Fiction' in *Studies in Canadian Fiction*, 15, 2 (1990).

24 *Grand Hotel*, directed by Edmund Goulding, MGM, 1932.

25 T. S. Eliot, 'The Hollow Men' in *Collected Poems 1909–1962*, London, Faber and Faber, 1962.

26 Pound, *The Cantos*, op. cit., LXXIV.

27 Findley, *Famous Last Words*, op. cit.

Chapter 21

1 Alessandro Baricco, *Omero, Iliade*, Milan, Feltrinelli, 2004.

2 Quoted by Diogenes Laertius, *Vies et doctrines des philosophes illustres*, traductions sous la direction de M.-O. Goulet-Cazé, Paris, Livre de Poche, 1999, IX: 1–6.

3 Celso, *El Discurso verdadero contra los cristianos*, introducción y notas de Serafin Bodelón, Madrid, Alianza, 1988.

4 Dante Alighieri, *De monarchia* in *Le Opere di Dante*. Testo critico della Società Dantesca Italiana, edited by M. Barbi et al., Milan, Società Dantesca Italiana, 1921/22, II: 5: 22.

5 *Odyssey*, XXII: 319–20.

6 Simone Weil, *The Iliad, or the Poem of Force*, translated by Mary McCarthy, Wellingford, Pennsylvania, Pendle Hill Pamphlet, 1956.

7 Herbert Read (ed.), *The Knapsack*, London, George Routledge & Sons, 1939.

8 *Iliad*, XV: 557.

9 *Iliad*, VI: 612.

10 Or perhaps it can. In *The Spectator*, London, 30 July 2005 ('Giving Thanks for Hiroshima') Andrew Kenny published an obscene defence of the bombing of Hiroshima, saying that, in the long run, it saved lives.

11 *Iliad*, VIII: 523.

12 Emile Zola, *Oeuvre critique*, Paris, François Bernouard, 1929, II.

13 *Iliad*, XVIII: 558–709.

14 *Iliad*, VI: 64–70.

15 *Iliad*, VI: 76–7.

16 *Iliad*, XXII: 183–8.

17 *Odyssey*, XI: 79–85.

18 Wallace Stevens, 'Phases', XI, in *Opus Posthumous*, edited by Samuel French Morse, New York, Alfred A. Knopf, 1957.

Chapter 22

1 Jorge Luis Borges, *El Aleph*, Buenos Aires, Losada, 1949.

2 *Iliad*, II: 935–6.

3 *Iliad*, VI: 530–33.

4 *Iliad*, IX: 385–8.

5 *Odyssey*, III: 263–4.

6 *Iliad*, XVIII: 126–7.

7 *Odyssey*, IX: 346.

8 *Odyssey*, XVII: 359–60.

9 *Odyssey*, XXIII: 343–53.

10 *Iliad*, VI: 591–2.

11 *Iliad*, XXIV: 740–44.

12 Quoted in F. Buffière, *Les mythes d'Homère et la pensée grecque*, Paris, Les Belles Lettres, 1973.

INDEX OF SUBJECTS

Note: Where more than one sequence of notes appears on the same page, notes of the same number are distinguished by the addition of 'a' or 'b'. Names of characters, MORTAL AND IMMORTAL, from *The Iliad* and *The Odyssey* are italicised.

INDEX OF CITATIONS

Also available in the *Books that Shook the World* series

The Bible
The Biography
KAREN ARMSTRONG

The Bible is the most widely distributed book in the world. Translated into over two thousand languages, it is estimated that more than six billion copies have been sold in the last two hundred years alone. In this seminal account Karen Armstrong traces the story of the gestation of the Bible to reveal it as a complex and contradictory document cre-. ated by scores of people over hundreds of years

Karen Armstrong tells of the development of both the Hebrew Bible and the New Testament, drawing on the disparate sources that formed these sacred texts. From the Jewish practice of Midrash and the Christian cult of Jesus to the influence of Paul's letters on the Reformation and the manipulation of Revelations by Christian fundamentalists, Armstrong explores the different ways in which these sixty-six books have been understood and identifies the social needs that they answered. In the process she demonstrates the Bible is a fascinatingly unfamiliar and paradoxical work. The result will permanently alter our understanding of this most crucial of books.

'Armstrong's great achievement is that, as well as leaving you with a clearer, more historically accurate picture as to what precisely the Bible is (and isn't), she also makes you want to go back and read it again with fresh eyes.' Peter Stanford, *Independent*

Atlantic Books
Religion
ISBN 978 1 84354 397 8

Also available in the *Books that Shook the World* series

Plato's Republic
A Biography

SIMON BLACKBURN

Plato is perhaps the most significant philosopher who has ever lived and *The Republic*, composed in about 375 BC, is his most famous dialogue. Its discussion of the perfect city – and the perfect mind – laid the foundations for Western culture, and has since been the cornerstone of Western philosophy.

In this exploration of Plato's *Republic*, Simon Blackburn explains its judicial, moral and political ideas, and shows why, from St Augustine to twentieth-century philosophers such as Whitehead and Bergson, Western thought is still conditioned by this most important of books.

'Beautifully written with cogency and flair… Compelling reading.'
A. C. Grayling, *The Times*

'A delight… Its contents illuminate, subvert and rejig the big ideas.'
Stuart Kelly, *Scotland on Sunday*

Atlantic Books
Philosophy
ISBN 978 1 84354 347 3

Also available in the *Books that Shook the World* series

Darwin's Origin of Species
A Biography

JANET BROWNE

No book has changed people's understanding of themselves more than Darwin's *Origin of Species*. Its publication in 1859 caused a sensation, and it went on to become an international bestseller. The theory of natural selection shocked readers, calling into question the widely held belief that there was a Creator.

Here, Janet Browne, Darwin's foremost biographer, describes with bracing clarity the genesis, reception and legacy of Darwin's theories, and how his work altered forever our knowledge of what it is to be human.

'Superb: easy to read but none the less intellectually exciting...
the perfect introduction to Darwin's thought.'
Adam Sisman, *Sunday Telegraph*

'A gem... Browne explains with absolute clarity and readability the
sources, nature, reception and legacy of *On the Origin of Species*.'
A.C. Grayling, *The Times*

'Browne relates the history of Darwin's ideas with a pellucid fresh-
ness that makes reading the book a continuous pleasure.'
John Gray, *New Statesman*

Atlantic Books
Popular Science
ISBN 978 1 84354 394 7

Also available in the *Books that Shook the World* series

Thomas Paine's Rights of Man
A Biography

CHRISTOPHER HITCHENS

Thomas Paine is one of the greatest political advocates in history. His most famous work, *Declaration of the Rights of Man*, is a passionate defence of man's inalienable rights, inspired by his outrage at Edmund Burke's attack on the uprising of the French people.

Since its publication in 1791, *Rights of Man* has been both celebrated and maligned, but here Christopher Hitchens marvels at its forethought and revels in its contentiousness. Above all, Hitchens demonstrates how Paine's book forms the philosophical cornerstone of the first democratic republic.

'A timely book.' Billy Bragg, *Observer* Books of the Year

'Christopher Hitchens is at his characteristically incisive best.'
A. C. Grayling, *The Times*

'A brilliant portrait of Paine.' Jonathan Rée, *Prospect*

Atlantic Books
Politics
ISBN 978 1 84354 628 3

Also available in the *Books that Shook the World* series

The Qur'an
A Biography

BRUCE LAWRENCE

Few books in history are as little understood as the Qur'an. Sent down in a series of revelations to the Prophet Muhammad, it is regarded by the faithful as the unmediated word of Allah.

In this definitive account, Bruce Lawrence describes the origins of Islam in seventh-century Arabia. He goes on to discuss the Qur'an's many doubters and assesses its influence in societies and politics today. He ultimately shows that the Qur'an is a work of profound importance that can only be properly understood in the context of its history.

'Admirably balanced and informative.' John Gray, *New Statesman*

'An exceptionally illuminating and balanced narrative.' Ziauddin Sardar, *Independent*

'Lawrence's work could not be finer.' Stuart Kelly, *Scotland on Sunday*

Atlantic Books
Religion
ISBN 978 1 84354 399 2

Also available in the *Books that Shook the World* series

On the Wealth of Nations
P.J. O'ROURKE

Adam Smith's *The Wealth of Nations* was first published in 1776 and was almost instantly recognized as fundamental to an understanding of economics. It was also recognized as being really long; and as P. J. O'Rourke points out, to fully understand *The Wealth of Nations*, the cornerstone of free-market thinking and a book that shapes the world to this day, you also need to be familiar with Smith's earlier doorstopper, *The Theory of Moral Sentiments*. But now you don't have to read either, because P. J. has done it for you.

In this brilliant and indispensable book P. J. O'Rourke shows us why Smith is still relevant and why what seems obvious now was once so revolutionary.

'Consistently funny, with cracking asides... O'Rourke is a glittering writer, light but punchy, wry and impassioned, witheringly witty one moment and rambunctiously sarcastic the next... If you're daunted by *The Wealth of Nations*, O'Rourke's riff on it is the next best thing.' Stuart Kelly, *Scotland on Sunday*

'P. J. O'Rourke has done the hard work for you by taking the 900-page masterpiece and compressing its ideas into a little over 200 breezy pages... His wit can be razor sharp.' Alex Moffatt, *Irish Times*

'Sophisticated and comprehensive... For those without the stomach to read the real thing, P. J. O'Rourke's book will provide an unusually enjoyable starting point.' Allister Heath, *Literary Review*

Atlantic Books
Economics
ISBN 978 1 84354 389 3

Also available in the *Books that Shook the World* series

Carl von Clausewitz's On War
A Biography
HEW STRACHAN

On War by Carl von Clausewitz was first published in Germany after the Napoleonic Wars. One of the most significant treatises on military strategy ever written, it is still prescribed at military academies today. Its description of 'absolute war' and its insistence on the centrality of battle to war have been blamed for the level of destruction involved in both the First and Second World Wars.

Hew Strachan's accessible and readable book challenges the popular misconceptions that surround *On War*. He dispels the notion that for Clausewitz policy necessarily shapes war, asserting instead that war has its own dynamic and that its reciprocal effects can themselves shape policy. Strachan returns to the very heart of *On War* to recover its central arguments; in the process challenging the received wisdom about this cornerstone of military strategy.

'So clear and comprehensive you might end up giving von Clausewitz's book itself a swerve.' Colin Waters, *Sunday Herald*

Atlantic Books
Military History
ISBN 978 1 84354 392 3

Also available in the *Books that Shook the World* series

Marx's Das Kapital
A Biography

FRANCIS WHEEN

Das Kapital was born in a two-room flat in Soho. The first volume was published in 1867 to muted praise, but, after Marx's death, went on to influence thinkers, writers and revolutionaries, from George Bernard Shaw to Lenin.

Francis Wheen's brilliant assessment traces the book's history, from Marx's twenty-year fight – amid political squabbles and personal tragedy – to complete his masterpiece, through to the enormous impact it has had on the course of global history. It is the perfect introduction to both the man and his legacy.

'As gripping and as readable as a first-rate thriller.'
A.C. Grayling, *The Times*

'Exhilarating... Wheen provides a vivid portrait of the man.'
Adam Sisman, *Sunday Telegraph*

'A brilliant account.' Jonathan Derbyshire, *Time Out*

Atlantic Books
Politics
ISBN 978 1 84354 401 2